THE EBONY COLUMN

THE EBONY COLUMN

CLASSICS, CIVILIZATION, AND THE AFRICAN AMERICAN RECLAMATION OF THE WEST

Eric Ashley Hairston

Classicism in American Culture
John C. Shields, Series Editor

The University of Tennessee Press / Knoxville

The Classicism in American Culture series is designed to bring to light works that examine the classical influences that lie at the heart of American literature, artistic production, and intellectual life. Long overshadowed by an emphasis on America's Christian origins, this often unrecognized classical heritage is a vital thread that helps define a distinctly American self.

Copyright © 2013 by Eric Ashley Hairston
All Rights Reserved. Manufactured in the United States of America.
Cloth: 1st printing, 2013.
Paper: 1st printing, 2016.

Library of Congress Cataloging-in-Publication Data

Hairston, Eric Ashley.
The ebony column: classics, civilization, and the African American reclamation of the west / Eric Ashley Hairston. — First edition.
        pages cm. — (Classicism in American Culture)
Includes bibliographical references and index.

ISBN 978-1-62190-230-0

1. American literature—African American authors—History and criticism.
2. American literature—Classical influences.
3. Classicism in literature.
I. Title.

PS153.N5H2226 2013
810.9'896073—dc23
2013001464

To
Graham Michael Naresuan Hairston,
Madeline Gabrielle Saengdao Hairston,
Joseph Solomon Hairston, and Ava Blair Hairston.
The first three hundred years of our family in this land are finished,
and the next are yours to command.

CONTENTS

FOREWORD

Regrettably, an attitude dominates in the land that all things classical are the exclusive property of white folks. To declare this anemic attitude a crock of creeping ignorantum hardly addresses the extent of the problem. Over ten years ago, I published *The American Aeneas: Classical Origins of the American Self* (University of Tennessee Press, 2001), in which I attempted to assuage a measure of the difficulty encountered in pressing for recognition of America's immense debt to ancient classicism. A few years after this volume appeared, with the help and encouragement of Scot Danforth, UT Press director, I proposed a series of monographs, Classicism in American Culture, once again to assist with the recovery of America's classical origins. Eric Ashley Hairston's *The Ebony Column: Classics, Civilization, and the African American Reclamation of the West*, we are proud to observe, showcases the objective of this series.

In this, the series' first volume, Hairston's very title, *The Ebony Column*, promotes a clearly militant approach, one that admirably captures the spirit of the entire series. Carl J. Richard, author of the excellent *Founders and the Classics*, has written of my *Aeneas* that "Shields's book reminds us that the classics have frequently been a vital resource for those seeking liberation and classical works belong to humankind, not to any one particular racial or ethnic group or gender" (reader's report on *The American Aeneas*). Hairston's volume demonstrates masterfully just how classicism can serve the quest for liberation, particularly for African Americans.

The title of Hairston's first chapter, "The Trojan Horse," once again highlights the author's militancy. With appealing cleverness, the author directs our attention to the Greeks' famous instrument of war, their wooden horse, which brought about their victory over the Trojan peoples. By deploying a martial narrative to describe the literary career of our first African American to publish a book (on any subject), Hairston moves far beyond *Aeneas*'s analysis of Phillis Wheatley's classicism. In his introduction, Hairston states provocatively that a classical education "invalidated the idea of an intrinsic black inferiority." The source of this understanding derives, of course, from the splendid example of Phillis Wheatley, whose pen served as her sword of freedom.

Hairston brilliantly positions Wheatley's 1773 *Poems on Various Subjects, Religious and Moral* as a "literary Trojan horse" which figuratively ambushes her predominantly white readers (patrons as purchasers of her volume). Indeed, her book "carried her inside the literal and intellectual walls of white, colonial American, and British society," while at the same time her *Poems* forever strategically challenged the racist idea that a black poet could not create highly sophisticated poems, thereby denying that blacks were only suitable to serve white folks. All of which is simply to say that Wheatley's literary Trojan horse defeated white oppression, if only for a time.

I say "if only for a time" because Wheatley's authenticity has endured over two centuries of attacks. Thomas Jefferson, our third president, is unfortunately merely the best known of her early detractors. Hairston is careful to point out that the famous Duyckinck brothers, George and Evert, coauthors of the immensely popular *Cyclopedia of American Literature* (2 vols., 1855, 1866, 1881) and literary editors and advisors to Herman Melville, fully recognized Wheatley's fine translation (replete with interpolations) of Ovid in her ekphrastic epyllion, "Niobe in Distress . . ." Yet, more recently, Wheatley studies have been beset by such contemporary commentators as Carla Mulford, who insists that Wheatley only knew the ancient classics in translation, or such as Rosemary Guruswamy, who seeks to minimalize Wheatley's striking classicism so as to exaggerate her allegedly orthodox Congregationalism.

These commentators and others like them wish to gainsay the plethora of evidence, first, that she did in fact know the Latin tongue and, second, that she exemplified a liberal, relaxed Christianity whose tendency toward inflexible dogma was tempered, in her case, by elements of Islam, hierphantic solar worship, and, of course, classicism. We should hope that we are past the era when we might expect mainstream scholars to suggest that Wheatley, as an African, was incapable of learning Latin. However, we must still be vigilant against the tendency to knowingly and deliberately refuse to grant Wheatley the latitude of having possessed classical knowledge because it absolves contemporary scholars—usually bereft of substantive classical training—of having to do the old-school and not particularly fashionable intellectual work required to meet Wheatley on her level. In other words, they themselves do not have to take the trouble to learn Latin well enough to grasp Wheatley's ability to read Ovid, or indeed Virgil, Horace, Terence, and Tacitus proficiently, so as to perform her own translations.

Among the many erudite particulars of new knowledge Hairston delivers to us in the remainder of *Ebony Column* is a carefully crafted description of how Frederick Douglass mastered his "gift" of oratory. This so-called "gift," Hairston shows us, was acquired by means of deliberate study, particularly of the works of such Roman orators as Cicero (in translation). Hairston notes as well his acquaintance with such accomplished scholars as James W. C. Pennington, a name which continues to appear numerous times throughout *The Ebony Column* at moments when Hairston wishes to provide us with illustrations from the career of a successful nineteenth-century intellectual.

I remark the example of Pennington because Hairston subtly teaches us how it was that nineteenth-century African Americans could rise into the highest ranks of American society through their achievement in the realm of classicism. Subsequent chapters treat such major, classically trained figures as Anna Julia Cooper (most of whose contemporary critics have ignored her classicism) and W. E. B. Du Bois (whose classicism in *The Souls of Black Folk* has also been largely passed over).

In the case of Cooper, Hairston holds that a lack of knowledge of Cooper's classicism prevents discovery of the origins of her enthusiastic feminism. Regarding Du Bois, Hairston poignantly informs us about his wise principle that "it is impossible to work alongside a white American population that does not recognize the value of its own Western past." Herein Hairston appears to levy a pointed admonition affecting the whole of contemporary American society.

The manner by which Pennington's biography is handled in two of our major biographical tools, *The American National Biography* (24 vols., Oxford UP, 1999) and *The African American National Biography* (8 vols., Oxford UP, 2008), suggests the need for the kind of admonition Hairston seems to be delivering. For example, the *ANB* article on Pennington by Clifton H. Johnson (vol. 6, pp. 300–301) studiously acknowledges that Pennington "became a proficient scholar in Greek, Latin, and German" (p. 300). The *AANB* piece on Pennington by Herman E. Thomas makes no mention of Pennington's knowledge of Latin, Greek, or German but does emphasize Pennington's pivotal role in the *Amistad* affair (pp. 303–5), a highly significant moment in Pennington's life and in the life of our country, which Johnson also elaborates. But I am left to wonder why Thomas finds Pennington's knowledge of Latin, Greek, and German not worth the remarking.

Pennington's career is punctuated by many instances of his celebration of classicism among his colleagues. One such celebration occurs, for example, in Pennington's enthusiastic endorsement of Ann Plato's obvious classicism in his introduction to her *Essays: Including Biographies and Miscellaneous Pieces in Prose and Poetry* (1841). Significantly, Plato's poems are closely imitative of several of Phillis Wheatley's. While the *AANB* treatment of Pennington ignores his essential classicism, Hairston repeatedly and often underscores Pennington's close association with classicism. I suspect there may well be a general anti-classicism afoot of the sort with which I opened this foreword. We can now say with a modicum of certainty that this anti-classical attitude has become unsettlingly apparent among the African American intellectual community. Given this context, one inimical, perhaps even hostile, to classical studies, I find myself eagerly praising and even celebrating Eric Ashley Hairston's courage in constructing a work in which he refuses to be intimidated by a destructive force in our midst.

John C. Shields
Illinois State University

PREFACE

In this book, I begin a new thread in a conversation about the influence of antiquity on American civilization and American education that has gone on for quite some time. While many of the scholars gathered around the topic have made exceptional observations about antiquity and the American experience, I have been continually frustrated by the regular elision of African American experiences with the classics, such that all classical influence appears to disappear. That omission across the history of the discussion is disturbing for a number of reasons, not the least of which is its longevity, through a period of overt stereotyping and institutionalized racism right up to the contemporary—and, one hopes, more cosmopolitan and enlightened—scholarly era.

Today's scholars still comment on African American writers and even anthologize them without any serious discussion of classical content, even when that classicism peppers a text such as W. E. B. DuBois's *The Souls of Black Folk* or Anna Julia Cooper's *A Voice from the South.* Perhaps most troubling is the commentary of some contemporary African American scholars, who even in the aftermath of John Shields's resonating rejection of black and white critics of Phillis Wheatley, still dismiss classical content in African American works as mimicry of white forms, brainwashing in Eurocentric ideas, or some meaningless code or badge of an elite college-bred population. At worst, the African American classicism that is misunderstood or not understood at all is covertly coded or overtly labeled as *not black.* In the cases I have observed, it appears that the critics are unfamiliar with the classics or not interested in what either the ancient or later authors are saying beyond what can be deployed for a specific partisan purpose. The works of past African American writers are mined endlessly for a "when and where I enter" or a revelation of "the Veil" passage. All else is far too often dismissed as unusable and worse—as *elitist*, a term whose use increasingly reveals not a haughty and oppressive exclusivity of the learned but instead an eviscerating anti-intellectualism and a radical limiting of the scope of African American letters.

Since my early conference presentations in the mid- to late 1990s and graduate writings on the substantial classical elements in African American literature, some new work on African American experiences with the classics have appeared. Tracey Walters's *African American Literature and the Classicist Tradition: Black Women Writers from Wheatley to Morrision* (Palgrave MacMillan, 2007), Patrice Rankine's *Ulysses in Black: Ralph Ellison, Classicism, and African American Literature* (U of Wisconsin P, 2008), and William Cook and James Tatum's *African American Writers and Classical Tradition* (U of Chicago P, 2010) are among the works that suggest increasing activity in studies of classical influence in African American intellectual history, especially as represented in literature. Of course, Michelle Valerie Ronnick's effort to salvage the work and legacy of black classicist William Sanders Scarborough has been a tremendous victory for African American letters. Still, it is interesting that most of these works and projects tend not to linger on the broad and deep relationships, perhaps over lifetimes, that their authors and black scholars more broadly have had with the classics or with each other, tending, rather, to move with some dispatch toward the twentieth century.

In his particularly intriguing work, Patrice Rankine explicitly and earnestly endeavors to bridge the gap between black studies and the classics, but he boldly constructs that scholarly span largely out of twentieth-century materials, without full attention to writers throughout the tradition—including many of the stodgy old lovers of things ancient who do not have the Afrocentric edge favored in much of the contemporary black-studies world. Ultimately, even Cook and Tatum's very recent work limits the scope of Wheatley's accomplishments, even demeaning her "Niobe in Distress" as being not a translation but instead a novice imitation that meets contemporary standards of plagiarism—an assessment that should strike Wheatley scholars especially as Jeffersonian in its derision. Their analysis also separates the phenomenon of Frederick Douglass from its classical elements and provides only a limited examination of even a tremendous celebrant of the classics such as W. E. B. Du Bois. These most recent examinations fail to establish the centrality of classical works to the African

American intellectual tradition. This tradition, I maintain, is a multigenerational attempt to reclaim the West for African Americans as part of their heritage, restore the African shore of antiquity to regular intellectual commerce, and reanimate the voices of people of African heritage within the Western discourse on virtue, citizenship, duty, and civilization.

In the pages that follow, I endeavor to provide a partial correction of the multigenerational and multiracial failure to chronicle the journey of African Americans in the West and within the experience of Western Civilization. I have attempted to move beyond the snobbish elision from historic scholarship of what Ronnick has termed *Classica Africana* or the mere observation of classical activity among African American writers or the half-amazed musing over the appearance of Greek and Roman mythology among more solidly ethnic prose, poetry, and politics. And, for certain, I reject the disapproving view of culture building and heritage reclamation that rightly critiques Afrocentrism (which often recklessly idealizes a black past and appropriates whatever is necessary to that vision) but threatens to sneer at all reclamation efforts. Similarly, I have noted and decried with others the racist rejection of black claims on the West and critiques of traditional classicism that surfaced in some attacks on Martin Bernal's work. Although I will leave to the cross-cultural sociologists, psychologists, and psychiatrists to execute the differential diagnosis and identify particular parameters of the condition, I fully intend to leave behind the phobia apparent in far too much scholarship that to embrace the West is to deracinate, fragment, or decimate blackness—to somehow disrupt the very molecular structure of cultural identity and the black experience. On the contrary, Marvin Gaye, W. E. B. Du Bois, the Wu Tang Clan, Alain Locke, Mos Def, Jay-Z, and Rita Dove can jointly exist in a mind and ethnic experience along with Cicero, Sappho, Homer, Catullus, Lucretius, Virgil, and Ovid. Briefly to exemplify the contemporary autobiographical impulse in scholarship, I will say that beyond all the ingrained stereotypical representations of African American life in the seventies and eighties—from double-dutch jumping in the streets to overlong church services to unhealthy relationships with purple Kool-Aid—there is another reality of black life. For instance, more than a few of us grew up with Cicero on the bookshelf beside Ellison and Cleaver. Some of us lay with feet dangling over a sofa arm, still in church clothes, reading Virgil or Homer for the cool battle scenes. Some of us visited a grandmother's house to find Shakespeare's *Antony and Cleopatra* on a bookshelf beside a United Methodist or Baptist hymnal and the *Odes* of Horace. Black is complex like that, and complexity has been known to frighten people—often into embracing and enforcing simplicity.

I have endeavored to make some contribution toward recovering classics fully, along with the West, for African Americans and demonstrating how generations of African Americans learned and deployed the works of that Mediterranean world of antiquity for their own purposes and edification, celebrating and reclaiming Greece and Rome, Carthage and Numidia, Egypt and Judea, and even Ethiopia as *their* ancient world and *their* West and not the private legacy of their white captors and adversaries—a complex heritage that belongs to contemporary African Americans as they make their way as citizens in this, our new American Rome.

ACKNOWLEDGMENTS

I would like to thank my family for all their support as I developed this book. Thanks as well to the local Durham, North Carolina, businesses that continue to make space for scholars lingering over meals and coffee to work. I greatly appreciate those close friends and colleagues who were part of those regular, varied, and provocative exchanges via telephones, texts, email, and the even richer but rarer engagements over coffee and in ambling or rushing wherever our next appointments demanded. Thanks to Dr. Cornel West for taking some time many years ago at the University of Virginia to walk with me and answer questions about the *various* classics, especially Lucretius and Richard Pryor. Thanks to Dr. Houston A. Baker Jr. for taking time over coffee in Durham to discuss academe and the influence of the classics. There is no sufficient measure of thanks for those who read, critiqued, and argued mightily for or against the various elements and drafts of this book, and here I must thank Dr. Crystal S. Anderson in particular.

I note my enduring gratitude to the scholars who contributed to the intellectual foundations of this project in various ways: Dean Patricia A. Johansson, Dr. Charles Lewis, Dr. Edwin G. Wilson, Dr. Doyle Fosso, Dr. Gordon Braden, Dr. Alan Howard, Dr. John C. Shields, and—

the late Dr. Allen Mandelbaum, who must, as is fitting, stand alone.

Quod Deus bene vertat.

INTRODUCTION
A MORE THAN PARTIAL GRACE

A PROLEGOMENON FOR AFRICAN AMERICAN EXPERIENCES WITH THE CLASSICS

African American writers have confronted a multitude of claims against black intelligence and humanity, lodged by white detractors and dating from the colonial period onward. They countered these assaults in numerous literary genres, notably Protestant evangelical sermons, political treatises, and the slave narrative tradition. Scholars have devoted considerable attention to these traditions, essentially turning the slave narrative into the emblem of African American literary history. But no counterattack devised by black writers has been more remarkable, yet consistently overlooked, than their deployment of Greek and Roman, and, periodically, Egyptian classical references.

The classics—mythology, epics, histories, rhetorical strategies, and philosophical meditations on the virtuous life—were a body of knowledge the command of which whites in Europe and America had historically recognized as a sign of highest academic achievement and humanity. Classical education existed in concert with ecclesiastical and university training and even underpinned it, with classicism existing, after Christianity, as the "central intellectual project in America before the late nineteenth century"[1]

They also contained philosophical, intellectual, literary, and moral under-standings that did not presume black inferiority but could provide a sub-stantive foundation for black cultural and intellectual growth. Therefore, the classics represented a key source of intellectual and cultural responses to racist evaluations of black humanity and intellectual capacity.

In this volume I have chosen to investigate selected classical elements in African American literature between 1772 and 1910. The body of Afri-can American literary productions in the United States is vast, and I do not claim to achieve a definitive evaluation of the influence of the classics across African American literary history. However, the years on which I focus are critical because they contain the beginning of African Ameri-cans' intellectual investigation of works of antiquity, the first discernable educational and political deployments of classical elements by African Americans, and eventually the clear theoretical articulation of classics as essential cultural tools for African Americans to build civic and spiritual virtue, encourage heroism, value and pursue civic equality, and cultivate artistic and intellectual life. I do not construe the "classics" simply in terms of their obvious association with mythology, elegies, encomia, epics, phil-osophical treatises, rhetorical manuals, or histories. Rather, I regard the classics as integrated, powerful, and enduring transmitters of cultural val-ues. I am particularly concerned with how these classical genres facilitated the definition, production, and dissemination of knowledge and virtue in the Mediterranean civilizations of antiquity. "Virtue," the Greek *arête* or Latin *virtus*, as well as manliness and heroism, are commonly understood as primary foci of classical texts.

Virtue takes on philosophical form in Plato, whose *Republic* and other Socratic dialogues give us the most famous classical treatment of individ-ual and civic virtue. In *The Republic*, Socrates outlines the nature of good-ness, the character of the good life, the virtuous education of youth, and the proper form of government for the virtuous state. Aristotle's *Nichoma-chean Ethics* challenges the single, universal virtue of Socrates and sug-gests a body of intellectual (learned by instruction) and moral (acquired by deliberate practice) virtues that lead men to a single end that is both in the personal and communal interest: *eudaimonia*, or the human good. *Pietas*, a concept that Americans have read both in terms of religious piety and civic virtue, also figures prominently in classical texts.[2] The Roman virtue of piety is articulated in *The Aeneid*, visible in the writings of Cicero, Marcus Aurelius, and Caesar, and perpetuated politically and legally in im-perial and senatorial activity, not the least of which is the conservative Au-gustan agenda inaugurating the imperial era. These terms *virtus* and *pietas* take on a historical emphasis in Herodotus and Tacitus, whose works recount the virtues and vices of the leaders and nations of the ancient world and the effects of those characteristics on regional politics and culture. The writings of Quintilian and Cicero, especially Cicero's *De Oratore* and Quintilian's *Institutio Oratoria,* examine the nature and aims of oratory. They take up the qualities of virtue and masculinity an orator must have and project, qualities through which a man literally embodies virtue and encourages it in individuals and civilizations. Further, Cicero's *On Duties (De Officiis)* and *Against Verres* illustrate the qualities of civic duty and Roman citizenship and their formation of superior civilization. Horace's writings offer a variety of thoroughly respectable and moderate views on living a good life—temperance exalted in elegant verse. Horace's temperance is a lesson amplified when taken in comparison to Ovid, whose life, writings, and sad exile provide a startling set of lessons on political virtue, which might well be to be wary of power and the powerful. While the *Metamorphoses* contend with transformation, they also provide lessons in piety, humility, and moderation, which were clearly not Ovid's goal in the *Ars Amatoria,* the provocative text at least partly responsible for his exile.

Worthy of special attention, the Homeric and Virgilian epics—*The Iliad, The Odyssey,* and *The Aeneid*—provide extensive treatments of martial and civic virtue, the proper making of masculinity, and the production of heroism, and they do so on a global stage. These epics of love, international relations, war, destruction, and nation building chronicle the experiences of heroes and nations over years of turmoil. Moreover, they provide rich, nuanced, and multilayered accounts of the specific rewards and consequences of virtue and vice for individual men, those immediately around them, and their nations. Consequently, these epics have become some of the most enduring classical works. They shaped the education of young men in antiquity and from the Renaissance through the late nineteenth century.

The epics go far beyond just investigating virtue over an extended period of time; indeed, they explore the particular complexity of exercising virtue, masculinity, and heroism in the face of uncontrollable human and divine events. As Martha Nussbaum illustrates in *The Fragility of Goodness,* the Greeks were acutely concerned with how to maintain virtue and the overall human good in the face of chance, changing political environments, and the intervention of the gods. Roman historians also alert us to the persistent conflict between sober republican virtues and imperial or barbarian excess. We might remember the young Achilles of *The Iliad,* first among the *agathoi,* sulking in his tent over a slight.[3] As Naoto Yamagata's work suggests, looking at a series of Greek terms common to the epics, one

4

can come to an interesting set of conclusions about the nature of virtue and morality in the Greek world. Terms such as *arête, agathos, esthlos, ameinon, areion, aristos, aristeus, aristeuo, kakos, kalos,* and *aischros* pepper the epics. They do not approximate Christian virtues, and in that regard their absorption into African American intellectual history is particularly interesting. The *agathoi* are the ruling elite, with *kakoi* encompassing the rest. This is not a smooth relationship, because the *kakoi* are subject to worldly hardships and abuses, known as *kaka,* that may derive directly from the *agathoi.* The *agathoi* are given *arête* by interfering gods (as favors or scheming) or as a matter of fate or *moira.* They do not receive *arête* by virtue, as it were, of outstanding morality, especially since part of the benefits package of being one of the *agathoi* is the ability to dole out *kaka* to *kakoi,* or to foes. The *agathoi* have a battlefield ethic and a peacetime code, and losing track of the proper venue often brings on disaster. In battle the *agathoi* can loot and pillage and kill, hurl children from battlements, strip enemies of armor and clothes, and take women as prizes with abandon; they cannot show pity or mercy to suppliants without generating opprobrium.[4] However, when this viciousness spills over into peacetime or into relationships within the community of *agathoi*—as in, for example, Agamemnon's theft of Achilles's Briseis, an act prompting Achilles to describe him as "shameless, armored in shamelessness" (I:175–176), or in Achilles's near regicide—disorder, if not disaster, is likely.[5]

Thus, the complexity of the celebrated sulking episode involving Achilles is more substantial than we generally imagine. Achilles is expected to be exemplary in personal and military matters in a conflict that is the dirty little war of the classical age, a conflict in the crumbling Mycenaean world for which there may be no virtuous reason in the first place. Perhaps Paris and Troy are being punished for a violation of *xeinia,* but it is clear as well that Agamemnon is on a cynical and avaricious quest. Similarly, young prince Aeneas of Virgil's *Aeneid* is expected to lead his people from the smoldering ruins of Troy to the founding of Rome, and he must do so with his virtue, manhood, and heroism intact. In this exodus, he must also remain true to the gods and their will and sustain *pietas.* Here too we have a flawed hero and a disturbing question.[6] How does one remain virtuous in a world in which the environment, foundation, and rules for virtue have been radically altered, are routinely shifted, or have been called into question in the aftermath of a holocaust and during a struggle for survival? If, as Martha Nussbaum argues, the fragility of goodness is such that it only can exist like flora, where the environment allows it to survive, how can virtue (and its variety of wisdom or intellect) survive in an inhospitable if not deadly environment? These questions are not unlike those faced by African Americans, who, torn from the African cultural and ethical context, had to contend with brutal enslavement, mass murder, vastly limited if extant citizenship, and demands that they adhere to nearly impracticable standards of virtue and intellectual capacity in order to have any possible claim to humanity.

African Americans have been vexed by the question of what is virtuous and valuable, the intellectual challenges of discerning virtue in religion, history, and politics filtered through the lens of white racism (and shaped substantially by New Testament Christianity and its heresies), and sustaining personal and communal goodness in the face of extraordinary and fundamental deprivations spawned by slavery and racism. These deprivations thoroughly complicated questions of virtue by creating pressing issues of survival and practical necessity.

Ultimately, the African American writers I examine in this text adopted a concept of virtue emphasizing secular classical intellectual and moral characteristics that could coexist with or augment Christian virtues. Like the founding fathers, who did not "segregate their Greco-Roman, Whig and colonial American tools in separately marked boxes," African Americans were able to use the classics pragmatically to craft more nuanced political, ethical, religious, and intellectual positions.[7] For example, the Aristotelian intellectual virtues of wisdom and intuitive good judgment—combined with the moral virtues of courage, temperance, greatness of soul, gentleness, honesty, wit, friendliness, righteous indignation, and justice—provided more robust virtue and clearer pathways to personal and racial happiness when Christian humility, faith, hope, and charity seemed ineffective or were thoroughly undermined by practical problems of racism. The Homeric ethic, although gingerly handled because of the raging Achilles, also suggested a battlefield ethic distinct from peacetime morality. Beyond the Greeks, the Roman writers of antiquity thoroughly revisited the issue of virtue: culturally in Virgil, irreverently in Terence and Ovid, and critically in Cicero, each providing a more nuanced evaluation of virtue than was commonly available through contemporary Christianity.

The qualities of excellence celebrated by the authors in this study included heroism and an ethic of heroic response to injustice, civic responsibility, commitment to civil rights, manliness, Christian piety, culture (in terms of the habits and activities of refined society and an appreciation for social, artistic, and humanistic enterprises), and profound and diverse knowledge aimed at discerning the meaning of life and the best and most abundant life for the individual and the race. In addition, while gender inflected their writings differently, each writer discussed here (including to a lesser extent Frederick Douglass), through personal action or literary activity, found ways to venerate the domestic sphere and traditional gender roles while contesting the traditional limitations of domesticity and gender. They rejected the growing materialism of America, as well as purely economic plans for improving the plight of their race. They embraced the martial foundation of classical virtue but sought a more nuanced reading of the battlefields on which virtue was attained and the ways in which women and men could share virtue. Whether or not African American writers fully embraced all of these elements, they routinely took historical, political, and literary models of virtue, as well as human exemplars of virtue, from the classical texts. African Americans' contemplations of virtue and value had to be conducted in the face of widespread European and American beliefs that blacks were incapable of understanding and reasoning on such concepts at the most basic level. In the colonial American discourse on African American humanity, detractors such as Thomas Jefferson argued that African Americans were essentially incapable of higher intellectual thought and cultural productions and were graced only with a talent for imitation and a penchant for slight religiosity. In his much-quoted *Notes on the State of Virginia* and letters to Benjamin Banneker and the Abbè Gregoire, Jefferson classified blacks as something other than human, relying on the Greek sense of differing *natures*. Eventually, Jefferson's breed of racist philosophical distinction mingled with nineteenth-century genetic science, spawned by Charles Darwin's publications, to produce a pseudoscientific rationale for black inferiority.

Interestingly enough, this intellectual assault on African Americans also has roots in the classics, albeit a decidedly imperialist application of the tradition that privileges conquest and subjugation over a policy of cultural enrichment and cultivating virtue. As Richard Waswo notes in *The Founding Legend of Western Civilization*, the European West continually advances a cultural mythology of a transforming and civilizing expansion, a mythos exemplified in the mythology of Roman origins and crystallized in Virgil's *Aeneid*. Accordingly, the European West advances and justifies imperial and colonial projects in part by philosophically and pseudoscientifically dehumanizing the indigenous or colored Other as devoid of *cultus* (culture) or *mos* (tradition). The arts and sciences of Western culture and tradition themselves become the very tools in a process heralded in the Middle Ages as *translatio imperii et studii,* or the transmission of empire and learning. In this process, the justification for subjugation or eradication of the Other rested in the Other being unlettered in these intellectual tools and *cultus,* existing instead as "some sub-, pre-, or proto-humanity not *quite* entitled" to the rights of civilized humanity.[8] Unenviably, Africans, and later African Americans, found themselves in the path of the European impulse to conquer, convert, and civilize—a sense of manifest destiny that was classically mythologized and justified on religious/evangelical/moral grounds. As Richard Beale Davis illustrates, the cultural foundation for Thomas Jefferson's colonial South was distinctly Graeco-Roman, with the Virginia or Carolina gentleman modeled on "the more admirable of the Greeks and Romans."[9] American governmental philosophy developed "strongly in the ancient republican image as it existed in the minds of James Madison and George Mason and Thomas Jefferson."[10] However, that image, especially for the well-read Jefferson, thoroughly ignored the qualities of Roman slavery and historians' assessments, like that of Gibbon.[11] Roman slavery was not absolute, and it certainly was not race-limited. "Hope, the best comfort of our imperfect condition," Gibbon famously observed, "was not denied to the Roman slave; and if he had any opportunity of rendering himself either useful or agreeable, he might very naturally expect that the diligence and fidelity of a few years would be rewarded with the inestimable gift of freedom."[12] The South's use of classical republicanism to gild a core of strong-arm oppression, is also thoroughly consistent with the imperialist model of the *translatio.*

This Western imperialist advance nonetheless offered sufficient reason not to expect a rigid caste system genetically linked to race. As Rogers M. Smith argues, there was every reason to suspect that a racial caste system might not always be in the interest of the British Crown, which preferred to link servitude to the fact that the men and women of the empire were all *subjects* of the King. British imperial expansion historically included an assumption of *cultural* superiority and the advancement of the *translatio,* but history also reflects that enslavement and impermeable racial barriers proved less palatable or productive to the empire than cultural conquest, political influence, and the policy of making the world an extension of England. Smith speculates that the American Revolution was in part a struggle over the course of the *translatio* and the character of Western expansion. The American process of challenging and separating from England included establishing both a cultural supremacy and physical control over all those people and institutions England had exercised control over or arrayed against the interests of white colonists. Therefore, looking to the text of the draft and adopted Declaration of Independence and the Constitution, we find that Native Americans, Tories, and Hessian mercenaries were all groups to be controlled. African American slaves, however, whom the British planned to free and recruit as an imperial army against the rebels (in what would be called "Ethiopian" regiments), posed a particular military and social threat.

Even after the Revolution, republican and Lockean democratic elements were jointly (and sometimes conflictingly) part of American political history, enough so that liberalizing philosophical tendencies were present in American political culture. Such tendencies would seem to be sufficient to offset the "ascriptive citizenship" hierarchies hardening along lines of race. But the tree of liberty (whose branches of universal rights and citizenship would be ruthlessly pruned so often in the American legal future) was initially altered by white America's insistence on grafting on to it the additional civic myth of racial supremacy. Explaining "why persons form a people, usually indicating how a political community originated, who is eligible for membership, who is not and why, and what the communities' values and aims are" is elemental to understanding the "ascriptive hierarchies" of American rights and citizenship.[13] Beyond the standard belief in cultural superiority, the civic myth of white (male) superiority in terms of culture, tradition, and civic worth immediately requires that one define the Other as "'lower races,' 'savages' and 'unassimilables,' slaves and servants, aliens, and denizens, 'unnatural' criminals and second-class citizens, wives and mothers."[14] As Martha Nussbaum reminds us, "Ancient Greeks imagined hypothetical barbarian lands where women ruled, or wantonness ran riot; Roman authors described a Germany that was the mythic inversion of Roman Africa. Likewise, the Africa imagined by Americans was an inversion of Puritan values, and Puritan America defined its worth by contrasting itself with the hypothetical bestial other."[15] In breaking from "tyrannical" England, Americans chose to draw the boundaries of citizenship with this civic myth. But they constructed a racial superiority, exceeding and rendering more harsh and terrible the Western cultural mythology and military expansion normally in action.

Colonial debates over the Declaration of Independence clearly addressed the rights of "men," the dangers of Native Americans savages, the horror of facing German mercenaries, and the barbaric threat of African slaves being used as soldiers against the colonies. If the expansion of white culture and the triumph of the American *translatio* depended on the civic myth of racial superiority, then Thomas Jefferson's philosophy of black subhumanity, civil inferiority, and intellectual deficiency outlined in the Declaration and *Notes on the State of Virginia* practically lit the path to conquest. The effect was long-lasting and devastating. Nineteenth and twentieth-century African American scholar and activist Mary Church

Terrell, who studied classics at Oberlin College, demonstrated how pervasive this view of black intellectual inferiority became. According to her 1940 autobiography, *A Colored Woman in a White World,* myths of black inferiority were globalized and infected some of the best minds of Europe:

> One day Matthew Arnold, the English writer, visited our class and Professor Frost asked me both to read the Greek and then to translate. After leaving the class Mr. Arnold referred to the young lady who read the passage of Greek so well. Thinking it would interest the Englishman, Professor Frost told him I was of African descent. Thereupon Mr. Arnold expressed the greatest surprise imaginable, because, he said, he thought the tongue of the African was so thick he could not be taught to pronounce the Greek correctly.[16]

Terrell was not the only black scholar to identify the classics, the foundation of the *translatio imperii et studii,* as a proving ground for African American intellect or humanity. Like her, Carter G. Woodson argued that the debate over African Americans' intellectual equality with whites, their ability to comprehend and live in civilization, and their right to do so rested on the answer to the questions: "[C]an a Negro master the grammar, language, and literature of Latin, Greek, and Hebrew? Can he learn to think? Can he understand the significant things of life as expounded by mathematicians, scientists, and philosophers?"[17] The argument put forth by proponents of slavery, from common citizens to slaveholders to clergy and political leaders, was that the "Negro" was clearly incapable of higher thought and was therefore unworthy of the freedoms enjoyed by the human race. It was this argument that African Americans had to disprove.

What specific role, then, could the classics play in the debate about black intelligence and humanity? The classics could offer a historical account of human civilization that invalidated the idea of racial superiority and undermined white claims to intrinsic intellectual supremacy. While Greek and Roman writers questioned and evaluated the differences among mankind, their assessments of tribe and nation and immigration status did not condemn or elevate on the basis of race.[18] The environmentalist theory common to many classical writers suggested that location on the globe and exposure to heat or cold added or detracted from the qualities of peoples and nations, a view that attributed a penchant for the exotic and passionate to inhabitants of southern climates.[19] If nothing else, the classics called into question the idea of assessing humans by race. As a student of the classics, W. E. B. Du Bois said, as perhaps no other of his generation, that as regards matters of intelligence, blacks were not the only group in question. Questioning the humanity of any one race exposed all races to charges of barbarism, since all races had experienced high and low points in their cultures and civilizations. As Du Bois put it, "[A] Greek of the age of Pericles might have put just as puzzling and unanswerable a query [about their humanity and intelligence] to the ancestors of the present Europeans who were crawling about the forests of Germany half-naked and periodically drunk."[20]

Unfortunately, this straightforward and lacerating historical point was not sufficient to incise deep-seated racism, which impaired the intellectual and historic operation of the classical world in the American mind during the period of this study. To dispute white convictions about African American intellectual inferiority, blacks would have to prove their humanity by displaying facility in intellectual fields privileged by whites. Since critics like Jefferson recognized the mastery of the language, thought, and works of the Greek and Roman civilizations as the mark of superior human intellect and virtue, African Americans had to demonstrate that they possessed allusive and interpretive power over the classics to claim humanity, freedom, and civic access. Without this link to the Greek and Roman classics, especially to the foundation texts of personal and civic virtue, black intellectual production would remain fully vulnerable to racist intellectual assaults. Subsequently, many African American literary, political, and educational projects through the early 1900s were deeply inflected by the classics. Projects that minimized or rejected the classics, most notably the industrial education and economic plans of Booker T. Washington, faced entrenched resistance from many black scholars and leaders such as W. E. B. Du Bois.

Even though many blacks with access to education embraced the classics and deployed the myths, epics, philosophy, and history of antiquity to address racist evaluations of black humanity and intellect, we cannot understand the deployment of the classics as merely a response to specific racist challenges. To do so would suggest that African Americans had only a superficial relationship with the classics and merely aped Anglo-American neoclassicism, which flourished in the seventeenth and early eighteenth centuries.

The elegant, stylized poetry and prose of Anglo-American neoclassicism reflected a high regard for tradition, reverence for the classics, distrust of innovation, and attention to artifice, rules, convention, decorum, and a "nature" defining permanent, fundamental ethical positions (virtue and vice). Alexander Pope's *Essay on Criticism* describes artistic rules as natural, "discover'd, not devise'd" and best articulated by ancients like

Homer and Virgil.[21] The latter, according to Pope, had to rein in pride (individual rebellion against nature and order and the primary threat to virtue and virtuous art) and "checks the bold design" of his *Aeneid*.[22] American colonials aggressively mined classical literature and history to help enrich early American ideas of the citizen and the state, virtue, and proper education, but doubts about the practical usefulness and industrial and commercial applications of classical knowledge persisted and grew. So too did the suspicion articulated by Benjamin Rush to John Adams: "Do not men use Latin and Greek as the scuttlefish [*sic*] emit their black ink, on purpose to conceal themselves from intercourse with the common people?"[23] And, we generally note that as the neoclassical era expired in the eighteenth century, American neoclassicism declined in quality and popularity to a mere (and unreliable) sign of social refinement among the masses or to an actual "pooling in the esoteric byways of elite, high culture."[24] Although Meyer Reinhold's argument for a precipitous decline of classical study and influence at the end of the eighteenth century is substantively parried by Carl Richard, it seems relatively clear that in the nineteenth century the tradition lost ground in terms of curricular emphasis and social and political value. In contrast, the scope and depth of African American classical use among writers such as Phillis Wheatley, Frederick Douglass, Anna Julia Cooper, and W. E. B. Du Bois suggest a significantly broader purpose over a more substantial period—depending generationally on the power of classical study to defend their identity as humans and rebuild their culture from slavery in classically inflected literature, oratory, history, and political philosophy.

Phillis Wheatley's unique neoclassical writing, measured by the number and scope of her classical references, suggests that she thoughtfully and purposely commented on neoclassical "nature" and Christian piety in ways which implied that assumptions of inherent black intellectual and spiritual benightedness and fitness for slavery were neither natural nor virtuous. "To Maecenas," "On Being Brought from Africa to America," and "To the Students at the University of Cambridge in New England," among others of her poems, establish her as a living refutation of the stereotype of black intellectual deficiency and argue that blackness is neither a natural mark of vice nor destined servitude. Classical references saturate Wheatley's *Poems on Various Subjects Religious and Moral* (1773).

Scholars like Walter Ong have reminded us that the old-style classical education advanced the tradition of polemic and dispute. Moreover, classical education has traditionally provided to its students an instruction in virtue, a strong sense of individual worth and power, rhetorical armament, martial inclinations, and political and literary ambition. No doubt exists that Wheatley studied the classics that were routinely included in standard classical education, so we may reasonably argue that, like any other student of the classics, she developed some of the same characteristics. Given the classical influence on her character and ambitions, we can also argue that Wheatley employed the classics in *Poems on Various Subjects Religious and Moral* as part of a demonstration of intelligence, virtue, and literary virtuosity representative of normal classical ambition. Political ambition resulting from classical study can also explain Wheatley's deployment of the classics and use of the cachet of classical allusions as an attempt to critique colonial British and American political and cultural policy on race. For example, she directly challenged King George to free enslaved subjects, prodded the Earl of Dartmouth to understand her ardent love of freedom as the result of her enslaved state, and instructed Christians and students at Harvard that Christianity equalizes all men. Wheatley's sizeable classical vehicle delivered subject matter that included challenges to slavery, to the use of Christianity to justify slavery, and to claims of African subhumanity. Moreover, her poems were addressed to Harvard students, New England notables, British nobility, and the King of England, an audience for whom educational training in the classics was a typical marker of higher learning, intellectual prowess, and advanced social standing.

Subsequent African American writers such as Frederick Douglass, Anna Julia Cooper, and W. E. B. Du Bois moved beyond Wheatley's skillful, targeted, but restrained critiques to locate and define cultural and intellectual tools in the classics that are valuable as more than limited mechanisms of response or display. Essentially, they rejected the traditional understanding of the classics as the exclusive foundation and cultural property of white European civilization as well as its role in encouraging and transmitting destructive imperialist and colonialist philosophies. Instead, they offered an alternative vision of the classics as a transforming set of ideals that could produce or develop an African American–inflected *cultus* (culture) and *civitas* (citizenship), and enable a black counter-transmission of a virtuous, intelligent, resilient humanity. Rather than be plowed under the soil (or relegated to its maintenance) in European cultivation, they planted their own new and resilient strain of civilization in African American literature that contains an alternative vision of African Americans.

African American writers in both secular and religious contexts argue and demonstrate that the classics are useful, if not essential to overall black cultural and intellectual development. Frederick Douglass encountered the classics in his youth and as a preacher and abolitionist lecturer, and he also found particular value in classical models as a vehicle for challenging claims against black humanity. He exposed the inconsistency of white supremacy with American democratic ideals, and he demonstrated the corruption of classical, Western virtue as a result of slavery. In *My Bondage and My Freedom* (1855), Douglass addressed his early experience with classical and classically influenced material. He credited Caleb Bingham's *Columbian Orator,* a rhetorical text infused with Cicero's and Quintilian's oratorical lessons, with adding to his rhetorical abilities and awakening his mind. Douglass's oratory reflected Bingham's classical lessons, which gave him a portion of the power so often chronicled by reporters and abolitionists. Moreover, Douglass punctuated his oratory with classical references, usually targeted against his enemies in ways that imply a lack of masculinity and virtue or that specifically undermine southern claims that their society was grounded in classical republican virtue. In speeches ranging from "No Union with Slaveholders" (1844) and "The Claims of the Negro Ethnologically Considered" (1854) to "Revolutions Never Go Backward (1861)" and his 1892 reports of his Grand Tour of Western Europe, Greece, and Egypt, Douglass employs classical strategies, figures, texts, and allusions to animate and strengthen his oratory.

Like Douglass, Anna Julia Cooper saw the production and dissemination of virtue and resilient culture as the primary needs of African Americans, and she mined the classical tradition for intellectual and cultural elements useful in forming and advancing the virtuous African American *cultus.* Cooper championed a classically oriented moral education for African Americans, arguing that the lessons of the "heart of the young Achilles" should influence blacks' plans for educating youth. In *A Voice from the South,* Cooper insisted that women are the primary teachers of virtue to young men. Accordingly, women had to be fully and classically educated in the literature and philosophy of the good, virtuous, contemplative, and heroic life. Ultimately, like the Roman Catholic Church, which civilized barbarian hordes in the wake of the fallen Roman Empire, Christian women would bring the peace of civilization to America by learning and teaching the virtues of the classics and Christianity to newly freed slaves and the defeated South. In *The Idea of the Renaissance,* William Kerrigan and Gordon Braden remind us that one could embrace Lorenzo Valla's argument that the "Roman *imperium* is wherever the Roman language rules" (which I read literally and figuratively).[25] This follows logically from the *translatio imperii et studii.* Cooper, a Latin scholar and teacher, suggested that a Renaissance could emerge in America and African America as easily as it did in Carolingian France and Italy, driven by both Christian conversion and education in the texts, culture, philosophy, and language of the *imperium.*

The only African American scholar more deeply committed to the transforming power of the classical texts than Cooper was W. E. B. Du Bois. In *The Souls of Black Folk,* Du Bois outlined the fundamental importance of classical education to African Americans and illustrated the intrinsic conflict between American racist, capitalist, materialistic culture and the cultural virtues found in the classics central to Western civilization. Alarmed by Booker T. Washington's capitulation to white political and economic interests and his policy of pursuing economic goals for blacks instead of civil rights and higher education, Du Bois insisted that African Americans faced mythical Atalanta's fate, losing freedom in the lust for gold. He plotted a different course for a race just emerging from enslavement, insisting that the goal for African Americans should be higher education and the pursuit of civil rights—the rights and privileges of enlightened civilization. According to Du Bois, industrial education might lead to some material wealth, but in the face of racism and an exclusion from *civitas,* any economic project would most likely fail (and leave blacks with nothing material, intellectual, or spiritual). Du Bois insisted that a more useful set of cultural tools lay in classical education, and he argued that the "true college will ever have one goal, not to earn meat, but to know the end and aim of that life which meat nourishes."[26] The shining model for African American education was "the college curriculum that was laid before the Pharoahs, that was taught in the groves by Plato, that formed the *trivium* and *quadrivium*" of learning.[27] Essentially, Du Bois argued for a sort of African American *translatio,* one that would transmit a nurturing, enriching, and empowering African American culture to each successive generation. Like Cooper, Du Bois envisioned a cultural quest for the "hidden beauties of life, and learning the good of living," but he included with that moral inheritance an abiding political philosophy of republican virtue and civil rights.[28] In the Du Boisian *translatio,* a black *cultus, civitas,* and *mos* would survive, regardless of the state of American racial politics or black economic strength.

Scholars from Wheatley to Du Bois found that, ultimately, the classics provided a vision of virtue, education, history, cultural unity, and governance that was not fundamentally clouded by racist suppositions about blackness or dependent upon blacks sacrificing basic civil rights. And, in the face of nineteenth-century attacks on black political and educational rights, that was certainly needed. Questioned in 1868 by the U.S. Senate Committee on Education and Labor about education and work among blacks in Georgia, African American educator Richard R. Wright gave a classically inflected response to questions about the inferiority of blacks.

Arguing that the great religions, the sciences, and alphabetic writing came from "colored races," Wright continued to deploy his contemporary understanding of the classical world:

> Now I take the testimony of those people who know, and who, I feel are capable of instructing me on this point, and I find them saying that the Egyptians were actually woolly-haired negroes. In Humboldt's Cosmos (Vol. 2, p. 531) you will find that testimony, and Humboldt, I presume, is a pretty good authority. The same thing is stated in Herodotus, and in a number of other authors with whom you gentlemen are doubtless familiar. Now, if that is true, the idea that this negro race is inherently inferior, seems to me to be at least a little limping.[29]

Wright made a particular point of suggesting that men of power, influence, education, and virtue, like the critical politicians before him, should be familiar with Humboldt and the classical world. He used the cachet of the classics to question the knowledge of his white interrogators, while he defended black intelligence. As Wright no doubt found, nineteenth-century attempts to abridge black civil rights, especially the right to vote, rested both on the argument that blacks were "ignorant generally, wholly unacquainted with the principles of free Government," and on the pseudoscientific premise that blacks were genetically inferior and unfit for citizenship.[30] According to Alexander Keyssar's *The Right to Vote*, Alabama petitioners to Congress begged not to be put under the "blighting, brutalizing and unnatural dominion of an alien and inferior race."[31] Congressional opponents of the 1869 Wilson Amendment, one of the versions of what would become the Fifteenth Amendment, did not hesitate to use the biological weaponry of eugenics in their arguments. According to Keyssar,

> James Doolittle of Wisconsin maintained that African-Americans were "incompetent to vote" and that Congress should not try to "enforce this natural inequality." James Bayard of Delaware voiced . . . the fear that conferring "political power on an inferior race" would lead both to racial conflict and the destructive commingling of "the negro and the Caucasian." Blacks, according to Bayard, were "more animal" and "indolent" than whites, and any "crossing" of the two races would lead to a degeneration of the "moral nature" and life expectancy of their offspring.[32]

More than a response was required for such virulent attacks: African Americans needed an appropriate intellectual and cultural vaccine. As James D. Anderson notes in *The Education of Blacks in the South*, African

American scholars of the nineteenth century understood that even though classical education was not specifically geared toward overcoming the degradation of American slavery, corrosive discrimination, and economic deprivation, it invalidated the idea of an intrinsic black inferiority. The classics did not suggest that blacks were an "alien and inferior race." Rather, many Africans had been part of the classical world and part of the Roman Empire, as had many of the ancestors of the present-day Americans. Moreover, the classics operated as an analytical tool, providing "a means to understanding the development of the western world and blacks' inherent rights to equality within that world."[33] In classical sources like Herodotus and Tacitus, African Americans had proof of both black historical presence and historical context. Homer, Virgil, Socrates, and Plato provided lessons on virtue, heroism, and the development of the state in *The Iliad*, *The Odyssey*, *The Aeneid*, *The Republic*, and dialogues. Plutarch contributed countless exemplars and historical accounts of Greek and Roman generals, senators, orators, and emperors. Demosthenes, Quintilian, and especially Cicero offered oratorical and rhetorical power in such works as *De Oratore* and *Pro Archia Poeta*. Horace gave practical advice on the good life. Moreover, the ready availability of specifically African classical forebears and the clear indication of an ancient recognition of black humanity helped enable the work of the authors I explore in this volume. African American writers could point to Hannibal of Carthage as an exemplar of military power. St. Augustine of Hippo and St. Cyprian of Carthage offered writings that spectacularly demonstrated historic African Christianity and offered lessons in Christian virtue. Augustine's and Cyprian's foundational church writings (Augustine's *Confessions* and *City of God* as well as Cyprian's *Ad Donatum* and *De Unitate*) also demonstrated Africans' *bona fides* in the history of Christian orthodoxy and their importance to early Christianity. The playwright Terence was a particularly useful example of a slave raised to freedom and fame because of the excellence of his art, which was celebrated from the Renaissance onward, including in the writings of some of the founding fathers, such as John Adams.[34] African Americans could even claim their own imperial dynasty in Septimus Severus and his Afro-Syrian line, who left such monuments as the Arch of Severus and the spectacular Baths of Caracalla for anyone on the gentlemanly Grand Tour to see.

As helpful as this line of writers, exemplars, and forebears appears, it also suggests a troublesome problem for black women scholars and writers. As Walter Ong points out in *The Presence of the Word*, the classical world was a man's world. The works of antiquity were almost exclusively dedicated to the exploits and experiences of men. The basic terms *virtus* and *virilitas* and their relationship to the English "virile" and "virility" suggest how essential maleness is to the classics. Virtue is martial at its core, demonstrated on the literal field of war or on the figurative battlefield of oratory and the contest of words. Even classical philosophy failed to escape martial imagery in addressing virtue.[35] There was no field or forum in which women could attain virtue, and the terms applied to the spoils of literal or figurative warfare were not generally used to describe women. The Greek *kleos*, or glory, is largely gender specific, as are the Latin *virtus* and *virilitas*. Not surprisingly, women were not routinely afforded classical education from the beginning of the *translatio* onward. Moreover, it was not widely assumed that women in general (and certainly not black women) were capable of mastering the classics. A central question for black women scholars in the African American classical tradition was, therefore, how to adapt a discourse, a tradition, and an educational form designed for men, and largely preserved for white men, to their lives as African American women. Furthermore, they eventually had to address the question of whether an unmarried woman, a woman not officially attached to male virtue, can be virtuous.

Shelley P. Haley argues that black women classicists such as Oberlin graduates Frances Jackson Coppin (1865), Anna Julia Cooper (1884), and Mary Church Terrell (1884) all "view[ed] classics as a challenge, a concrete way to disprove the prevailing racist and sexist stereotypes of their times."[36] While they deployed the classics for race-specific purposes, their classical learning also defied the belief that women in general were incapable of higher intellectual pursuits. Mary Helen Washington argues that the classics specifically served such projects as Anna Julia Cooper's *A Voice from the South*. To clear rhetorical space to add her "plea for the *colored girls* of the South" and "counteract the prevailing assumptions about black women as immoral and ignorant, Cooper had to construct a narrator who was aware of the plight of uneducated women but was clearly set apart from them in refinement, intelligence and training."[37] The intellectual imprimatur of classical training created the rhetorical and political space for Cooper's protofeminist project, while both the classics and her Christian mission endowed her with virtue. She was not immediately painted with the same brush of immorality and ignorance with which many of her subjects were, and she could not be easily dislodged from the discourse on women's roles by the usual rhetorical weaponry. With an obvious tie to the tradition of the European *translatio* and a commitment to the oppositional African American classical tradition, Cooper had the rhetorical equipage and intellectual right to comment on the role of black women. In *A Voice from the South*, Cooper responded to the masculine exclusivity of *virtus* in part by lionizing women as the earliest cultivators or transmitters of virtue and culture. Cooper also added women to the list of figures traditionally used to exemplify virtue. Classical, medieval, and Renaissance women emerged as part of the *translatio* and examples of virtue. Cooper deployed the poet Sappho, St. Helena (Emperor Constantine's mother), Joan of Arc, and Cleopatra; and she even located a military exception to the male world of virtue by recalling the legendary Amazon warriors, recasting them as symbols of power and virtue instead of as the emblems of disorder the Greeks imagined.

Relying on this growing multitude of classical sources and exemplars, male and female African American writers developed important themes and strategies for a growing literary tradition. Moreover, following Phillis Wheatley's initial foray into eighteenth-century poetry, black writers continued the synthesis of classics and African American political agendas by contributing classically inflected strategies for cultural development to the educational and political discourse of the nineteenth and twentieth centuries. By initially locating the issue of black interaction with the classical world in the context of Phillis Wheatley's eighteenth-century classical themes, I intend to move beyond the particularly nasty and exhausting controversies surrounding contemporary Afrocentric, apologist, and conservative arguments about the classics that attempt to immediately revise, reassess, or ruthlessly maintain the cartography of classical source material: dates and locations of historical events, the existence and scope of cultural exchanges and influence, and the family tree of languages. Martin Bernal's *Black Athena*, for example, attempts to definitively establish African influence and contributions in the classical world by interrogating racist and orientalist philological management of classical source material. It also institutes an expansive, but problematic, revisionist reading of historical and linguistic evidence underpinning classical translations and the regional historical context from which the works of antiquity emerged. And, as Jacques Berlinerblau has demonstrated in part, Bernal's critics have responded in ways that have uncovered some legitimate errors and simultaneously revealed some suspicious and disturbing qualities about the academic establishment in classical and Near Eastern studies.[38]

Women classicists have argued also that classical philologists have been notoriously resistant to contemporary critical approaches and suspicious of postcolonial, feminist, and otherwise revisionist projects that explicitly offer to illuminate the multiethnic face of Rome or amplify the voices of classical women.[39] Traditionally, questions about who is speaking, for whom, and with what motivations or agendas have not been regularly asked. Moreover, the traditional list of classical writers has been a relatively fixed one, generally male. Contemporary critical methodologies are often odious to philologists, precisely because they have an activist component. They are imagined to contaminate an allegedly pure and apolitical translation of classical works with specific political and social agendas.[40] Despite this resistance, scholars in search of the ethnic and female Other in the classical world have demonstrated that they can confront racist and sexist translations of the eighteenth and nineteenth centuries by attacking conservative and recalcitrant philologists head on. African American classicist Shelley P. Haley demonstrates this in *Feminist Theory and the Classics*, in which she retranslates a passage of the Augustan-age work, *Moretum*. Using a standard Latin lexicon, she effectively deploys a (re)vision of blackness and the female body. Her main target in the critique is pioneering African American classicist Frank Snowden, whose 1970 translation of the passage detailing the African woman, Scybale, is particularly unflattering. Haley uses him as an example of a translator seemingly unaware that his philological practice was infected with European stereotypes and racist stigma. Here is a sample passage, followed by Snowden's translation:

> *Erat unica custos*
> *Afra genus, tota patriam testante figura,*
> *torta comam labroque tumens et fusca colore,*
> *pectore lata iacens mammis, compresior alvo,*
> *cruribus exilis, spatiosa prodiga planta* (*Moretum* 31–35).

> African in race, her whole figure proof of her country—her hair tightly curled, lips thick, color dark, chest broad, breasts pendulous, belly somewhat pinched, legs thin, and feet broad and ample.[41]

Snowden continues to blithely suggest that this description is similar to the modern vision of the Negro in E. A. Hooton's 1946 text *Up From the Ape:* "Narrow heads and wide noses, thick lips and thin legs, protruding jaws and receding chins . . . flat feet and round foreheads, tiny curls and big smiles."[42] Haley's translation offers a fuller and markedly different image:

> She was his only companion,
> African in her race, her whole form a testimony to her country:
> her hair twisted into dreads, her lips full, her color dark, her
> chest broad, her breasts flat, her stomach flat and firm, her legs
> slender, her feet broad and ample.[43]

A More Than Partial Grace

Although Haley pushes her translation to some questionable contemporary frontiers (we may reasonably question the classical legitimacy of dreadlocks), she clearly illustrates how irritatingly insufficient canonical translations can be. Haley also demonstrates that scholars can challenge the philological misreadings or stereotypical representations of black and female classical figures armed only with basic philological tools. Responsibly and accurately recasting the entire, already murky history of the ancient world, as Bernal attempts, is a considerably more intricate, uncertain, and Olympian task.

My argument avoids *Black Athena*'s Scylla and Charybdis of classical source material by focusing on how African Americans conducted their exploration of the classics. I address the issue of philology in terms of how African Americans investigated, applied, or chose to translate classical writings and how their choices influenced black literature and culture. For example, as a result of Phillis Wheatley's early, public success through the classics, African American scholars and leaders were able to recognize a historic rhetorical and political value in the field. Some pointed directly to Wheatley as an important exemplar and racial entrée to classical study. Others followed Wheatley's lead indirectly when they pursued classical literature, philosophy, and oratorical exercise, all hailed by increasing numbers of black scholars as a traditional standard. Still more scholars took up the ancient subjects in an independent recognition of the intrinsic value of classical study. As Alfred E. Moss illustrates in *The American Negro Academy: Voice of the Talented Tenth,* by the end of the nineteenth century, educated African Americans had greatly integrated academic, religious, political, and social activity. Many scholars and clergy had been educated in the classics. These African Americans also made numerous attempts to crystallize their informal associations and focus their collective cultural and political power through formal organizations. The American Negro Academy was founded in 1897, and its weighty cultural and academic mission of using its members' "skills and abilities as a means of both leading and protecting their people and as a weapon to secure equality and destroy racism" rested on the shoulders of a membership significantly involved with the classics.[44] Among the founding members was William Sanders Scarborough, the first black member of the Modern Language Association, a member of the American Philological Association, and the chairman of the Classics Department at Wilberforce University. Scarborough, an accomplished translator and teacher, published his *First Lessons in Greek* in 1891 and saw the text used in a number of black and white institutions, including Yale University.[45] Scarborough regularly lectured before the APA, starting with an 1884 lecture on "The Theory and Function of the Thematic Vowel in the Greek Verb."[46] Ironically, at the 1885 APA meeting, Washington and Lee University Professor James A. Harrison's evening paper "Negro English" was followed by Scarborough's morning lecture, "Fatalism in Homer and Virgil.[47] Remarkably, Scarborough offered an 1892 APA lecture at the notoriously genteel but racially inhospitable University of Virginia in 1894 on the "Chronological Order of Plato's Dialogues."[48]

In addition to Scarborough, founding members Richard R. Wright and William H. Crogman were classmates at Atlanta University and took the lead in organizing the American Negro Academy. Crogman was professor and translator of Greek and Latin at Clark University and later its president. Edward A. Clarke was a Greek and Latin professor and translator at Wilberforce. W. E. B. Du Bois had been a classics professor at Wilberforce and sustained a tremendous investment in the classics. Lewis Baxter Moore was an instructor of Latin and pedagogy at Howard. Professor J. E. Jones taught homiletics and Greek at the Baptist Seminary in Richmond, Virginia. Among these figures, Crogman in particular argued that the academy should be considerably more selective in finding soldiers for the cultural and scholarly army being assembled. His January 1897 letter to founding member John Wesley Cromwell expressed his hope that "that Tom, Dick and Harry *et id omne genus* will not be admitted."[49] In addition to the members of the ANA, the blossoming field of African American colleges and universities consistently deployed the classics as the foundation for their "classical" tracks and even some "normal" school curricula. G. F. Richings's *Evidences of Progress among Colored People* illustrates the vast number of African American scholars and institutions including classics in their institutional curricula and social community. Ultimately, the emphasis on the classics permeated the Talented Tenth. Classicist Michele V. Ronnick points out that Sarah Jane Woodson Early, Countee Cullen, Zora Neale Hurston, Charles Chesnutt, and Paul Robeson all displayed substantial allusive or philological facility with the classics. From established scholars to artists, African Americans studied, translated, and deployed the classics in their cultural and academic work. Phillis Wheatley's training was private study and indirectly from the Cambridge, Boston, and Harvard communities, and Douglass drew his knowledge from *The Columbian Orator*'s use of Cicero and Quintilian, as well as from other sources. Anna Julia Cooper obtained her early training at St. Augustine's College and Oberlin in the classical course reserved for male seminarians. She finished her training with advanced work at Columbia University and a PhD from the Sorbonne. Du Bois was put through his paces at Fisk, Harvard, and

Friedrich Wilhelm University in Berlin. The new vision of the classics we get from these quite traditionally educated writers is filtered through only one "activist" lens: the unquestioned humanity and equality of people of African descent. Through this oculus we are able to see a unique African American experience with the classical world and provide a firmer foundation for contemporary critical evaluations of race as it intersects with classical scholarship.

The relative independence of the black classical tradition also suggests another of its notable characteristics. "Neoclassical" describes the use of classical themes after antiquity, but it also suggests the unchecked degradation and fragmentation of those ideas as well the superficiality arising from the social currency of the classics in the centuries following the Renaissance. While "neoclassical" may accurately describe the mainstream uses of classics in the nineteenth and twentieth centuries, it does not appropriately define the character of African Americans' use of the classics. Especially in the case of African Americans with access to education, classics were a main source from which the columns of culture were quarried.

By the eighteenth century, the classics were a *sign* of erudition and the imprimatur of privilege for white men. But, especially in the rugged Americas, one could rarely be sure of the depth of one's classical training. We know that many men of the British and colonial American upper class, including a number of the founding fathers, had classical training. Thomas Jefferson had Latin grammar school training before attending the College of William and Mary, while George Washington and Patrick Henry employed a social Latin despite their scant educations.[50] But the lack of a centralized or institutionalized American educational system to sustain classical education combined with the fundamental needs of a frontier colony to make classical education impractical for many. Even Benjamin Franklin's 1751 Philadelphia Academy emphasized vocational training more than classical education, and Jefferson too came to favor a less classical foundation for education.[51] In *Democratic Eloquence*, Kenneth Cmiel alerts us to the contentious argument over education and speech in an America where democratic rule began to at least superficially alter class distinctions and require leaders with a less aristocratic language and bearing. The trappings of classical education still held social significance, but the practical substance had begun to give way to decoration.

Since classical elements had been partly reduced to an intellectual calling card of the elite and no longer truly represented absolute command of the "empire of the mind," recommending the classics to African Americans as the essential measure of humanity was, in part, a cynical act. However, the African American response to white civilization's challenge was a sincere acquisition of the classics as both a claim to humanity and a source of cultural renewal. With the exception of Wheatley, African Americans did not adopt the styles of the classical masters. They did look to the classical world for virtues, lessons, and tools that could help them interrogate the contemporary world and build culture. This resonates as something far more substantive and "classical" than what is traditionally called "neoclassical." African Americans of the nineteenth century extended and intensified mainstream voices of civic concern. They critiqued the decline of American civic virtue and the threat to republican ideals posed by the moral decay of slavery, industrialization, and the pursuit of material wealth. Douglass took up the matter in earnest in "What to a Slave is the Fourth of July," when he questioned whether the descendants of the virtuous founding fathers were a degenerate offspring. The decline of American virtue is also a significant theme in *The Souls of Black Folk*. Therefore, with an eye toward this independent and often exceptionally orthodox commitment to the *translatio*, I speak of African American classicism or the classical tradition.

This classical column not only underpinned the critique of white America but also supported both secular and religious discussions of virtue within African American culture. This included endeavors to socially, politically, and economically "uplift" the black population, a project that consumed the latter half of the nineteenth and early twentieth centuries and manifested itself in a number of forms. The uplift message resided in novels of middle-class respectability, Christian piety, and the virtuous comportment of men and women as demonstrated in the works of such writers as Pauline Hopkins, Frances E. W. Harper, and Emma Dunham Kelley. It also surfaced in texts like Anna Julia Cooper's *Voice from the South*. The strain continued in direct educational arguments and thinly veiled eugenic suggestions in Du Bois's *The Souls of Black Folk* and the *Crisis*.

While a contemporary examination of classical influence in African American literature beyond Du Bois would enlarge my project past practical limits, I must still mention the classical strain that continued through the Harlem Renaissance in works such as Nella Larsen's *Quicksand* and Jean Toomer's *Cane*. Moreover, it enjoys a healthy, if modest, life in contemporary investigations of African American intellectual history, the black religious and secular oratorical traditions, literary productions of and about African Americans, and the literary productions of Africans in the Americas. Martin Bernal's *Black Athena* prompts us to interrogate the historical reading of African contributions to the classical world, while

24

Shelley P. Haley's contribution to *Feminist Theory and the Classics* alerts us to the colonialist and imperialist translations of the classics that have enabled and fueled racism and sexism in classical studies. Classical elements are also visible in the work of Rita Dove and Toni Morrison, the criticism of John Shields and Alice Walker, continuing sermonic traditions of African American clergy, and contemporary orators like Cornel West, who envisions the black intellectual tradition as a synthesis of "Socratic doubt and enquiry" with a "Jerusalem-based" spiritual and liberation tradition.[52]

Practical limitations aside, evaluating classical influence on African American literature between Phillis Wheatley and W. E. B. Du Bois offers rich possibilities and rewards. Scholars such as John Shields and Henry Louis Gates Jr. have successfully rehabilitated Phillis Wheatley and her classically inflected poetry. David Blight, Gregory Lampe, and Deborah McDowell have shed some light on Frederick Douglass's oratorical roots and masculinized rhetoric, and John Blassingame masterfully chronicled the numerous and revealing classical references by and about Douglass in *The Frederick Douglass Papers.* One very notable and recent exception to the silence on black classical activity is classicist Patrice Rankine's *Ulysses in Black* (2008). Rankine explores the broad influence of the Ulysses myth and its particular resonance in a select group of later black writers, including Ralph Ellison, and explicitly attempts to identify connections between black studies and classical study. However, the roots and influence in broader African American literary history are not fully articulated. Despite this recent scholarly activity along the shoreline of the classics, the main currents of classical use in African American literature remain uncharted. Neither black nor white scholars have given sustained and comprehensive attention to the presence of classical elements in black thought and writing, even though the investment in the classics is unmistakable in a writer as widely known and esteemed as Du Bois and clearly visible in a major text like *The Souls of Black Folk.* The presence of the classics in African American literary and social history should not register as surprising, given the global scope of the classical tradition and its presence in canonical American literature. Ultimately, with so many writers and primary texts infused with classical elements, scholars of literature, history, education, and classics could reasonably expect to undertake no less ambitious a project than fully reconsidering the entire *corpus* of African American literature.

CHAPTER ONE
THE TROJAN HORSE

PHILLIS WHEATLEY

In 1772, at the commencement of a revolutionary season, a youthful Phillis Wheatley sought to publish a collection of classically pastoral, epic, religious, and elegiac poetry. Revolutionary in her own right, the young poet disrupted established assumptions about black literary authorship in eighteenth-century America and challenged broader European and colonial doubts about African humanity and intelligence by producing a book of verse. So unique was her accomplishment that the primary obstacle to its publication was neither expense nor the quality of the verse but the suspicion of authorial fraud. Consequently, a historic authentication of Wheatley and her work and a subsequent public attestation by eighteen of Boston's most prominent white citizens launched the fledgling poet's career.

The list of examiners comprised some of the brightest stars in the New England firmament, including the governor and lieutenant governor of Massachusetts and John Hancock. This remarkable event has been reduced mostly to a historical footnote, but such scholars as Henry Louis Gates Jr., Karla Holloway, and John C. Shields have fixed on the authentication as a historic test of African American intelligence and humanity. Kirsten Wilcox has proposed that this interrogation of Wheatley's talent was a series of parlor performances before royalists and future rebels. Gates suggests that interrogators pressed Wheatley to reveal the depth of her knowledge in the classical themes she deployed in her poetry.[1] The nature and depth of Wheatley's education have been at issue since the colonial era. We know that it included "astronomy, some ancient and modern geography, a little ancient history, a fair knowledge of the Bible, and a thoroughly appreciative acquaintance with the most important Latin classics, especially the works of Terence and Ovid."[2] This is consistent with the strong neoclassical stream that more generally saturated the intellectual environment of early America. Increasingly, scholars have noted the breadth of that stream in literary sensibility, religious expressions, the political philosophy of the founding fathers, and fine art such as the sculpture of Horatio Greenough.[3]

Although many writers have repeated the standard account of Wheatley's education, few have substantially explored its historical and intellectual significance. William Robinson and John Shields have been the most thorough commentators, illustrating how carelessly we have read Wheatley. With these exceptions, scholars have not added significant detail to the early account of Wheatley's education. They have left unanswered the question of what value a slave could find in even a thoughtful use of the classics. Why would a young African slave address antiquity and invite its presence in her New World existence? Contemporary scholars have failed to consider her work in light of what a classical education has traditionally been said to produce: ingrained virtue, a strong sense of individual worth and power, rhetorical armament, martial inclinations, literary celebrations of warfare, and political and literary ambition.[4] The historic underestimation of Wheatley's classical education has led scholars to misunderstand her importance and misjudge the depth of her poetry. To accurately evaluate Wheatley's work, reveal the power of her poetics, and understand her contribution to the African American literary tradition, scholars must reexamine her intellectual training.

The Spanish, French, and British established European-styled schools in their colonial territories, and religious instruction was common. The British also transplanted the ideas of apprenticeship programs, elementary schools, Latin grammar schools, and colleges. Unlike the British home system, which included private schools catering largely to the wealthy and nobles, American schools included charity- and church-supported education.

Despite their accessibility or more philanthropic goals, these schools still pursued firmly traditional ends. If they did not specifically continue the intellectual and spiritual battle with "The Old Deluder Satan," the general "educational aims of colonial schools and teachers represented stability, tradition, authority, discipline and preordained value systems that were marks of realism and classical idealism," ideas linked to Plato and

Aristotle.[5] Traditional class distinctions were also far from irrelevant to colonial American education. Educational opportunities gradually increased in the colonies, but class position routinely governed who received what sort of instruction. Latin grammar schools and theological institutions were the domain of the upper classes, while for a long period lower classes were fortunate to achieve modest literacy in rudimentary schools. Harvard College's early class rolls and final rankings were even organized by social class, making some kind of grade inflation an old American tradition.[6] Vocational schools that catered to the commercial middle class—Benjamin Franklin's Philadelphia Academy, for example—became the educational middle ground. Some free schools did develop in the South, but many southerners, like Virginia's Governor Sir William Berkeley were deeply suspicious of public education: "I thank God, *that there are no free schools or printing,* and I hope we shall not have them these hundred years, for *learning* has brought disobedience, and heresy, and sects into the world, and *printing* has divulged them, and libels against the best government."[7]

Limited southern educational options included tutorial schools, which routinely made teachers of willing Anglican ministers and Scottish indentured servants who were trained in Latin and Greek. Limitations aside, these schools served as preparatory academies for British colleges and private schools. Thomas Jefferson finished Latin grammar school training under the Reverend William Maury before attending the College of William and Mary, the only colonial southern college. James Madison, George Rogers Clark, and others of note finished Donald Robertson's boarding school near Dunkirk, Virginia, as well, but as a rule such academies were rare in the region.[8] This was largely because of underpopulation in the South and the restriction of education to the upper classes. With classical education largely geared toward producing a super-literate male ruling elite, women found it extremely difficult to obtain more than a rudimentary education. One rare exception to women's scholarly exclusion was Theodosia Burr, whose father, Aaron, insisted that she learn Latin and Greek and maintained lofty expectations for her progress. Generally, women were dependent upon the indulgence of parents or the material advantage that afforded them access to one of the few schools educating women.

The lack of institutionalized or centralized education in colonial American society and the traditional restrictions on access to the classics limited access to civic life and discourse. Given these limitations, it was already improbable that a woman would acquire extensive knowledge of the classics or produce literature utilizing that knowledge at a complex level. The odds of finding a colonial slave in that position were infinitely long. In

"Of Natural Characters" (1753) and *Observations of the Beautiful and Sublime* (1764), Enlightenment philosophers such as David Hume and Immanuel Kant raised serious doubts about Africans' humanity and intelligence.[9] Yet, despite the developing philosophical criticisms of black intelligence, some religious groups took steps to educate slaves. Colonial religious groups made early and brief attempts in the seventeenth century. As early as 1704, the French Huguenot Elias Neau and the Society for the Propagation of the Gospel in Foreign Parts ran a New York school for blacks and Native Americans.[10] However, such formal arrangements were exceedingly rare and made rarer still by the complications of educating slaves raised for slaveholders. According to popular logic, slaves could be ruined by education by being given knowledge and ambition that made them difficult to subjugate. Education for slaves and free blacks depended largely on indulgent slaveholders and unique local circumstances. Southern states passed a series of laws throughout the antebellum 1800s that prohibited the education of slaves, and after these legislative actions, educating slaves required a significant act of defiance. Even in New England, where the politics and economics of servitude created slaves of ambiguous "quasi-person" status, one could find in Phillis Wheatley's lifetime no record of black students among the eight hundred studying in Boston's two Latin schools and three vocational schools.[11] Nonetheless, such exceptional religious, political, and educational circumstances as were necessary existed to produce the classically educated Phillis Wheatley.

Wheatley's first classical cues might well have come from her own name. Scholars have long presumed that Wheatley was named after the *Phillis*, the ship that transported her to Boston, but Wheatley's name also has classical mythological resonance as the name (Phyllis) of the abandoned, suicidal lover of Theseus's son Demophon.[12] The name was a regular feature of the classical poetry of writers like Horace. It reemerged in neoclassical poetry and frequently appeared as an English Christian name by the sixteenth century. Phyllis (Greek for "foliage") was a natural name for the pastoral genre and a recurrent name in English poetry preceding Wheatley's era. For instance, Thomas Lodge (1556–1625) wrote two poems to a beloved "Phillis."[13] Wheatley's more formal classical education gave her a rare opportunity to flourish in the era's cultural nursery for cultivating white, masculine intellect and virtue, and we reasonably gather that Wheatley's education followed at least in part the standards of the exclusively male Latin grammar schools of the time. This educational model emphasized reading classical epics, histories, verse, and philosophy and translating between vernaculars and Latin (often called "making Latin").

The curricula of the grammar schools, such as Boston Latin School, included Cato, Ovid, Cicero, Virgil, Horace, Terence, Homer, Isocrates, and Xenophon. Where Wheatley's makeshift education under the Wheatley children ended, there is good reason to believe somewhat more substantive Latin instruction began for her to attain the oft-quoted "thoroughly appreciative acquaintance" with major Latin classics. Beyond the more generic classical references, Wheatley made a significant investment in the work of Horace, Homer, Virgil, Terence, and Ovid. In *Poems*, John Wheatley's letter to the publisher stated that Phillis Wheatley's English and biblical skills came from study in his household, and her writing came of her own curiosity. Of her Latin learning, he wrote that she "has a great Inclination to learn the Latin Tongue, and has made some progress in it." Both Shields and Robinson have pointed to the case of a local Boston instructor in Latin and French, a Mr. Delile, as a possible tutor. As the 1773 publication emerged in Boston in 1774, the *Boston Weekly News Letter* included the rapturous Delile's request that four celebratory lines of Latin verse appear beneath the frontispiece of the book of poems.[14]

Scholars agree more uniformly that Wheatley was frequently in contact with learned men and women from Boston and its environs. These learned people, either through curiosity or genuine interest, took part in her education. Clergymen, politicians, and tutors visiting the Wheatley household routinely brought gifts of classical and contemporary texts to the young prodigy—an attention from the literati noted by early biographer Margaretta Odell.[15] In her 1784 elegy on the death of clergyman Samuel Cooper, Wheatley admits that he was a literary mentor, "A Friend sincere, whose mild indulgent grace / Encourag'd oft, and oft approv'd her lays." Cooper was the pastor of the Brattle Street Church and the minister who baptized Wheatley into the Old South Church in 1771. Clergyman Mather Byles is roundly argued to have been a significant mentor, since Wheatley sought out his and Cooper's advice on her verses.

There is evidence that Wheatley had good access to libraries that contained significant holdings in the classics and other literature. Reverend Thomas Prince left his renowned library to Wheatley's Old South Church upon his death in 1758. With the Wheatley family's staunch Congregationalist standing, Phillis Wheatley's exceptional circumstances, and her attendance at the church and baptism into the Old South Church's congregation in 1771, it is reasonable to suppose that she had access to its rich library holdings. The more than two thousand volumes that survived a fire at the church now reside in the Boston Public Library and include works by Horace, among them his *Odes*, as well as works by Homer, Virgil,

Ovid, Lucan, Caesar, Suetonius, Plutarch, Dante, Milton, Pope, and a host of early American religious writers. This library alone would have been enough to form the classical, literary, religious, and historical foundations for Wheatley's work. Interestingly enough, the only local libraries that rivaled Thomas Prince's in size and depth were those collected by the Reverend Mather Byles and Governor Thomas Hutchinson, who were both signatories to the attestation of Wheatley's authorship. In 1765, a mob, enraged over Hutchinson's intention to enforce the Stamp Act and the Sugar Act, ransacked his Garden Court Street mansion in Boston, stole his furniture and other household goods, and made off with his books and papers.[16] Wheatley, who arrived in 1761, learned English by 1763, and penned her first known (but nonextant) writing in 1765, when she was twelve, was unlikely to have used his library. Although Hutchinson examined Wheatley and knew the Wheatley family well, there is no indication in what remains of Hutchinson's diaries and papers that he met Wheatley when she was between the ages of seven and twelve.

Mather Byles knew Thomas Prince well (Prince officiated at Byles's marriage to Anna Noyes) and shared the title of most learned man in the colonies with him. Byles had inherited the bulk of the Mather family library (now held and largely uncatalogued by the American Antiquarian Society), which contained between fifteeen hundred and three thousand volumes in Cotton Mather's lifetime and included extensive holdings in the classics and theology. Cotton Mather, who had a formidable command of the classics, added significant numbers of classical texts to the library.[17] Byles shared Cotton Mather's familiarity with the classics, and like Mather, who reportedly gave away as many as a thousand books in one year, Byles made a habit of lending books. He was also an active figure in Boston, a notorious wit, practical joker, and satirist, which makes his love of Alexander Pope unsurprising. Byles wrote to Pope in 1727 and after expressing his great love for *The Rape of the Lock* and other works, asked for "the favour of a few lines." Although he had nothing to say to Byles, Pope did send him a copy of his *Odyssey* when it was published. Byles and Wheatley also shared an interest in Pope's classical translations. There is a record of Byles lending the book, so the text did circulate in Boston.[18] Both Wheatley's critics and supporters have pointed to Pope as one of her models, and his translations of Homer were among her favorite reading. While Wheatley was in England, the Earl of Dartmouth gave her money to buy books, and she bought her own copy of the 1766 Pope translation of *The Odyssey* and the nine-volume set of Pope's *Works*.[19] Wheatley knew Cooper, Byles, and Hutchinson personally, and they are almost certainly among the visitors to whom Odell refers. Most of the influential men who signed the attestation knew each other well or were related to each other by blood or marriage, so they represented a remarkable block of support for Wheatley. Many had literary and theological interests that overlapped with Wheatley's. Any one of these men could have been among Wheatley's continuing supporters, and some are recorded as mentors of varying importance and the subjects of Wheatley's poems and letters.

Whatever Wheatley's connections to the Boston and Harvard elites, the attempt to publish her poems in America failed for racial and political reasons. Perhaps because few believed that a slave wrote verse, she was unable to secure sufficient numbers of subscribers. Equally problematic was the fact that the angry population of Boston in the early 1770s was in no mood for genteel poetry, especially from a slave.[20] In England, Wheatley's reception was much warmer, and her poems were significantly more successful. While her audience there was relatively small, it was still significantly larger and more classically and religiously educated than the one in Boston; and it was familiar with the structure, course, and expectations of a classical education, including the virtuoso performance. Moreover, Wheatley's English readers were immensely curious about her African presence and performance in such an elite intellectual and social space. This was due in part to successful marketing of the prodigy and the poems. Kirsten Wilcox suggests that Wheatley's real agency in *Poems* ended with writing the verses. She was forced to arrange or to see *Poems* arranged to mute her political and social opinions. Wilcox's reading downplays significant facts about Wheatley's assessment of the publishing environment and her own political and social position, for there is evidence that Wheatley was not only a gifted poet but also reasonably astute in the legal and financial ways of the world. In her October 18, 1773, letter to David Wooster, penned from Boston, she indicates that she has secured her freedom. According to the letter, her manumission is in part "at the desire of [her] friends in England. She notes that the legal "[i]nstrument is drawn, so as to secure me and my property from the hands of Executvs. [sic] [,] administrators, &c. of my master, and secure whatsoever should be given me as my Own."[21] More interesting is that Wheatley's newfound freedom influenced the strategy for marketing her poems. She seems to have had both full knowledge of the plan for marketing and publication and a role and stake in its creation and execution:

> I beg . . . that you use your interest with the Gentlemen and Ladies of
> your acquaintance to subscribe also, for the more subscribers there are,

Phillis Wheatley

the more it will be for my advantage as I am to have half the Sale of the Books. This I am the more solicitous for, as I am now upon my own footing and whatever I get by this is entirely mine, & it is the Chief I have to depend upon. I must also request you would desire the Printers in New Haven, not to reprint that Book, as it will be a great hurt to me, preventing any further Benefit that I might receive from the Sale of my Copies from England. The price is 2/6d Bound or 2/Sterling Sewed. If any should be so ungenerous as to reprint them the genuine Copy may be known, for it is sign'd in my own handwriting.[22]

Wheatley seemed interested in the basic economics of publication. She was personally invested in the marketing of the poems, because she would gain half of the proceeds. Moreover, she was worried about protecting herself against unauthorized copies of her book and unabashedly concerned about the impact bootleg copies would have on her profits. Wheatley's nineteen-year-old entrepreneurial acumen is remarkable, but it also suggests both that the same marketing and profit concerns would have affected which poems composed the London edition and that Wheatley is likely to have influenced those decisions. She certainly would have had reason to choose the poems carefully, if she had any inkling that marketability, high sales, fame, and public pressure might help pay for her freedom, as they seem to have done. William Robinson notes that as the publication emerged, John Andrews, a Boston merchant and early admirer of Wheatley's work, wrote to William Barrell in Philadelphia, "[A]fter so long a time have at last got Phillis' poems in print. . . . These don't seem to be near all her productions. She's an artful jade I believe and intends to have the benefit of another volume. "[23] Andrews's comments point to a shrewd and ambitious poet, not the puppet imagined by Wilcox.

Wilcox attributes much of the agency in the marketing process to Susannah Wheatley, who doubtless orchestrated Wheatley's meetings with Bostonians and some of the London notables. She points out that Susannah Wheatley's marketing strategy for Phillis Wheatley and the poems manipulates her access to the noble and literate public to create publicity and a literary name for Wheatley. Selina Hastings, Countess of Huntingdon, arranged for Wheatley to have a series of audiences with significant British nobles and citizens. Wheatley's letter to Wooster reveals that she met with the Earl of Dartmouth, Alderman Kirkman, Lord Lincoln, a Dr. Solander, Lady Cavendish, Lady Carteret-Webb, rhetoric professor Dr. Thomas Gibbons, Israel Mauduit, Benjamin Franklin, and Grenville Sharp, among others. Sharp also escorted her on a tour of London.[24] In both Boston and London, the "series of drawing-room performances before Susanna Wheatley's ever widening circle of influential friends" and the meetings with British nobles put her name in conversation among the male literary elite and gave "her name meaning in the context of print."[25] The Boston publication proposal did not showcase Wheatley's classically influenced work. Rather, it included her more provincial work, regularly referring to local Boston and New England affairs. Wilcox aptly notes that the book of poems offered to the English publisher reflects the kind of literary expectations that a refined, educated audience maintains for an author attempting to make a name for himself (or herself): "London publication brought with it certain belletristic expectations that affected both what Wheatley printed there and how her literary authority would be construed."[26]

As true as this might be, the changes reflected more than superficially belletristic concerns or attempts to mute Wheatley's opinions. Wilcox's position assumes that replacing poems that addressed local Boston issues with classically influenced verse (for example, "Niobe" and "To Maecenas") silenced opinion, as though the classics are merely window dressing— politically neutral and socially unthreatening. Intellectual history does not support that assumption. The classically influenced poems projected Wheatley's voice beyond provincial Boston into a broader Western discursive space regularly employing the classics artistically and politically and known by various European elites. This might well have amplified Wheatley's positions. Moreover, the Wooster letter suggests that Susannah Wheatley was not the exclusive force behind the creation of the marketable Phillis Wheatley. At the very least, the poet was capable of comprehending the salient issues involved in advancing her fortunes, and Wheatley's words suggest that she took action to safeguard her interests. Moreover, Susannah Wheatley was not in London with Phillis Wheatley as she made the Grand Tour of private parlors and tourist sights. Neither was Selina Hastings in London to guide Wheatley. She arranged for her to meet with English nobles and subjects, but whatever advances Wheatley made by diplomacy, charm, wit, guile, and intelligent conversation were her own.

Wheatley did travel with her owners' son, Nathaniel, who has remained largely voiceless in the history of Wheatley and *Poems*. He was so voiceless that Benjamin Franklin expressed annoyance that during his visit with Phillis Wheatley, Nathaniel did not come downstairs to greet him.[27] Some have suggested that the question of Wheatley's liberty was so uncertain in the aftermath of the Somerset legal decision that Nathaniel was not comfortable meeting with visitors in England. Wheatley's reputation and open discussions of slavery in England might well have exposed him to difficult inquiries about her. In any case, there is no historical evidence that he could be considered a guiding voice or moving force behind Wheatley's accomplishments.

The marketing for the text, including Wheatley's 1773 London tour, specifically presents Wheatley as a practitioner in the line of literary tradition, offering a poetic display unusual for one who is a black slave. Wheatley emerges as the "practicing poet concerned with the display of her belletristic mastery and engaged with other kinds of literary and artistic productions" that Wilcox suggests.[28] But she also emerges as a visibly ambitious and self-aware black poet—one who would not only perfect her craft but also use its conventions and its audience to her own ends. Bell, the London publisher, broadcasts Wheatley's access to elites and unexpected knowledge as part of her allure, allowing subscribers to share in her access to noble and learned classes. He is quick to note that Wheatley "wrote upon a variety of interesting subjects, and in a stile [sic] rather to have been expected from those who, to a native genius, have had the happiness of a liberal education."[29] Moreover, she had ascended to heights where it was possible for her to have been "conversed with by many of the principal Nobility and Gentry of this country, who have been signally distinguished for their learning and abilities."[30] Like the Roman playwright Terence, whom she celebrates in "To Maecenas," Wheatley displays a mastery of the higher arts beyond her station and is called to sit at the side of the nobles as a result. When *Poems* is shipped back to the colonies, it has the imprimatur of not only Boston Brahmin but also of the nobles of the British Empire and the tradition of classical education, a combination that wins her manumission.

Wheatley's historic penetration into the realm of the literary and social elite was not roundly hailed as a success. Generations of critics from Thomas Jefferson to Amiri Baraka and William Robinson have suggested not only that Wheatley's poetry was unremarkable but also that the verse itself reveals a stunning insensitivity to the horrors of slavery. Wheatley's tenuous position as a slave and her dependence on the support of white patrons limited her ability to criticize American slavery directly. Moreover, the marketing of her poetry "deliberately directed readers away from the interpretive frame supplied by her servitude."[31] Nevertheless, these critics fail to offer even a modest evaluation of the classical resonance of her work or the nature of her classical literary exercises. They certainly do not consider how effective her use of classical source material was in helping her transgress boundaries of race, class, or gender, or the importance of her success in undermining Enlightenment notions of black inferiority in the colonial and European intellectual establishment.

We could evaluate Wheatley's success in terms of the critical responses she generated that challenged the prevailing claims and assumption of Enlightenment thought. Wheatley's poetry was provocative enough to prompt a number of responses during her time, many focusing on both her intelligence and her enslavement. As early as 1772, Thomas Wooldridge wrote to the Earl of Dartmouth, in a tone of profound surprise, of his encounter with Phillis Wheatley:

> While in Boston, I heard of a very Extraordinary female Slave, who had made some verses on our mutually deceased friend [Rev. George Whitefield]; I visited her Mistress, and found by conversing with the African, that she was no Imposter; I asked if she could write on any Subject; she said Yes: we had just heard of your Lordships Appointment; I gave her your name, which she was acquainted with. She immediately wrote a rough Copy of the inclosed [sic] address & letter, which I promised to convey or deliver.[32]

Benjamin Rush included in his 1773 commentary on slaveholding a reference to Wheatley, whose "singular genius and accomplishments are such as not only to do honor to her sex, but to human nature."[33] Anonymous notices of the poems appeared in London publications. The *Gentleman's Magazine and Historical Chronicle* reprinted "On Recollection" and expressed outrage that Wheatley remained a slave, according to the attestation:

> Youth, innocence, and piety, united with genius, have not yet been able to restore her to the condition and character with which she was invested by the Great Author of her being. So powerful is custom in rendering the heart insensible to the rights of nature, and the claim of excellence![34]

The *London Monthly Review* refused to see Wheatley's poems as proof of broader African intelligence and something other than their "deadness of invention." However, it did see her unique accomplishment as noteworthy, arguing that she has "written many good lines, and now and then one of superior character has dropped from her pen; as in the Epistle to Maecenas." Moreover, the writers, irritated that her singular genius had not earned her freedom and clearly seeing a chance for an intercontinental rhetorical jab at the rebellious colonists, complained that

> [w]e are much concerned to find that this ingenious young woman is yet a slave. The people of Boston boast themselves chiefly on their principles

of liberty. One such act as the purchase of her freedom, would, in our opinion, have done more honour than hanging a thousand trees with ribbons and emblems.[35]

George Washington responded to Wheatley's letter and celebratory poem in frequently reprinted letters to his private secretary and to Wheatley herself. Struggling to find an appropriate form of address for an African woman slave who had provided "new evidence of [her] genius," Washington settled on a compromise between the uncomfortably genteel and the awkwardly racist: "Miss Phillis."[36] The secretary of the French Legation to the United States, François Marge de Barbe-Marbois (for whom Jefferson prepared his *Notes on the State of Virginia*), Ignatius Sancho, Thomas Clarkson (the English abolitionist), Richard Nisbet, and many others in the eighteenth century commented favorably on Wheatley's poetry and used it as evidence of reason and sentiment in Africans. It is notable that two years after Wheatley's death, Benjamin Franklin, as the president of the nation's first abolitionist society, penned his "Address to the Publick," which argued for the publicly funded emancipation and education of slaves. Thomas Jefferson, ignoring what should have appeared to a classically educated gentleman and polymath of the era as competent uses of the classics and the tenets of Christian faith, dismissed her work. Faced with reports of the black prodigy, Jefferson offered these comments among others in a larger discussion of the physical and moral inferiority of blacks in *Notes on the State of Virginia:*

> Misery is often the parent of the most affecting touches in poetry. Among the blacks is misery enough, God knows, but no poetry. . . . Religion, indeed, has produced a Phillis Whately [*sic*]; but it could not produce a poet. The compositions published under her name are below the dignity of criticism.[37]

Jefferson found Wheatley inconvenient, since as part of his classical whitewashing, he needed to claim the classics, sentience, and access to civic culture for the white American population. In *Notes on the State of Virginia*, Jefferson addresses what he considered necessary postrevolutionary changes to British legal statutes that were "relative merely to that form of government, or inculcating principles inconsistent with republicanism."[38] Among the amendments that later proved unsatisfactory was a provision for the manumission, public education "*according to their geniuses*," and removal of blacks to an unspecified place of colonization outside the existing colonies. According to Jefferson, the incorporation of blacks into the state as equals was prohibited by "[d]eep-rooted prejudices entertained by the whites; ten thousand recollections, by the blacks, of the injuries they have sustained; new provocations," and "the very real distinctions which nature has made." All of this Jefferson feared would lead to "extermination of one or the other race." The distinctions of nature in Africans were for Jefferson wide ranging, from lack of beauty to bad odor, but they included deficient mental capacity.[39] After dismissing both Wheatley and Olaudah Equiano, Jefferson insisted that, in the allegedly "more deplorable" conditions of Roman slavery, genius still emerged: "Epictetus, Terence, and Phaedrus, were slaves. But they were of the race of whites. It is not their condition then, but nature, which has produced the distinction."[40] Most troubling in Jefferson's claim that "nature" had determined differences between the races is that contemporary theories of biological race had not developed by his era and would not appear until the late nineteenth and twentieth centuries. Therefore, Jefferson's claims on nature were in the ancient Greek sense, that two things differing in nature are essentially different. An African could not be equal to a European, for he was not of the same nature or form that constituted mankind. Following this line of reasoning, Jefferson claimed Terence, obviously, as white, as well as all the slaves ancient Homer chronicled as exceptional men.

Wheatley found a capable defender in Voltaire, who entered the discussion of African American intelligence and countered claims like Jefferson's —that Africans were incompetent to engage in the higher intellectual activities:

> Genius, which is rare everywhere, can be found in all parts of the earth. Fontenelle was wrong to say that there would never be poets among Negroes; there is presently a Negro woman who writes very good English verse (She is named Phillis Wheatley and died in 1787. She lived in Boston, but her works were published in England under the title Poems on Various Subjects Religious and Moral, London, 1773). The Empress of Russia, who is diametrically different from Negro women, writes in prose as well as her chamberlain in verse, and both astonish me equally.[41]

Other, more recent writers of the nineteenth and twentieth centuries followed Voltaire and have disagreed with Jefferson, notably Evert and George Duyckinck, who were careful enough to recognize and comment on Wheatley's original translation of Ovid when evaluating her work.[42] But, like Jefferson, a number of twentieth-century black and white critics have claimed that Wheatley's poetry is mediocre. Richard Wright and Amiri Baraka dismissed her as a mere neoclassical mimic. Vernon Loggins weakly echoed the Duyckinck brothers with a lukewarm acknowledgment that "Niobe in Distress" was one of her better productions. Such critics as William H. Robinson and Julian Mason treated Wheatley more evenhandedly, even if they did not fully apprehend or concede the depth of her work. None gave significant attention to her classical references. Mason insisted that Wheatley was "not really a poet in the classical Greek sense of maker, seer, creator," an assessment ironically corresponding to Jefferson's distinction of "race" in the classical Greek sense.[43] He labeled her as more mere craftsman than poet and the maker of too many common elegies. Mason's surpassingly superficial comment offers a stark vision of the poet as maker, seer, and creator in a narrow sense and reduces the elegy to mere and common craft. This, of course, ignores the place of the elegy in literary history. But Mason's narrowness shares something in common with Jefferson's racial hoarding of Epictetus, Phaedrus, and Terence. Jefferson and Mason both had a stake in narrowly construing the boundaries of intellect, scholarly excellence, racial achievement, and the literary canon. Jefferson could not abide an African whose intelligence invalidated his tenuous defense of slavery. Admission to the African American literary pantheon has long depended on the visible commitment of an author—quite frequently male—to protest against slavery, racism, and its continuing effects. Moreover, that protest usually has to be constructed with a limited and easily recognizable literary toolbox, of which the classics and New England Congregationalist training are not a part.

Although many scholars from Jefferson onward have failed to recognize value in Wheatley's use of classical literature, figures, and themes, it is clear from history that classical education animates imagination, intellectual adventure, and both political and poetic ambition. We cannot dismiss poetic ambition in Wheatley, since it is a primary concern of poets from the classical era through the Renaissance and well beyond Wheatley's time. Poetic virtue, classical or Christian, has always competed with or been accompanied by poetic ambition. Renaissance versifiers from Petrarch to Milton openly contended with that tension throughout their works. For Wheatley to use the classics as a tool to enhance her name while she publicly meditated on virtue would not be unnatural for a poet. Moreover, the classics support poetic ambition and adventure in a way that Christianity does not. Piety and humility provide Wheatley with a specific aura of Christian virtue and a shield against excessive criticism, but Christianity does not emphasize pride, ambition, and ostentatious display as virtues. The classics arm her with intellectual weapons and opportunities both to mount ambitious ventures and to openly display her prowess. The lament of the London-based *Gentleman's Magazine and Historical Chronicle* that youth, innocence, and piety, combined with genius, had not freed her highlights the key qualities that empowered Wheatley. As she later pointed out, the influence of her friends in England hastened her freedom. Poetic ambition would also not be necessarily overridden by the marketing interference of a slaveholder such as Susannah Wheatley. Phillis Wheatley's access to classical education produced something entirely new in the nation, a black intervention in Anglo-American literature and thought not again matched until the middle of the nineteenth century. The wonder and power of this "millennial, if not quite apocalyptic force" of a moving African American pen could not have escaped Wheatley's sensibilities.[44] Wheatley's letters to David Wooster and Samson Occum, John Andrews's epistolary assessment of her as "an artful jade," and her facility in charming and using British and American elites indicate that beyond the notoriety her classical applications gained, her study authorized her to live and write in a fashion unimaginable to black slaves and most whites. It also fired her ambition to approach and transgress intellectual, social, and political boundaries of gender and race.

If classical education held such promise to fructify ambition, produce poetic power, and create an alternative to traditional constraints of race and gender, then we should expect to see significant uses of classical texts, authors, and themes in Wheatley's poetry. The amount of classical influence visible in Wheatley's poetry is certainly prodigious. Of the thirty-nine poems in the 1773 volume, at least twenty-five (64 percent) contain classical allusions, ranging from the mere mention of the Muses to Wheatley's translation of Ovid's myth of Niobe from the *Metamorphoses*. As Shields notes, some form of the word "muse" appears at least forty-one times in Wheatley's poems.[45] "To Maecenas," "Goliath of Gath," and "Niobe in Distress" immediately reveal their debt to major textual antecedents and such writers as Homer, Virgil, Horace, Terence, and Ovid, but other poems possess classical connections also. The body of poems that address classical deities and creatures, including Neptune, Phoebus (Phoebus Apollo), Tithonus, Aurora, the Nereids, and the Muses, is substantial: "To the University of Cambridge in New-England," "Thoughts on the Works of Providence," "To a Lady on the Death of Three Relations," "To a Clergyman on the Death of His Lady," "An Hymn to the Morning," "An Hymn to the Evening," "Isaiah LXIII. 1–8," "On Recollection," "On Imagination," "To Captain H——d of the 65th Regiment," "To a Lady on Her Coming to North America. . . ," "To a Lady on Her Remarkable Preservation. . . . ,"

"On the Death of Dr. Samuel Marshall. 1771," and "To a Gentleman on His Voyage to Great Britain...." Wheatley's classical references are also visible in "An Hymn to Humanity," "To ... a Child of the Name Avis...," "Ode to Neptune," "To S. M. a Young African Painter, on Seeing His Works," "To His Honour the Lieutenant-Governor, on the Death of His Lady. March 24, 1773," "A Farewell to America," "A Rebus," and "An Answer to the Rebus." When we add to this list not only classically inflected work but also the poems in which Wheatley neoclassically personifies Christian themes or admirable qualities such as virtue, chastity, goodness, and greatness, then virtually all her poems reflect direct or indirect classical influence.

Wheatley's poems do a great deal to challenge, complicate, and transgress the normal boundaries and requirements of her eighteenth-century world. "To Maecenas" presents us with both tradition and transgression. The title immediately signals Wheatley's knowledge of Horace, recalling Horace's poetic conversations with his patron, Maecenas, which he initiated with his first ode. One can reasonably conjecture that among her gift texts, loans, and library volumes, Wheatley encountered Horace. Horace was a standard of eighteenth-century classical training, from Boston Latin School through Harvard College. He was seen as both a source of classical virtue that made good contemporary morality and as a font of practical advice for living.[46] He would have been one of the classical authors foremost in the minds of those who attested to Wheatley's poetic skill. Almost all of the men who signed the attestation in *Poems* were Harvard graduates who would have shared specific texts as the foundation for their educations: the grammar school authors in further depth, plus Sallust, Caesar, and the Greek New Testament.[47] Horace provides an example of how realizing what texts were available to Wheatley gives us insight into what encouragements she might have had and what classical influences we should expect to find in her poetry.

Shields has adeptly alerted us to what other scholars have missed routinely, the Horatian connections to "To Maecenas" and "Ode to Neptune." He does not report the interesting fact that two of Horace's *Odes* actually include references to "Phyllis."[48] It is doubtful that either link would have eluded Byles, Hutchinson, and others of Wheatley's admirers steeped in Horatian texts. Nor would they have failed to entice, intrigue, and even encourage Wheatley. Reading the *Odes*, Wheatley would have encountered "To Xanthias" (II.4) and might have been inspired by Horace's account of the virtuous and beautiful slave, "Phyllis":

> *Nescias an te generum beati*
> *Phyllidis flauae decorent parentes;*

regium certe genus et penatis
maeret iniquos.
Crede non illam tibi de scelesta
plebe delectam, neque sic fidelem,
sic lucro auersam potuisse nasci
matre pudenda.

How do you know that your blond Phyllis isn't
Descended from highborn parents? Why, she must
Have come down from *kings!* Surely your Phyllis grieves

Because the unkind gods have brought her down
From what she was to this her present station.
You can be sure of this: a person like her,

So without guile or greed, so faithful and selfless,
Must be the worthy child of a worthy mother.[49]

Among other things, the poem diminishes the shame of slavery and celebrates ancient Phyllis's attributes of guileless grace, lack of greed, faithfulness, and selflessness—traits celebrated in Wheatley's own poetry. Wheatley might also have found in the *Odes* an equally intriguing poem, the remarkably named "To Phyllis." In this poem (IV.11), Horace seeks to entice a young "Phyllis" away from her beloved and into his arms. Horace's signature on "To Maecenas" also introduces an element of transgression. Gaius Maecenas—minor poet, soldier, and the trusted personal and political agent of Caesar Augustus[50]—was the legendary protector of Horace and Virgil, who was famously victimized by Roman power. Horace's opening lines (I.1) celebrate Maecenas's aid as he navigated the dangerous political waters of a Roman republic running rapidly toward empire:

Maecenas atavis edite regibus,
O et praesidium et dulce decus meum,
sunt quos curriculo pulverem Olympicum
collegisse iuvat metaque fervidis
evitata rotis palmaque nobilis
terrarum dominos evehit ad deos;
. . . Me doctarum hederae praemia frontium
dis miscent superis, me gelidum nemus
Nympharumque leves cum Satyris chori
Secernunt populo, si neque tibias

Phillis Wheatley

Euterpe cohibit nec Polyhymnia
Lesboum refugit tendere barbiton.
Quodsi me lyricis vatibus inseres,
sublimi feriam sidera vertice.

Maecenas, you, descended from many kings,
O you who are my stay and my delight,
There is the man whose glory it is to be
So famous even the gods have heard the story
Of how his chariot raised the Olympic dust,
The dazzling wheel makes the smoking turn;
. . . What links me to the gods is that I study
To wear the ivy wreath that poets wear.
The cool sequestered grove in which I play
For nymphs and satyrs dancing to my music
Is where I am set apart from other men—
Unless the muse Euterpe takes back the flute.
Or Polyhymnia untunes the lyre.
But if *you* say I am truly among the poets,
Then my exalted head will knock against the stars.[51]

Like Horace, Wheatley gives her Maecenas the mantle of nobility, but hers is the prince of poets. What inspiration and talents the great poets possess, Maecenas's "equal genius shares / In softer language, and diviner airs." Wheatley also hungers after the same literary aid and renown that Horace desires from the Muses and Maecenas, but Wheatley seems not to expect a crown of laurels, despite her talent or success. The ivy crown of learning Horace desires is curling round Maecenas's head in Wheatley's poetry, and as a slave, she must obtain by guile and theft what should be hers by merit:

Thy virtues, great *Maecenas!* shall be sung
in praise of him, from whom those virtues sprung:
While blooming wreaths around thy temples spread.
I'll snatch a laurel from thine honour'd head,
While you indulgent smile upon the deed.

Wheatley makes a number of additions to the Horatian ode to Maecenas, among them a pastoral flourish, a demonstration of her familiarity with classical epics, an assessment of her own position as an enslaved poet, and a very pointed request for protection.

Shields observed that as early as George Puttenham's 1598 *Arte of English Poesie* we see that the pastoral, which Wheatley employs, often serves as a political device and a sufficient mask for far deeper concerns than singing shepherds or woodland gods. Also, African American writers have long employed signifying to infuse otherwise innocuous words, allusions, or conventions with multiple politically and culturally charged meanings. In this context, the Augustan convention of *recusatio*, a feigned inadequacy to the epic deployed in non-epic poetry, fails to capture the full range of Wheatley's African American poetics in "To Maecenas." In the poem, Wheatley couches her ambitious pursuit of literary laurels in pastoral terms, suggesting some of the imagery from Virgil's *Eclogues*. Wheatley casts Maecenas "beneath the myrtle shade," reclining in some poetic Elysium when she interrupts him. She expresses awe at the work of the ancients, with lightning streaking the skies and thunder that "shakes the heav'nly plains." This respectful admiration within the pastoral setting is predictable and safe—the humble servant singing in the glade. But, after walking into the poetic countryside to seek Maecenas's aid, Wheatley goes on to declare her intent to rival the ancients and sing of virtues, even with her alleged "grov'ling mind" and "less happy state." Wheatley goes a bit further to declare her intent to "snatch" a laurel while Maecenas and her readers look with "indulgent smil[ing] upon the deed." Immediately after boldly declaring her intent to commit the grand theft of poetic voice and literary power, Wheatley resumes her humble pose and closes with a pastoral image of flowing streams, reposing naiads, celestial bodies, and her own grateful appreciation of Maecenas's aid. Wheatley uses the pastoral mode both to court her audience's support and to brashly stake out poetic territory among the great poets of virtue and political commentary. The verse continues with Wheatley's description of the features of Homeric verse and his potent abilities:

> While *Homer* paints lo! circumfus'd in air,
> Celestial Gods in mortal forms appear;
> Swift as they move hear each recess rebound,
> Heav'n quakes, earth trembles, and the shores resound.

Beyond celebrating Homer's ability to animate the word, she also indicates her deep emotional reaction to his poignant scenes. Relegating the poem to mere *recusatio* would make Wheatley's choice of scenes meaningless, but to a black slave writing under physical threat, with the threat of censorship, and with ambitions for access, critique, and possibly liberty to mask and manage, the choice of authors, scenes, characters, and exploits can reasonably be expected to have more intent, meaning, and political value. The scene she selects from Homer is fascinating, since it is an episode involving masking and assumed identity. Wheatley celebrates the famously tragic episode in Book XVI of *The Iliad*, when Patroclus, eager to join the battle and rally the Greeks, asks to fight using Achilles's armor. Patroclus takes the field only to be slain by Hector, who ignobly mocks him as he delivers a death blow, strips him of Achilles's armor, and attempts to decapitate the body and feed it to the Trojan dogs. Patroclus, eloquent even in death, cuts Hector with his final poetic lines. Wheatley earnestly desires to join the literary fray, donning as much of the armor of the ancients as she can, assuming the role of a poet, and braving the dangers of her position as a slave to offer as many eloquent lines as possible.

In the midst of her praise, Wheatley indicates the special power over the human soul she sees in the array of gods and legendary epics, a power so great in the case of the ancients that even in her era the world still drew its ideals and virtues from the poetic tales of both immortals and mortal struggles. She also reveals that she desires to count herself among the great poets and acquire their power. She understands that if "[she] could rival thine [Homer's] and Virgil's page / Or claim the Muses with the Mantuan Sage" the "same beauties" and "same ardors" in her own soul might well enable her song to "in bolder notes arise" and "all [her] numbers pleasingly surprise."[52] Mirroring the talents of the ancients, Wheatley might protect herself with the skill of Maecenas or have the same educative cultural influence that Homer or Virgil achieved. She might exert that influence on the Africans who constituted "all [her] numbers" or generate the pathos in her white readers that Homer produced in his "gentler strains." We must ask if Wheatley masks her desires and hides her ambitions for freedom, abolition, or Christian equality in a homeric Trojan Horse of classicism and eighteenth-century verse. At the pinnacle of artistic possibility would have been her ability to produce poetry that would contain the eternal, redeeming virtues generations of scholars could imbibe and use to redeem a less than virtuous world. One can easily argue that *The Iliad*, *The Odyssey*, and *The Aeneid* at the very least have served precisely this end in the West, as have many of the subsequent texts directly descended from the ancient epics.

Beyond the triumphant epics of antiquity, the authors to whom Wheatley alludes also provide ways of critiquing or complaining safely, lessons that Wheatley learned well. The poets Maecenas protected, like Virgil, often suffered under the Romans. Virgil was not a beloved babe snatched from his home; tradition indicates that he had his ancestral home confiscated by Caesar Augustus. Within that tradition, his *Aeneid* is a work partly designed to regain his home by favor and flattery. Further, as scholars like Allen Mandelbaum have pointed out, despite the early critical tendency to glorify *The Aeneid,* the epic that canonized the ascension story of the empire also contains an undercurrent of pain and complaint. We might see "the ache and the bite of *The Aeneid,* ever less—as we read more— a triumphant poem in the praise of the *imperium* of Caesar Augustus." Mandelbaum notes that "for me, it was chiefly through Ungaretti that I saw in *The Aeneid* the underground of denial—by consciousness and long- ing—of the total claims of the state and history: the persistence in the mind of what is not there, as a measure of the present."[53] What exists neither in Wheatley's "To Maecenas" nor in any of her other poems is unbridled enthusiasm for British or American civilization. Nor does she embrace the earthly church with abandon. Just as Virgil refuses to fully and uncriti- cally embrace the Roman *imperium,* Wheatley retains the position of an instructor in virtue, a lecturer on piety and Christianity, and a messenger of recollection. She periodically reminds her readers that she is "less happy," "an Ethiop," and in need of defense. Wheatley does seem quite painfully aware in "To Maecenas" that she is in a precarious position as an Afri- can slave. She ends her celebration of Horatian and Virgilian poetic power, with a plaintive assessment of her predicament: "But here I sit, and mourn a grov'ling mind / That fain would mount and ride upon the wind." She later laments that Maecenas is free to burn with the "immortal fire" of poetry, but "less happy" Wheatley "cannot raise the song, / the fault'ing music dies upon my tongue." In the final two stanzas, Wheatley praises Maecenas and implores him to "Hear me propitious, and defend my lays."

Wheatley does not ask for protection merely on the merits of her own verse or the basis of her desire to rival the ancients. She offers an example of another African who has given similar evidence of literary talent and proven a boon to his patron. The "less happy" poet reminds the reader and Maecenas that the Roman dramatist Terence "all the choir inspir'd, / His soul replenish'd, and his bosom fir'd." She makes a special note beneath the poem that "He was an *African* by birth," and continues to ask,

> But say, ye, Muses why this partial grace
> To one alone of *Afric*'s sable race;
> From age to age transmitting thus his name
> With the first glory in the rolls of fame?

At least two remarkable developments emerge from this passage. Wheatley is the first African American writer to deploy European heraldic elements to describe and valorize African heritage. Sable, the heraldic tincture of constancy and grief, defines Africanity as fidelity, *gravitas,* and mourning—characteristics visible in *Poems.* Furthermore, Wheatley seizes on and underscores Terence's African birth in Carthage to create a classical literary forebear of African descent.

Suetonius Tranquillus, whose works were present in the Thomas Prince library, details Publius Terentius Afer's life in the fragmentary work *De Viris Illustribus.* In the section *De Poetis,* he provides a biography of Terence (*De Vita Terenti*). The singular evidence of his race comes from Suetonius' description of Terence: *"Fuisse dicitur mediocri statura, gracili corpore, colore fusco"* ("He is said to have been of moderate height, slender, and of dark complexion").[54] *Fusco* is variously translated as "swarthy," "dark," or "dusky." Betty Radice, for instance, translating Terence's plays, describes him as "slight, dark, and good looking."[55] Wheatley clearly intends to claim Terence as African by geography and "by birth." Enlightenment scholars regularly claimed North African Romans as white; Kant and Hume left no room for blacks of antiquity. Jefferson argued that unlike Roman slaves, blacks gave no evidence of intelligence, and he included Terence as an example.

Wheatley would have gotten her information about Terence from Suetonius or a mentor who was familiar with Suetonius, and she chose to make an issue of *colore fusco.* Her reasons for doing so are understandable. Terence was one of the most widely studied and respected classical writers during the colonial period. In *Classica Americana,* Meyer Reinhold points out that Terence was the only dramatist of antiquity read with any regularity in America. John Adams lectured his son John Quincy to read Terence because "Terence [was] remarkable, for good morals, good Taste, and good Latin." He also recommended him to his grandchildren in 1816, saying that "[t]he six plays of Terence are valuable [for a number of reasons, including] the Maxims and Proverbs, which are now and have been for 2000 years common place expressions of all civilized nations."[56] But the issue of *colore fusco* is not easily settled. Terence was not widely imagined to be African in the sense that colonial slaves were African, and letters and commentary from Jefferson to Adams and beyond declare or assume that Terence was African by geographic birth but not by race. Even twentieth-century translators have often gone out of their way to dismiss the possibility of racial Africanity (part of a larger problem of scholars in classics and other disciplines that is dealt with in excruciating and controversial detail in Martin Bernal's *Black Athena* and responding texts).[57] But African American writer Joel Augustus Rogers, who produced two volumes on historical figures of African ancestry, made a philological decision to translate in favor of blackness. He argued that he called Terence a Negro for the following reasons: he was from Africa; he was a slave; and Suetonius (A.D. 98–138) describes his color as "fusco" (dusky, very dark). Had he been, say of a mulatto color, Suetonius might have said he was "subfusco." For instance, Ammianus, fourth century historian, says of the Egyptians of this time, "Homines autem Aegyptii plerique *subfusculi* sunt et atrati" (The men of Egypt are, as a rule, somewhat swarthy and dark of complexion).

Terence was also called 'Afer.' The *Century Dictionary* says of this, "The ordinary terms for African Negro or Africans were Ethiops and Afer." *L'Encyclopedie Franciaise* [*sic*] says similarly, "The Latin, Afer, which was both ethnic and geographical, sufficed at a time when Africa was little known to designate its inhabitants by that characteristic which was almost typical of them and most apparent, namely color." (vol. VII, I, 46, 6)[58]

With her Latin training, it appears that Wheatley made a specific philological choice in translating *colore fusco,* perhaps for the reasons Rogers noted. Wheatley was certainly aware of Terence's influence in her world as a model of moral excellence, a font of good sense, and a source of excellent language. As a fellow African, Terence also released Wheatley from the bonds of uniqueness, served as a racial literary ancestor, and provided a racial link to the classical world. Houston A. Baker Jr. insists that these links between authors, the "sound of precursors," orient African American writers and allow them to comment thoughtfully on issues of race.[59] By penning Terence into her eighteenth-century discourse, Wheatley connected herself to a world beyond American slaveholding culture and found an experience that gave new meaning to her own. In Terence, she could identify a fellow African slave who employed the pen (or stylus) to defy the limitations of slavery and gain his freedom.

Wheatley peers out thoughtfully from the frontispiece of *Poems on Various Subjects Religious and Moral,* in Scipio Moorhead's now famous portrait of her. One might imagine her reviewing the classical texts of her study, searching, remembering those ancient myths and great figures whose words and lessons can alternately veil and amplify her critical appraisals of eighteenth-century America and give power to the verse and letters she sends abroad. In acknowledging Moorhead in *Poems,* Wheatley also demonstrates the presence of another black prodigy and more evidence of black intelligence. However, the verses to Scipio Moorhead must operate as more than just an admiring and instructive poem, for Scipio (Publius Cornelius Scipio Aemilianus Africanus Numantinus, or Scipio

Africanus the Younger) is also the name of one of Terence's patrons and friends, the general responsible for ending the Punic Wars and conquering Terence's Carthage.[60] It cannot have escaped Wheatley's mind that the destroyer of Carthage and adopted grandson of the initial conqueror of Roman Africa would become the patron and friend of a Carthaginian slave. If Terence was, as has been popularly held, born in Carthage after the end of the Second Punic War, then selecting him was a consummate signifying gesture—the invocation of the incisive, insightful comedies (which regularly included precocious and provocative slave characters) of an African antecedent native to the empire that nearly dethroned Rome and changed human history. The studious Wheatley must have been aware of the biographical similarities between Terence's position and her own. Handsome young Terence, dressed in rags, so impressed the comic master, Caecilius Statius that he was called to sit at dinner with the honored guests—a beginning similar to Wheatley's that would have resonated both with the poet and many of her learned readers.[61]

Like a contemporary Terence, Horace, or Virgil, Wheatley created within her book of poems the role of Maecenas, her indulgent patron. However, she cultivated fruitful acquaintances and relationships with any number of powerful men and women who could freely imagine themselves as Maecenas. In addition to creating a desirable identity for her readers, one that could encourage even greater support from them, she could also thank her actual, indulgent patron in the process. The question of who Wheatley's Maecenas was remains unanswered, but it was the aegis of the many patrons or mentors who collectively played Maecenas that made it possible for Wheatley to address audiences otherwise outside her reach. The imprimatur of the Harvard alumni who signed her attestation provided the authorization for her to lecture the scholars who were the target of "To the Students at the University of Cambridge in New England." Wheatley seems fully invested in following the ancients' example by exhorting the students to virtue. The poem is third in the volume behind "On Virtue," continuing the theme of piety, morality, and practical advice that Horace and Virgil help her establish in "To Maecenas." She immediately identifies her own motivation as the "intrinsic ardor that prompts her to write." The belletristic flourish of the Muses descending to assist her verse quickly reinforces her authority to speak. Their appearance, however, also precedes her admission that she is from the "land of errors and *Egyptian* gloom." The first lines take in hand the practical problem of trying to address virtue as an African woman slave by pitting the mythological convention of enlightened literacy against the myth of African benightedness. The intrinsic virtue that inspires the poet, the high literary convention of the Muses, and the Christian redemption of the "Father of mercy" disrupt the powerful social conventions of race, slavery, and gender that might otherwise silence her. What emerges from the Trojan Horse of piety, humility, and classical convention is a lecture. When she turns her verse to the students, the lesson she offers is one of preserving virtue against sin. In making her case, she argues that, like blooming plants, they are vulnerable to destruction:

> Ye blooming plants of human race divine,
> An *Ethiop* tells you 'tis your greatest foe;
> Its transient sweetness turns to endless pain,
> And an immense perdition sinks the soul.

Wheatley lectures as a pious preacher of Christian virtue and a classically educated poet with the spiritual and intellectual authority to instruct the students, many of whom are barely older than she. She also overtly signals her race with one of the terms routinely used to identify black Africans in the classical world. "Ethiop" leaves no doubt that an African is the author and lecturer in the poem. Moreover, by making reference to "Egyptian gloom," Wheatley accomplishes two things. First, she affirms her Christian orthodoxy by embracing her redemption and separation from pagan Africa. However, by illustrating this point with Egypt, she also subtly reminds readers of Egyptian civilization's place in the classical world. This ranges from the writings of Herodotus to Memnon's place in *The Iliad* to the Pharoahs, stretching to Ptolemaic Cleopatra, whose ethnic identity has been a subject of debate among scholars.[62] As she does with Terence, Wheatley writes Africa back into the classical world with her poetic reference to Egypt.

"Ethiop" also carries with it a resonance beyond the Roman identification with Africanity. It also recalls Psalm 68:31, "Princes shall come out of Egypt; *Ethiopia* shall soon stretch out her hands unto God." With Ethiopian and Egyptian references, she also seems to foreshadow nineteenth-century African American Ethiopianist and Egyptological movements within black nationalism. Encompassing the period from the middle of the nineteenth century until the Harlem Renaissance, black nationalism included both intellectual and spiritual ideological prongs. Cultural, intellectual, and political uplift of both the African American and African populations (often imagined under the aegis of a great hero or great man) formed one. The spiritual foundations rested on the prophecy of Psalm 68:31, and the message was amplified, interpreted, and directed by the various denominations of the powerful African American church. African colonization enterprises, "civilization" projects, and even dreams of an Imperial Africa sprang from the movement, most notably in Marcus Garvey but also from figures such as Alexander Crummell and W. E. B. Du Bois.

Wilson J. Moses describes the black nationalist impulse embedded in these movements as both separatist and resting on the idea that European civilization was more advanced.[63] However, Phillis Wheatley deploys African Terence, the Egyptians, and "Ethiop" to establish blacks' place in the ancient and Christian worlds as equals. Blacks have a place in the ancient world, and Wheatley employs that vehicle to move toward both Africans' restoration in history and personal advantage. She rhetorically and incredulously inquires why Terence would be the only talented African. Her affinity for elite Western culture does suggest her familiarity and comfort with European civilization. Her Christian rejection of pagan Africa also suggests strong affiliation with the culture. However, her continual positioning of herself as a lecturer, teacher, and pious critic of the culture militates against concluding that she believed in white cultural superiority. In "Students," for instance, Wheatley refers to the students' advantages as mere "privileges" that they should improve and refine while they existed. There is no evidence in her poetry that she desired anything other than to recover Africans' place in the free world—certainly not separation.

While the aegis and influence of a collective Maecenas gave Wheatley freedom to write, there is reason to believe that Wheatley signaled to an individual who had given her special aid. At least a portion of the title of Maecenas must go to Mather Byles, who shared with Maecenas a short poetic career. Byles's library was available for Wheatley, and his influence is visible in a number of features Wheatley's poetry shares with his *Poems on Several Occasions*. Both Byles and Wheatley included hymns ("An Hymn to the Morning" and "An Hymn to the Evening"), poems recognizing artists ("To PICTORIO, on the Sight of his Pictures" and "To S. M. a Young African Painter"), and a treatment of the biblical David and Goliath story ("Goliath's Defeat" and "Goliath of Gath"). Moreover, Byles joined the classical Muse and the Christian Heaven in his elegy "To a Friend on the Death of a Relative," a conscious combination that Wheatley makes throughout her poetry. John Shields notes this syncretism of classical and Christian themes in Wheatley, and this relationship between the Christian and classical is visible in Wheatley's version of the Goliath story. While Byles's "Goliath's Defeat" follows the biblical story closely, only once deploying the term "Knight," Wheatley's account reflects classical influence throughout. "Goliath of Gath" recalls the epic and violent accounts of battles in the works of Homer and Virgil, even as it addresses the classic Christian story. Like Homer and Virgil, her first lines call to the gods and the Muses and announce her tale:

> Ye martial powers, and all ye tuneful Nine,
> Inspire my song, and aid my high design.
> The dreadful scenes and toils of war I write,
> The ardent warriors and the fields of fight:
> You best remember, and you best can sing
> The acts of heroes to the vocal string:
> Resume the lays with which your sacred lyre
> Did then the poet and the sage inspire.

Immediately, there is a remarkable combination of Christian and classical pagan elements. Wheatley's invocation to martial powers suggests not only Mars but also the host of Olympians who participated in wars of both *The Iliad* and *The Aeneid*. Next, Wheatley arrays the forces of Israel and Philistia, following Virgil's and Homer's pattern of metaphorically describing soldiers' ranks as natural forces. She spends considerable time giving detailed descriptions of the combatants' deportment and armor, again matching Homer and Virgil. Wheatley emphasizes elements described in the "Essay on Homer's Battels" that precedes Book V of Pope's translation of the *lliad*, Wheatley's working volume. Pope focuses on Homer's attention to the variety of deaths of the warriors, the record of the "Age, Office, Profession, Nation, Family &c." of the characters and the attention to characters' clothing "and the Singularity of his Armor."[64]

There is reason to characterize this biblical tale as an epic foray, an *epyllion* or short epic, by the ambitious poet.[65] While both the Bible and Byles record Goliath's insults to the Israelites, Wheatley's boastful, insulting Goliath echoes the mocking Numanus Remulus of Virgil's *Aeneid*, Book IX 576–604. Ascanius (Iülus), the young son of Aeneas, who has not been involved in battle, hears Numanus' taunts against the Trojans and their gods.

> . . . For Numanus
> had stalked before the front lines, shouting things
> both worthy and unworthy to be spoken . . .
> and boasting as he swaggered, bellowing:
> "Twice conquered Phrygians, are you not ashamed
> to be hemmed in again by siege and ramparts,

to set up walls between yourselves and death?
Look, those who want to take our brides by battle!
What god brought you to Italy or what
insanity?"[66]

Numanus continues, bellowing that the Trojans dress like women (with "robes of saffron," and bonnets with ribbons) and adore dancing and laziness. Finally, he advises the Trojans to "leave arms to men, you have had enough of swords." Goliath sounds little different, swaggering and mocking.

> The monster stalks, the terror of the field.
> From Gath he sprung, Goliath was his name . . .
> He strode along, and shook the ample field,
> While Phoebus blazed refulgent on his shield.
> Through Jacob's race a chilling horror ran,
> When thus the huge enormous chief began:
> "Say, what the cause, that in this proud array,
> You set your battle in the face of day?
> One hero find in all your vaunting train,
> Then see who loses, and who wins the plain.
> For he who wins, in triumph may demand
> Perpetual service from the vanquished land:
> Your armies I defy, your force despise,
> By far inferior in Philistia's eyes:
> Produce a man and let us try the fight,
> Decide the contest, and the victor's right."

Like *The Aeneid's* Ascanius, who lets fly an arrow through Numanus's head, the young David chides the mocking enemy and then brings down the great warrior, after pious words, with his first martial projectile. With Goliath's shattered brain and severed head, among other images, Wheatley also matches the regular gore of classical battle scenes:

> Just o'er the brows the well-aimed stone descends;
> It pierced the skull, and shattered all the brain—
> Prone on his face he tumbled to the plain.
> Goliath's fall no smaller terror yields,
> Than riving thunder in aerial fields:
> The soul still lingered in its loved abode,
> Till conquering David o'er the giant strode:

Goliath's sword then laid its master dead,
And from the body hewed the ghastly head. . . .

Pope's translation of Homer's *Iliad* Book XVI provides a good comparison: "Next *Erymas* was doom'd his Fate to feel, / His open'd Mouth receiv'd the *Cretan* Steel: / Beneath the Brain the Point, a Passage tore, / Crash'd through thin Bones, and drown'd the Teeth in Gore: / His Mouth, His Eyes, his Nostrils pour a Flood; / He sobs his Soul out in the Gush of Blood."[67] The combination of Christian and classical elements is especially vivid in the battle scenes echoing the epics of Homer and Virgil, and we can identify lines of poetic influence from the classical writers and Pope to Wheatley. However, looking at *Poems on Various Subjects Religious and Moral* as a conversation between Wheatley and Byles, like that between Horace and Maecenas in the *Odes*, further illustrates how the classics can unlock Wheatley's poetics.[68]

Thirty-two years ago, John C. Shields provocatively argued that Wheatley's frequent references to the sun and solar progress—Phoebus Apollo, Aurora, "round the central sun," and so on—signified a remnant memory of African solar worship mixed with Islam.[69] Furthermore, he argued that Wheatley was affected by her enslavement to the point that her circular, solar references were evidence of both memories of syncretized African animist and Islamic religious practices and the Jungian Mandala Archetype. Margaretta Odell's biography reports that Wheatley recalled her "mother poured out water before the sun at his rising." We can reasonably accept with Shields that the Islam of the Arab invaders, who conquered and converted remnant Roman African civilization at the tip of a scimitar, blended with a local animist and fetishist tradition in some cases. However, with only a reference to a single, fragmentary memory, we can yet resist the temptation to rest the entire discussion on these tantalizing conclusions about what Wheatley's memory and circular themes mean for her work and psychological state.

Shields is unconvinced that Christian sources for this circular or solar imagery provide sufficient explanation. However, Christian relationships between the Son and the sun, to which Shields alluded, are not the only historic Christian uses of solar or circular imagery. From the early preoccupation with the music of the spheres, concentric ranks of angels, and the celestial order to the Dantesque circles of *Inferno*, *Purgatorio*, and *Paradiso*, or even the Renaissance fascination with the ovoid form as a representation of perfection (we should remember the prevalence of egg-shapes in Renaissance painting), circular and spherical forms have been central to Christianity and Western literary representations of order. Moreover, a Newtonian sense of clockwork organization in Nature, created by a mechanistic God, permeated the Age of Reason, in which Wheatley lived and wrote. Ordered reason and virtue were thought to unlock the secrets of the rational Creation. Among the era's neoclassical literary creations, solar imagery and the representative gods of sun, moon, dawn, and dusk were commonplace enough to be subjects of the wit of the day. Richard Steele's *Tattler* No. 106 for December 13, 1709, includes a humorous report of a poet desiring to go into business selling his literary wares. Among his offerings are "about fifty similes that were never yet applied, besides three-and-twenty descriptions of the sun rising, that might be of great use to an epic poet."[70] Wheatley's Maecenas, Mather Byles, also includes a substantial amount of solar imagery in his *Poems on Several Occasions.* For instance, Byles's "To the Memory of a young Commander slain in a Battle with the Indians 1724" includes references to dawn, radiant streams from the sun, and shining stars. His "To PICTORIO, on the Sight of his Pictures" contains these lines: "An hundred Journies now the Earth has run, / In annual Circles, round the central Sun." His poem on "Eternity" includes the line "Before this System own'd the central Sun; / Or Earth its Race about its orbit run." These lines are strikingly similar to Wheatley's verse in "On Recollection": "Now eighteen years their destined course have run / In fast succession round the central sun." Wheatley is surrounded by a culture obsessed with neoclassical balance and reason, Christian conventions of godly order, and a Western tradition in which the sun-centered universe long endured as a metaphorical analog of Christian order radiating out from the Creator God.

If we are inclined to apply contemporary knowledge and intelligently speculate about Wheatley's cultural influences or psychological state as a slave, then the Jungian explanation of Wheatley's psychological state may bear reconsidering. Time has rendered the Jungian Mandala Archetype a somewhat Byzantine explanation for attributes that can also be elegantly explained by sound contemporary psychiatric trauma theory. The mandala form is essentially the basic form for the entire Jungian model of the psyche, with the Mandala Archetype (see accompanying illustration) as the emerging archetype for the psyche in need of wholeness and healing.[71]

The Jungian mandala and Mandala Archetype, as appealing as they are to some contemporary spiritual and cross-cultural projects, exist primarily as theory, with little practical application to contemporary psychiatric analysis or therapy.[72] Its most significant remnant is the widely known Myers-Briggs Type Indicator personality test. Both the Freudian and Jungian projects deconstruct the rigid rationality and order of the Enlighten-

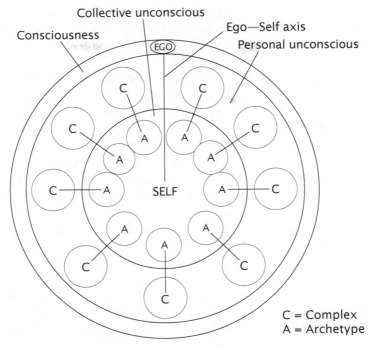

Collective unconscious

Consciousness

Ego—Self axis

Personal unconscious

C = Complex
A = Archetype

Jungian psychic apparatus: self, archetypes, complexes, collective and personal unconscious, consciousness, and the ego. From STEVENS, ANTHONY; *ON JUNG; UPDATED EDITION WITH A REPLY TO JUNG'S CRITICS.* © 1990, 1999 Anthony Stevens, pub. in U.S. and Canada by Princeton Univ. Press. Reprinted by permission of Princeton University Press.

ment, exposing the influence of the subconscious mind and demonstrating that Man is not even master of his own house, much less a rational evaluator of an ordered universe. However, descendants of Freudian analysis, contemporary neuropsychological or psychobiological approaches, give more practical analyses of the function of the subconscious and the effects of environment, biology, and experience on the conscious mind.

In assessing the psychological landscape of Wheatley's poetry, we might take into account Margaretta Odell's report that Phillis Wheatley suffered from a kind of short-term memory loss. The Wheatleys had to place a candle or lamp nearby so that she could record her inspirations whenever they emerged, even in the middle of the night, because she could not retain her immediate thoughts for extended periods. This inability could indicate the aftermath of significant trauma, which a seven-year-old child experiencing the Middle Passage no doubt endured. Contemporary psychiatry clearly articulates a series of neuropsychological responses to various kinds of trauma, and a range of memory impairments is among them.[73] Contemporary researchers have found that early childhood trauma has marked, cumulative, and often permanent effects on the developing brain. Using magnetic resonance imaging (MRI) and electroencephalography (EEG) tests, researchers have determined that childhood trauma does visible damage to the hippocampus, one of the primary verbal and emotional memory centers in the brain, as well as to the amygdala and other brain structures. Moreover, it has an impact on the production and dispersal of neurotransmitters. In short, childhood trauma can open a Pandora's box of problems, not the least of which can be various forms of memory impairment in registration, retention, and recall.[74]

Wheatley's literary productions and artfulness in the social and business arenas related to publication give ample evidence of her reason, intelligence, and talent. However, it strains reason to imagine that Wheatley emerged from the Middle Passage unscarred, given what we now know of trauma. It is extremely likely that some remnant memories of her African life, abduction, and Middle Passage captivity haunted Wheatley, and her poetry offers evidence of the experience. The poem to the Earl of Dartmouth strongly suggests that her "love of Freedom sprung" from the trauma of being "a babe belov'd" who was "seiz'd" from her father. Although the pain is projected onto the parents in the poem, Wheatley intimates that the true horror of the event can be understood by those with "feeling hearts alone." In fact, Wheatley's poetry is filled with a pattern equally recognizable and resonant as the circular, that of memory. She uses the classics to explore memory, especially as it relates to virtue. In "On Recollection" Wheatley extends earlier themes of virtue, piety, and reflection on sin and judgment. In this poem she describes memory's role as a repository of reasons to resist the temptation to do evil and illustrates memory's capacity to terrify evildoers as they meet judgment. Wheatley calls to Mnemosyne, often called the mother of the Muses, to initiate the verse. Then she calls on all nine Muses to animate this particular verse and inspire their "vent'rous *Afric* in her great design."

> MNEME begin. Inspire, ye sacred nine,
> Your vent'rous *Afric* in her great design.
> *Mneme,* immortal pow'r, I trace thy spring:
> Assist my strains, while I thy glories sing:
> The acts of long departed years, by thee

Recover'd, in due order rang'd we see:
Thy pow'r the long-forgotten calls from night,
That sweetly plays before the *fancy's flight.*

As an adventurous African, Wheatley seems intent upon revealing acts of the past, enshrined in memory and played in dreams vivid enough to rival modern cinema. Wheatley points to the "pomp of images" given in dreams to the "high-raptur'd poet," and the "heav'nly phantom" that "paints the action done / by ev'ry tribe beneath the rolling sun."

Carla Williard argues that Wheatley was used as a tool by colonial audiences who needed evidence for their own social or political projects— patriot publications, royalist papers, and even race theorists like Thomas Jefferson. Moreover, since none of these audiences had the positive qualities Wheatley attributed to them, she created ideal "fictive audiences" and created speaking heroes, such as Wooster and Whitefield (who owned slaves), to act out the qualities she desired.[75] Although Williard credits Wheatley with attempting a "heroic entrapment" of audiences, she does not contend with the classical models Wheatley deploys who are not part of her audience. Nor does she address poems such as "Goliath of Gath," "Niobe in Distress," and "On Recollection," which address pride and obduracy in the face of God's will, the obvious presence of evil, or recollection that recalls and illuminates good and evil. The revelatory and echoing capacity of recollection is double-edged, "sweeter than music to the ravish'd ear, / Sweeter than Maro's entertaining strains," but "dreaded by the race, / Who scorn her warnings and despise her grace." Again we can note an intriguing commentary on race and power visible within Wheatley's verse. Mneme is portrayed as a combination of memory and conscience, both classical in origin and vaguely Christian in application. Recollection seems to be the forceful arm of conscience, the internal moral compass that "enthron'd within the human breast, / Has vice condemn'd, and ev'ry virtue blest." Moreover, the voice of memory is sweeter even than that of Virgil's lauded verse when great and virtuous acts are recalled, but for the race guilty of vice and crime, memory's voice is dreaded and "her awful hand a cup of wormwood bears." The "race / Who scorns her warnings and despise her grace" could apply broadly to the world of sinners, in which Wheatley includes herself:

Now eighteen years their destin'd course have run,
In fast succession round the central sun.
How did the follies of that period pass
Unnotic'd, but behold them writ in brass!

Phillis Wheatley

In Recollection see them fresh return,
And sure 'tis mine to be ashamed, and mourn.

However, Wheatley clearly repents of her folly and appeals to Virtue to guide her. That still leaves the unrepentant and unnamed race "the wretch who dar'd the vengeance of the skies," to face the final reward of evil and perish as they recall their sins and repent too late. Emerging from Wheatley's apparent Trojan Horse of pious introspection may be an attack on white slaveholders, who make excellent candidates for this unnamed group. The race arrogantly and unrepentantly engaged in evil is, like Goliath, unmoved by conscience, God's word, or recollection. Moreover, they may be unresponsive to the virtuous words of Wheatley, the high-raptur'd poet armed with Mneme's revelation of history, guided by Virtue, and capable of "chang[ing] the scene." Their fate is clear, unless they turn to virtue as the poet has. As she does with the students at Cambridge, Wheatley takes the opportunity to instruct the reader in virtue. She begins with a standard flourish, invoking the Muses to aid her, and she displays her own piety by interspersing meditations on her own virtue between criticisms directed outward. In "On Recollection," Wheatley emerges as being in league with or possessed by the Muses, their vent'rous Afric. But the vent'rous Afric of "On Recollection" is not the only transformation we see in Wheatley.

This theme of transformation—from benighted soul to Christian poet, Negro black as Cain to member of the angelic train, thief of laurels to poetic Patroclus, and vent'rous Afric to Infant muse of the "Answer to the Rebus"—may be the most thoroughgoing theme in *Poems on Various Subjects Religious and Moral.* Despite the obvious presence of the circular and solar or even recollection and Memory, the longest sustained classical project in *Poems* is a verse translation of an author focused on transformation. Ovid's *Metamorphoses* provides the original text for Wheatley's "Niobe in Distress." The Latin Ovidian metanarrative is the dominant secular force at play in the writings of Dante, Petrarch, Shakespeare, ad infinitum. Not surprisingly, an Ovidian myth, which in some translations ends "[a]nd, as will happen, new tales bring back old" (*Metamorphoses,* VI), serves as the basis for one of Wheatley's longest poems. The 224-line meditation "Niobe in Distress . . ." is an extended poetic treatment of the pride and later mourning of the Phrygian queen, "all beautiful in woe," who dared to count her splendor equal to the gods. After all her family and splendor are destroyed, she turns to stone.[76]

Wheatley's treatment of the Niobe myth is also likely the first translation of any kind by an African in America. It certainly appears to be the first African American philological project in the classics. Translating the work of a major classical author is an ambitious undertaking by an African American slave in any case, but Wheatley's ambition is considerably more developed than this. She alters the Ovidian narrative to add her own signature in making another, longer, and more personal foray into the frontiers of the epic, crafting an epyllion in "Niobe" that brings her within sight of her epic idols. Ovid opens with Niobe's arrogant disregard for the lesson of her friend, Arachne, her boasting, and her usurping Latona's glory. Wheatley, on the other hand, invokes the Muses and focuses on the wrath of Apollo before addressing Niobe. Apollo's indignant slaughter gets special treatment from Wheatley, who embellishes Ovid with additional lines:

> With clouds incompass'd glorious *Phoebus* stands;
> The feathered vengeance quiv'ring in his hands . . . .
> Then didst thou, *Sipylus*, the language hear
> Of fate portentous whistling in the air[.]

Wheatley also removes the touch of mercy Apollo showed to Niobe's Ilioneus, who prayed to all the gods to spare him. His brothers had died of arrows that tore out flesh, spouted "streams of purple gore," and left blood "darting upward." Ovid wrote that Apollo was moved by Ilioneus's appeal, and Pope's translation, which Wheatley almost certainly consulted, showed the touch of sympathy and mercy:

> *Ilioneus*, the last, with terror stands,
> Lifting in pray'r his unavailing hands;
> And, ignorant from whom his griefs arise,
> Spare me, o all ye heav'nly Pow'rs, he cries:
> *Phoebus* was touch'd too late, the sounding bow
> Had sent the shaft, and struck the fatal blow;
> Which yet but gently gor'd his tender side,
> So by a slight and easy wound he dy'd.[77]

Wheatley coldly declares, "Thou too, O Ilioneus, are doom'd to fall, / The fates refuse that arrow to recal."

Wheatley's alterations to Ovid amplify the wrath and vengeance of the gods who punished Niobe's excessive pride in her fine lineage and progeny. Unlike the comparably long "Goliath of Gath" (in which one cannot miss the striking resemblance of the young David to Miss Wheatley), "Niobe" does not have a premiere role for the humble warrior to launch powerful words and stones at a boastful giant; rather, it contains a self-reflexive warning about recklessly succumbing to comfort and poetic pride. "Niobe" emphasizes in its treatment of Ilioneus, whose prayerful but "unavailing hands" do not forestall his slaughter, that even piety, which has been part of Wheatley's aegis, does not always save the pious. Written in reaction to a painting by Welsh artist Richard Wilson, "Niobe in Distress" seems to contain and display all of Wheatley's fears about her essential vulnerability and the downfall awaiting her if her ambition and classical weavings of verse ever make her too enamored of her African self. The excessive mourning Niobe displays also suggests that the added folly of immobilizing grief is something neither the reader nor the author can afford. If Niobe errs in not learning from Arachne's ignominious downfall, then the readers and writer of so many elegies can err if they fail to learn from the lives of the departed and "take [them]" (as Wheatley suggests in "Whitfield") for their lessons of faith or folly.

Interestingly, Apollo is the god associated with music, poetry, and finer cultural attainments, and he is the agent of Niobe's destruction. The unfortunate Niobe is excessively proud of her productions, fourteen children of beauty and strength (not unlike the fourteen lines of a sonnet). Also, when ordering Latona's worshippers to disband, she commands them to remove the laurels they wear to honor the goddess. Here, snatching a laurel, which is Wheatley's announced intent in "To Maecenas," is a precursor to annihilation. For Wheatley, the balance between ambition and endearing piety is an important and precarious one. Both *The Iliad* and *The Aeneid* contend with the virtues and dangers of pride and ambition. Excessive pride is not a quality she can afford to display. In "Elegy on the Death of a Late Celebrated Poetess," Wheatley writes, "O! How vain the wish that friendship pays, / Since her own volumes are her highest praise," and she outlines the dangers of self-praise in "Niobe" by contrasting the celebrated and proud queen—

> Niobe comes with all her royal race,
> With charms unnumber'd and superior grace:
> Her Phrygian garment of delightful hue,
> Inwove with gold, refulgent to the view,

—with the devastated Niobe of the final stanza, who is bereft of even the freedom of movement, that which Phillis was generally allowed as a pampered slave.

Wheatley's commentary on the lessons of death and mourning is particularly useful in considering her elegies. Many of them encourage mourners to focus on the virtues of the departed, and she often uses the classics to illustrate those virtues and their heavenly reward. Even in an elegy like "To a Gentleman and Lady on the Death of . . . a Child of the Name Avis . . . ," Wheatley mines the smallest classical vein for its value. In "Avis" she plays on the unfortunate child's Latinate name for both metaphors of heavenly flight and bird-like feeding on the eternal fruits of heaven, Wheatley's version of ambrosia:

> Thine *Avis* give without a murm'ring heart,
> Though half thy soul be fated to depart.
> To shining guards consign thine infant care
> To waft triumphant through the seas of air:
> Her soul enlarg'd to heav'nly pleasure springs,
> She feeds on truth and uncreated things.

The elegiac form that Wheatley relied on to memorialize Avis, console mourning families, and extol the real or imagined virtues of the dead may itself be construed as a classical influence. The elegy functioned as more than a funereal poem for classical writers, and it routinely expressed political positions. The primary Augustan tension was between the elegy as individual and indulgent versus Cicero's and Octavian's vision of Roman unity or *tota Italia* (the whole of Italy). Wheatley's elegies created community by drawing local Boston together in corporate mourning for admirable or pitiable members of the community. But she also used the elegy as a Trojan Horse to make herself a valued member of the community—as elegist and fellow mourner—in an era when blacks, especially slaves, would normally be excluded from the community. Moreover, with the prerogative of the elegist, she *interprets* the virtues of the deceased. Wheatley's elegy to Whitefield is constructed to seemingly echo the teachings of the preacher, but it also allows her to echo her own sentiments of Christian equality voiced just two poems before in "On Being Brought from Africa to America": "Remember, *Christians*, Negros, black as *Cain* / May be refin'd, and join th' angelic train." The elegy admonishes the people of America to heed Whitefield's words. To her own race Wheatley declares that the Savior he offered is their Savior too:

> Take him, ye *Africans*, he longs for you,
> *Impartial Saviour* is his title due:
> Wash'd in the fountain of redeeming blood,
> You shall be sons, and kings, and priests to God.

Phillis Wheatley

Wheatley's focus on recollection, impious pride, death, and mourning also suggests that she is particularly aware of the dangers she and others face from their own folly and from simple fate. It is clear that Wheatley had reason to be vigilant about her balance of piety, ambition, and pride. Wheatley's poetic critiques and classical adventures did not go unchallenged, as the long history of criticism during and after her era attests. And while she admits the limits of her poetic freedom and ability in such poems as "On Recollection," "On Imagination," and "Niobe in Distress," she insists that she is neither an African aberration nor a fraud. She subversively situates a poem of praise for fellow slave and artist Scipio Moorhead among the last poems. Furthermore, she includes a light-hearted but intriguing commentary on her own knowledge as the endpiece(s) of her work. "A Rebus, By I. B." and "An Answer to the Rebus" demonstrate both that Wheatley is again under examination and that she is transformed from the supplicant of "To Maecenas."

By the end of *Poems on Various Subjects Religious and Moral,* Wheatley has joined the ranks of the Muses. In the "Rebus" and the "Answer," Wheatley responds to a series of classical tests, now believed to have come from James Bowdoin, the founder of Bowdoin College and one of those who attested to her authorship. According to Wheatley, "The poet asks, and *Phillis* can't refuse / To shew th' obedience of the Infant muse." Wheatley demonstrates her memory of classical, Christian, and heraldic lore in the set of poems. As she initiates her response, she metamorphoses from the "Ethiop" or even the vent'rous Afric of the Muses to a younger sister of the Nine, the Infant muse.

Colonial British and American readers accepted Wheatley's poetry as it appeared: an appropriately respectful, properly attested, belletristic literary oddity that left white readers in control of their relationship with the black writer. Wheatley's relationship with the ancient poets and the Muses developed throughout the text of the poems, from her attempts to rival Homer and Virgil and snatch laurels to her appeal to the Muses to aid *their* vent'rous Afric and her evolution into Infant muse. But her relationship with her audience also developed, literally and in the literary world of *Poems on Various Subjects Religious and Moral.* She allowed herself—gave herself—to be transformed by each Maecenas, reader of an elegy, fellow Christian, celebrant of the classical masters, or examiner of her classical bona fides into something unique but greater than the limited and despised form of the black slave.

This overall transformation reveals the strategic ambush of Wheatley's literary Trojan Horse. The scheme that was Wheatley's verse—not mere pastoral, mere *recusatio*, nor mere mimicry—carried her inside the literal and intellectual walls of white, colonial American, and British society. Wheatley used the classical models, pastoral repose, Christian and poetic humility, and wealthy patrons—familiar and accepted elements of belletristic literature and colonial culture—to achieve extraordinary access to colonial elites, mask her ambition, acquire the power to critique colonial civilization, and secure her freedom. In "To Maecenas," the poet begged the solicitude of the reader, pled the weakness of her poetic voice, and longed for the power of the epic masters—playing down any sense of her own power. But in the same poem she used the classics to penetrate the white intellectual world, and Terence in particular, to inject a resonant black presence there that authorized her own presence. Subsequently, she used her impeccable Christian credentials to lecture young students at Cambridge and celebrate redeeming virtue. She parlayed her virtuous verse into commentary on freedom and enslavement and a direct appeal to King George and rewrote the rolls of heaven to include blacks in the angelic train. The audience for whom she mourned the dead also found itself including her in the local community and subject to her assessment of the virtuous life. She moved beyond Horace to position herself near the epic masters, whose lasting influence she envied, by transforming the David and Goliath story into a first epyllion (taking care to chastise an unrepentant race seeking to enslave others) and then daring to alter Ovid into a second epyllion. By the end of her woven verse, the young poet, who needed authentication to begin her poetry, protection from patrons, and guidance from ancient teachers, had not only successfully arrogated to herself the role of teacher but also that of "infant muse"—an inspiration herself.

CHAPTER TWO

THE VIRTUOUS VOICE OF FREDERICK DOUGLASS

Frederick Douglass's extemporaneous speech in 1841 at the Nantucket Athenaeum inaugurated his historic career as a national abolitionist orator and, combined with subsequent early speeches for William Lloyd Garrison's antislavery society, transformed abolitionist oratory. Before Douglass, abolitionists had sought to enhance the authority and credibility of their attack on slavery by including African Americans as orators. However, they were neither able to overcome educated free blacks' often dry rhetoric, which was suspect because it came from those who had not been slaves, nor use effectively the impaired oratory of escaped slaves who "could not get 'the hang of the schoolhouse.'"[1]

Douglass's astonishing personal narrative, combined with his fluid oratorical style and sonorous voice, animated the stentorian but barren abolitionist rhetoric of the era. Moreover, he gave a heroic, visible form to what was for many white Americans and Europeans the abstract figure of the African slave. Although Douglass's eloquence also spawned accusations that he had never been in bondage, multitudes of auditors were enchanted by Douglass's seemingly immaculate conception of oratorical skill and erudition.

Countless news reports, letters, and other writings from Douglass's era onward have advanced the popular myth of him as the noble hero who miraculously emerged from harrowing slavery with a natural oratorical skill superior to those with university training and material advantage. However, it would be particularly unwise to assume that the popular, cultivated image of Douglass as a miraculous and natural possessor of these qualities is fully accurate.

In *My Bondage and My Freedom,* Douglass declares that he "had no preparation" for his inaugural speech as a Garrisonian lecturer in Nantucket. He wryly quips, "'[I was a] graduate from the peculiar institution,' Mr. Collins used to say, when introducing me, '*with my diploma written on my back!*' The three years of my freedom had been spent in the hard school of adversity."[2] Nonetheless, an examination of Douglass's life both before and after Nantucket suggests that he had more training in the beginning of his career than has been popularly assumed and a wealth of influences afterward. He did not spring fully formed like Athena from the forehead of Zeus (or William Lloyd Garrison, for that matter) onto the Athenaeum's podium. Frederick Douglass was a product of multiple intellectual, religious, and rhetorical traditions—substantively coalesced and refined by the lessons of antiquity—the experience with which allowed him to understand, master, and deploy a rich multicultural and multiethnic oratorical style, one unheard in America up to his emergence and of a kind only conceptualized in formal rhetorical study in the twentieth century.

Given the legendary power and influence of Douglass's oratory, scholars have expended considerable energy to discuss its content and the source of its power. Fewer have focused on his education and oratorical preparation. Although a number of researchers have identified fragmentary evidence of Douglass's education and oratorical background, most have offered little to replace his legend with a more substantive explanation of what has been widely and historically recognized as devastatingly effective oratory. Professor James M. Gregory's *Frederick Douglass: The Orator* (1893) was the first attempt to collect and comment on Douglass's speeches. Both Gregory, a Howard University Latin professor, and noted African American classicist William Sanders Scarborough, who contributed a substantial introduction, extracted from the narrative what became the standard report of Douglass's education. In Gregory's words:

> At the age of ten he was sent to Baltimore to live with Mr. Hugh Auld, whose wife Mrs. Sophia Auld, was his first teacher, and she continued her instruction until objection was made to it by her husband. Frederick, however, found other means of accomplishing his desire. Having procured a spelling book he learned to read through the assistance of his

white playmates whom he met in the streets. When about thirteen years of age he bought a book entitled the "Columbian Orator," with money earned by blacking boots. The speeches of Sheridan, Lord Chatham, William Pitt, and Fox, which he read in this book increased his information and supply of words, enabling him to give expression to the thoughts that now began to form in his mind.[3]

Gregory notes Douglass's frequently mentioned encounters with other slaves, as well as activists like journalist, bookseller, and staunch educational proponent David Ruggles,[4] cultivated businessman Nathan Johnson,[5] and the classically educated clergyman James W. C. Pennington. However, Gregory's and Scarborough's assessment of Douglass differs considerably in approach from those of many of the works that follow. They contextualize Douglass's oratory by measuring it against the oratorical commentary of Socrates and Marcus Tullius Cicero and attribute to him the qualities of oratory admired by Horace.[6] They also repeatedly refer to Douglass as "hero" and "orator" and compare him to the classical orators Themistocles, Pericles, and Demosthenes as well as to contemporary orators, including Abraham Lincoln, Ulysses Grant, Charles Sumner, and William Lloyd Garrison. Gregory goes further, noting that visits to Douglass's home found him immersed in numerous cultural refinements, which included reading the classics:

> He said he was engaged in reading the writings and speeches of Rome's ancient senators and statesmen, referring to his own book-strewn table. In his reading, he observed one thing in particular—the profundity and incisiveness of their style. Such laconic brevity is scarcely observable in the utterances of modern Statesmanship. The Roman senator cracks the nut and gives you the kernel.[7]

Gregory's discussion of Douglass's home studies also suggests that Douglass viewed the proposed assembly of his own writings and orations into comprehensive volumes as the African American version of the Roman cultural and intellectual record. After pointing to his reading of the Roman works, Douglass noted that he hoped to arrange for the publication of his works to address the criticism that "[i]f the negro were sunk in the depths of the sea, all that the negro has done and the negro himself would be forgotten within twenty years."[8]

Benjamin Quarles's *Frederick Douglass* (1948) retained none of Gregory's classical comparisons but briefly recounted Lucretia Auld's abortive attempt at teaching Douglass, his purchase of *The Columbian Orator*, and his participation in the East Baltimore Mental Improvement Society. However, Quarles does not probe the historical and intellectual significance of nineteenth-century self-improvement societies, which facilitated black political, intellectual, and social activity, including classics and rhetoric, in urban areas from Baltimore to New York to Chicago. The five volumes of Philip Foner's *The Life and Writings of Frederick Douglass* continued both to build Douglass's legacy and to recover more of his work. However, little if any new information on Douglass's education emerged from the copious collection. Both authors stripped Douglass's words and career of their classical elements and detached him from that ancient tradition. David Chesebrough's *Frederick Douglass: Oratory from Slavery* clearly identifies ethos, pathos, parallelism, and mimicry as ancient rhetorical tools that Douglass consciously mastered and used, but he virtually ignores how these tools were part of the classical tradition consciously transmitted in *The Columbian Orator*.

Present-day scholars John Blassingame, Gregory Lampe, and David Blight have done the most to add depth and nuance to our scholarly understanding of Douglass's education, popular appeal, and oratorical power. This accomplishment is largely linked to their reexamining the same basic information about specific educational episodes and locales provided in the autobiographical works. *The Frederick Douglass Papers*, edited by Blassingame, has provided the most comprehensive collection of Douglass's speeches, debates, and interviews, including a faithful reconstruction of his travels and speaking itinerary. This collection of speeches reveals a crescendo in Douglass's direct classical references and sustained passages on classical subjects beginning in 1847.[9] Volume 1 (1841–1846) has zero, but the second volume (1847–1854) has twelve Greek and Roman classical references. This volume also includes an extended treatment of Egypt (among other classical states) in "The Claims of the Negro Ethnologically Considered." In that speech Douglass uses Herodotus, among others, to argue for the humanity and equality of the Negro. He insists that blacks have a founding role in Western civilization and the Greco-Roman world:

> The fact that Egypt was one of the earliest abodes of learning and civilization, is as firmly established as are the everlasting hills, defying, with a calm front the boasted mechanical and architectural skill of the nineteenth century. . . . Greece and Rome—and through them Europe and America—have received their civilization from the ancient Egyptians. This fact is not denied by anybody. But Egypt is in Africa.[10]

The classics are quite visible in volume 3 (1855–1863), which has eighteen classical Greek, Roman, or Egyptian references. Volume 4 (1864–1880) has twenty-eight, and volume 5 (1881–95) has ninety-seven—plus extensive references to Egypt, as well as references to Shakespeare's *Julius Caesar*, the Holy Roman Empire, and Addison's famous drama *Cato* (so important to the Founders and the revolutionary environment of colonial America). Douglass quotes playwrights Aeschylus, Aristophanes, and Sophocles, along with historians Herodotus, Plutarch, and Thucydides. He deploys the names, narratives, and exemplary accomplishments or crimes of a number of Roman rulers and emperors, including Julius Caesar and the emperors Augustus, Tiberius, Caligula, Nero, Titus, Trajan, Caracalla, Diocletian, and Constantine. Statesmen, politicians, and orators such as Marcus Vipsanius Agrippa, Marcus Antonius, Marcus Junius Brutus, Catiline, Cato, Cicero, Herod, and Pontius Pilate are prominent as well. Scientists and philosophers Archimedes, Aristotle, Plato, and Socrates are included, as well as sages, poets, and writers Aesop, Homer, and Virgil. The gods and oracles make rare appearances in the speeches, including Nemesis, Vesta, and the Oracle at Dodona. There are numerous references to the Roman Empire, Roman Republic, early and Ptolemaic Egypt, Ethiopia, Abyssinia, Carthage, and cities and architectural wonders throughout the ancient West and Asia Minor. When indirect classical references to the ancient world, references to North Africa and Ethiopia, references to classical Christian figures, or references to Shakespeare's classically grounded plays such as *Julius Caesar*, *Troilus and Cressida*, or *Antony and Cleopatra* are included, the numbers from 1847 onward swell significantly.

Blassingame downplays Douglass's attention to the majority of nineteenth-century rhetorical manuals, but he points to the particular influence of *The Columbian Orator*. Gregory Lampe's *Frederick Douglass: Freedom's Voice, 1818–1845* suggests that Douglass owed a portion of his rhetorical power and training to a tradition of storytelling, wordplay, and moral education among slaves. David Blight's bicentennial edition of *The Columbian Orator* revisits and illuminates the influence of the text on the orators of the era, including Douglass. Together, Blassingame, Lampe, and Blight argue that a knowable rhetorical framework exists beneath the mythology of Douglass, built of his plantation experience, his A.M.E. Zion ministry, and his readings in rhetoric and nineteenth-century popular and political literature.

While these scholarly projects have partly investigated the myth of Douglass's miraculous oratorical prowess to reveal the equally impressive truth that he masterfully combined African American, Christian, and formal secular oratory, only David Blight has recovered and reconsidered some of what nineteenth-century classicists Gregory and Scarborough must have known and taken for granted when they wrote of Douglass. They understood as a matter of course that *The Columbian Orator* was a text steeped in the classical tradition, including significant portions of rhetorical instruction taken directly from the writings of Cicero and Marcus Fabius Quintilian. Blight argues that a judicious evaluation of Douglass's relationship with the *Orator* must emphasize that Douglass mastered skills discussed in the book and present in classical oratory: mimicry, political humor, and "subversive theatrics."[11] Moreover, the *Orator* clearly demonstrates and defines manhood, heroism, human rights, and virtuous government, and evaluates the legitimacy of slavery.

Scholars have not inquired about what influence a classical rhetorical tradition grounded in ancient understandings of masculinity, heroism, virtue, and both civic and religious *pietas* had on Douglass's speeches, which addressed those issues repeatedly. The bulk of his speeches, including some of his most famous and regularly studied—"What to the Slave is the Fourth of July" (1852), "The Trials and Triumphs of Self-Made Men" (1860), and the various "Slaveholder's Sermons" (1842, 1846, and thereafter)—clearly include a multitude of these themes and display these recognizable rhetorical strategies. Moreover, such speeches as "The Claims of the Negro Ethnologically Considered" (1854), "The Significance of Emancipation in the West Indies" (1857), "Revolutions Never Go Backward" (1861), and "Fighting the Rebels with One Hand" (1862) specifically deploy classical allusions to illustrate the presence or absence of virtue, reason, manhood, *pietas*, loyalty, treason, barbarism, and civilization.

In today's era, in which the sword-and-sandal epic and classical themes are alive and well on multiplex screens, cable and satellite television, and even the minds of the masses, few scholars have been motivated to explore why so many of Douglass's auditors reached for classical, regal, martial, and heroically masculine images and names—"Spartacus," "manly," "colossal," "majestic, "master of every weapon," "with the dignity and grace of a courtier, and the bearing of a king," "[with a] voice that rang out like a clarion"—to describe the orator and his power, even though he was an A.M.E. Zion exhorter whose secular oratory regularly addressed Christianity and the church.[12] Nor have they asked how Douglass could attack the established church so ruthlessly and consistently and still be hailed as a virtuous voice. Moreover, scholars have failed to ask why the first serious examination of Douglass and attempt to collect his speeches came from an African American professor of Latin and included a significant introduction from the most noteworthy African American classicist, William Sanders Scarborough. Academe has also been slow to ask why Douglass is a "hero" to these classicists and why they choose to compare him to Themistocles, Demosthenes, and Cicero. As Blassingame makes clear, even popular press accounts of Douglass's era utilized martial or classically artistic terms to describe his language: "[His sentences] are so many thrusts which enter the vital parts of the enemy," opined the *New York Times* in 1872, while the *Auburn (NY) Cayuga Chief* wrote that Douglass's "language is classically chaste, not groaning under the flowery ornaments of school boy declamation, but terse yet eloquent, like a piece of finished sculpture beautiful in every outline of its symmetrical and unadorned simplicity.'"[13]

Recognizing the classical influences on Douglass's thought and oratorical strategies does help clearly demarcate the boundaries and limitations of much of the scholarship on Douglass. Moreover, it should prompt us to consider that as a result of those scholarly limitations, countless students read an anthologized, critically examined, and critically annotated Douglass, who is contextualized in American literature with little or no mention of any debt to the classics, despite the longstanding scholarly appreciation of classical influences in American literature, politics, and history.[14]

The implications for reading the work of an African American writer and orator like Douglass in the context of classical influence are significant. Reading Douglass's treatment of virtue, his critique of slavery, his narrative accounts of vicious slaveholders and abused slaves, or his declamations on slavery and the nature of the American republic as understandings and political positions grounded in the classics offers new insights on the rationale, appeal, and power of Douglass's work. It will also demand a new response from Douglass scholars, since academe has regularly championed Douglass as the quintessential man of his period and a unique champion of African Americans without analyzing his debt, beyond religious training, to an ancient tradition of oration, statesmanship, historical chronicle, and protest. Collections and commentaries that catalog and analyze Douglass's speeches and narratives as abolitionist documents, seminal protest documents, and declarations of women's rights, without considering any classical influence or inflection, will prove markedly incomplete.[15] Even the scholarship that has partly explored Douglass's rhetoric and challenged us to see his canonical position as one built upon the whipped backs of bound black women slaves, modeled on a questionable idea of exemplariness, and erroneously designed to valorize manliness must be understood as inadequate, having elided the ancient foundations of the period's understanding of manliness, exemplariness, and virtue.[16]

It will be far more fruitful to see Douglass's brief descriptions of his general education and experience with *The Columbian Orator* not as satisfactory and definitive statements but as grounds for more probing questions about education in nineteenth-century America, the influence of classics among African Americans of the period, and what Douglass received or contributed to the use of the classics during this period. No substantive analysis of Douglass's oratorical power, style, influence, and legacy can be complete without examining his exposure to the classics via primary and inflected texts, discerning his reliance on classically educated mentors, finding when and how he used classical and classically inflected rhetorical and literary material in his oratory, and gauging the reactions of his auditors to his rhetoric. Education in nineteenth-century America was in transition, both in terms of the general population's access to education and the kind of education preparatory academies and colleges dispensed. From the beginning of the century to 1860, the number of colleges grew from approximately 20 to nearly 220. Most of the new growth occurred after 1830, and by 1860, the eighteenth-century educational haven of New England had fewer colleges than either the South or the Midwest, with sixteen thousand students enrolled nationally by the beginning of the Civil War.[17]

The primary religious sponsors of education in the eighteenth century—Congregationalists, Episcopalians, and Presbyterians—lost ground to Baptists and Methodists, who founded their own institutions. Oddly enough, with the increase in church-affiliated colleges, the sciences flourished in the curriculum as what Harvard professor Jacob Bigelow called in his 1829 *Elements of Technology* "science as useful knowledge."[18] Despite gradually accepting science and more "practical" pursuits geared toward commercial, industrial, and financial success, the vast majority of colleges retained their classical focus. American collegians devoted half their study to the classics through the late 1900s.[19] However, common pre-college education became more accessible to the masses and changed to meet their needs. The availability of blossoming varieties of education, the growth of newspapers and readerships, and the popularization of politics during the revolutionary period added to the culture's general literacy and exposure to richer and more complex language. The oddity of the historical and educational moment is never more apparent than when one compares the lives and educations of two American presidents who were born in 1767 and governed in the early years of the republic: John Quincy Adams and Andrew Jackson. Educated at Harvard and in Europe, Adams was thoroughly versed in the classics. He was the president of the American Academy of Arts and Sciences, Boylston Professor of Rhetoric at Harvard, master of seven languages, and a poet. His study of the classics was impressive and daunting enough to unsettle the common population and damage his political fortunes.[20] Andrew Jackson was none of these things. As many historians have indicated, Jackson was practically uneducated, but he was also politically sensitive to the sentiment of the unlettered masses. He happily polished his plebeian image and celebrated his rough, rustic, and uncultured simplicity.[21]

The paradox of nineteenth-century American education was that democratic education had to raise the understanding, refinement, and ambitions of citizens, uphold civic virtues of the democracy, and remain useful to common men without fragmenting the nation along class lines. In addition, a useful education had to disseminate a national language that could serve as both a sign of education and a tool of common discourse without essentially dividing citizens by class or hearkening back to the old regime. By the nineteenth century, the very coin of language that an eighteenth-century writer like Phillis Wheatley used had gradually lost a considerable amount of its currency. While still very much concerned about the *pietas* so resonant in Revolutionary poetry and politics, Americans were equally concerned with acquiring practical knowledge and language that were useful for economic and personal advancement. Of course, early critics of traditional education, including Benjamin Franklin, Benjamin Rush, Thomas Paine, and Noah Webster, had feared that the standard model of classical education might not be suitable for the mainstream education of the American population. As Caroline Winterer notes,

> They argued that "dead languages" were useless to farmers, mechanics, and merchants; that they wasted the most important, formative years of a student's life in quickly forgotten grammatical niceties; that the Greek and Roman myths made boys into "Pimps" by reciting lascivious tales offensive to Christian morality; that the time spent in classical language education might be more profitably spent learning more useful subjects, such as English; that the classical languages conferred social cachet for no good reason.[22]

This public debate over the proper substance and effect of education was no less present in academe, where teachers argued over the most effective method of teaching Greek and Latin in the new nation. They feared that badly educated students would be both classically ignorant and shirkers of their civic responsibility. Effete scholars might "pollute the republic with the vice of pedantry."[23]

Responses to academic and broader societal criticisms of classical education emerged from the ranks of classicists, many of whom decried the pedagogical techniques of repetition and rote memorization that dominated academy and university study. Humanists and philhellenes of classical academe engineered major changes in classical education. They insisted upon a fuller, nuanced, and contextualized understanding of the classical world, one that did not tear classical authors and works from their historical and cultural contexts simply for the sterile purpose of translating them. Critics charged that young men knew how to translate narrow passages but knew nothing substantive of Greek and Roman civilization, where the true vitality and richness lay. Their admiration and celebration of the cultures were shallow and illogical because the cultural contexts of the nations and their works had been reduced to unintelligible fragments. "[Alexander Adam's] *Roman Antiquities* did for Roman life what the grammar did for Latin literature," writes Winterer, "parceling the past into discrete bits of information to be memorized."[24] The *Graeca Majora* had much the same impact on the understanding of Greek culture.

In the context of criticisms of classical training, it is even more interesting that we find descriptions of Frederick Douglass like those Blassingame notes. They extol the virtues of his elegantly simple delivery, a style that reaches beyond the dry, overwrought, logically questionable, and allusion-filled orations of formally trained speakers; it is a style that possesses instead the enlivened, romantic inspiration attributed to the progressive and German influences on classical education. Douglass emerged within a world in which the public and the scholarly classicists were clamoring for an enlivened experience with the classics. Many were influenced by a German romanticism that had unbound the classics and made it possible to explore new ways to experience the cultures and thought of the Greeks and Romans and develop a more complex, nuanced relationship between antiquity and the American experience. There was a flexibility and fluidity in classical study that made it possible again to unleash the urge to understand and experience the empire of the mind and create again those orators and leaders who would seek to turn that intellectual conquest into earthly power.

Edward Everett, George Bancroft, and Robert Bridges Patton published classical textbooks on Greek that helped transform American classical study into a more lively pursuit that eschewed mere rote memorization and sterile translation. Meanwhile, Bancroft's and Everett's student Cornelius Felton (as well as the young German Charles Beck) invigorated the study of Latin. While elevating German romantic philhellenes above dry British and error-prone American classics scholars, they used the newly enlivened texts to link Greek history and literature to the democratic ideals of the United States. Increasingly, American scholars celebrated what Winterer calls

"the noble spirits of Germany" who could appreciate the "moral sublime" of the Greeks. American scholars admired a number of things about ancient Greece. First, with democracy ascendant in America, fifth-century B.C. Athens became more acceptable as a model for young men to emulate in preparation for citizenship. As early as 1824 George Bancroft, in an article praising a new Greek grammar from Germany, looked to Homer and Herodotus as being favorable to "virtue and liberty."[25]

Democratic Greece was a considerably more comfortable object of admiration than Rome because of the latter's precipitous decline into empire and monarchy in all but name, political states with which the young republic was understandably uncomfortable. It would be inaccurate to say that Rome disappeared from the American mind, for it remained a formidable rhetorical tool for innumerable scholars, politicians, and clergymen. However, it is by no mere accident that during this historical period, Edgar Allan Poe penned the words that have characterized the American assessment of the classical world: "glory" as the legacy of Greece and "grandeur" as that of Rome. Contemporary Greece also helped marry ancient Greek and modern American democratic ideals. From 1821 to 1829, an America increasingly engulfed in Hellenism celebrated the Greek revolt and independence from the Ottoman Empire. Poetry, college activism, and popular pro-Greek societies developed, as Americans absorbed talk of liberation and drew comparisons between the rebirth of modern, Christian Greece from Ottoman Islamic near-slavery and their own revolution. The seeds of this interest in the old and new Greece flowered in the literature of the American Renaissance and even in the neo-Hellenic (Greek Revival) architecture so celebrated in the antebellum American South.

While Greek liberation was a national fascination, black liberation was paramount in the minds of African Americans. As it was in the eighteenth century, education was a significant part of the project. For African Americans, the paradox of finding an educational model that produced exceptionality in scholars and addressed the practical realities of the allegedly egalitarian republic would have been even more vexing. They could have ill afforded to abandon a tradition of training and praxis that immediately identified one as a possessor of education and intellect, especially when belief in blacks' baseness was rampant among both the white masses and a large part of the educated elite. African Americans' ability to embrace the "common man" and the cult of practicality was severely limited. This was especially true during a period when the most critical determinations about their humanity, intelligence, freedom, and right to remain in the country were being made at the highest governmental, theological, and scholarly levels in the United States and also debated internationally.[26] African Americans had to contend with the fact that the infancy of the American republic was also the era during which the nation enshrined slavery as an institution and sacked the remaining philosophical and legal architecture of black humanity. The construction and ratification of the American Constitution, fundamental American liberty, a healthy postwar economy, and the cultural sense of Americanness had depended mightily on the disposition of Africans in postcolonial America. The continuing racial policy of the state and the culture was elucidated in the nineteenth century, which saw the institutionalization of race-based slavery and dispossession of blacks in law and custom, a development that rigidly installed blackness as a proscription against citizenship, education, humanity, and the blessings of liberty.

A series of important legislative moves and U.S. Supreme Court cases from 1793 onward set the legal and discursive tone for the era. *Dred Scott v. Sandford* is generally the most well-known and most important of these cases. However, from roughly 1806 in *Scott v. Negro London* (and more important, the 1810 *Scott v. Negro Ben* case)[27] to *Dred Scott v. Sandford*,[28] the structure of American racial reasoning crystallized. One notable exception to the formal rejection of African American legal rights was *United States v. Amistad,* in which Associate Justice Joseph Story ruled that the African slave trade was illegal under Spanish law and that a group of Africans were free and eligible to return to Africa.[29] Despite *Amistad,* this line of cases culminated with twin blows to black liberty: the *Dred Scott* decision and the 1859 *Ableman v. Booth* case.[30] Together, these several cases indicated that the legality of slavery and ownership of individuals as slaves would not be invalidated by fraud, mistake, or the failure to fulfill legal formalities and that the public policy preference of the state and default at law was to preserve slavery. Moreover, African Americans were not citizens and had no rights at law, not even grounds to petition the court. This end to redress through the courts was underscored by the specific linking of rights with race. Additionally, there would be no American haven for the escaped slave, running from bondage on any continent. The world was truly a global village where slavery was concerned, and manhunters could ply their trade in America, above contrary local and state laws, with rights and immunities perhaps exceeding those of diplomats.

African Americans met these events with intellectual, political, and military responses that resulted in escalating racist legislation and judicial intervention.[31] The calamitous nature of this era ensured that African Americans would need to defend their humanity at the highest levels of American government as well as in the lofty regions of national and international intellectual exchange. Moreover, with the environment so hostile to African American education, if the liberty of the masses of African Americans were ever to be secured, it would likely depend upon an elite class of exceptional men and women who were free, well-educated, and able to engage the battle at the necessary levels. Finally, this group of unique leaders would have to develop and rely upon a tradition and vision of blackness that could compete with the prevailing cultural mythology of racial hierarchy and white superiority. This need for a specific cultural vision shaped African Americans' nineteenth-century experience with the classics into a search for intellectual enrichment, a usable past, civic guidance, and cultural virtue, not the ponderous grammatical exercise reviled by so many in the era. A number of prominent black thinkers hoped to mine the intellectual veins for useful cultural riches for African Americans, even if they valued differently what they found. Douglass and Alexander Crummell agreed that the development and mastery of language, literacy, and the power of the word held the greatest opportunity for African Americans and the making of men. Douglass found value and power in the vernacular, the utterances of the common man, and the unlettered and painful past of slavery, as well as the high linguistic, cultural, and literary productions dating back to antiquity (all properly critiqued and contextualized). Crummell represented another view of the value of the word and placed his complete faith in the transforming and civilizing power of formal language, high intellectual achievement, and the riches of classical culture. "Synthesis" was in Douglass's vocabulary (as he demonstrates in his orations on self-made men) but not in Crummell's.[32]

Though few in number, a small body of classically educated secular and semisecular scholars did emerge, including John Mercer Langston, Samuel Ringgold Ward, Henry Highland Garnet, Richard T. Greener, James McCune Smith, Lewis G. Reason, George B. Vashon, and William G. Allen. Many of these men were prominent orators, Douglass's companion voices on the abolitionist circuit, and shared the dais or the planning for a multitude of social and cultural enterprises with him. Others, like Smith, were devoted auditors of Douglass's oratory. Reason, Vashon, and Allen all taught Latin and/or Greek at New York Central College, a coeducational, multiracial institution surviving in McGrawville, New York, from 1849 until 1861. Lower local schools, such as the African Free Schools, were important initial educational experiences for many scholars. Oneida Institute and Oberlin College were key providers of higher education that accepted African Americans. James McCune Smith, who worked with Frederick Douglass to establish the National Council of the Colored People and wrote the introduction to Douglass's *My Bondage and My Freedom*, had three degrees from the University of Glasgow, including the M.D., and he "frequently drove home a point with a Latin phrase."[33] He actually ends his introduction to *My Bondage and My Freedom* with a Latin farewell, "Reader, *Vale!*"[34] Shortly after Smith graduated in 1837, Francis L. Cardozo began a three-year course at Glasgow, winning prizes in Latin and Greek.[35]

While the African American secular scholarly community was admirable in its own right, it was a community of exceptional cases and few in number. It could only be politically and socially effective in conjunction with another sizable community of blacks. The one body of African Americans large enough and comparably suited to this crucial role of defending African American liberty, intellect, and virtue was the Christian clergy.[36] Generally speaking, ecclesiastical education in the mainline Christian denominations (through which a large number of black clergy achieved their training before and often after major black churches splintered from unfriendly white denominations) was synonymous with classical education through the middle of the nineteenth century. As a result, nineteenth-century African American scholars and educated clergy were largely indistinguishable from each other during the period. Religious study certainly demanded attention to the substance of moral lessons in addition to the rigorous standards of grammatical training and repetition so common to the Western tradition of classical education. The earliest and subsequent American colleges were largely committed to producing ministers and uniformly included classics in their training. "The Greek [New] Testament remained a staple of American college admission requirements and of collegiate study for more than two hundred years," notes Caroline Winterer.[37] Even after colleges broadened their focus beyond producing ministers, the clergy retained the most solidly classical training in the United States outside classics departments in major universities. Routine training included instruction in Greek, Latin, and Hebrew, with a concentration on translating the Greek Gospels and relevant Latin works of church fathers. Moreover, the Greek and Latin works of antiquity were regularly part of the course of study.

Although scholars habitually distinguish between Christian and secular classical works, it is well worth noting that the Synoptic Gospels, the Gospel of John, and the words of Christ (written and recorded between roughly 50 A.D. and 110 A.D.), are as "classical" as any works of the period. Theirs is the same late republican and early imperial Rome of Cicero, barely cold from the purges of the Second Triumvirate in 43 B.C., Virgil, who died, prematurely, in 19 B.C., Ovid, who died in 18 A.D., and of those who follow, such as Petronius (died 66 A.D.) and Tacitus (died 117 A.D.), who records the death of Christ in Book 15 of his *Annals*. The rhetorical considerations of the writer(s) of the Gospels also alert us to the fact that they are literary works intended to persuade, either by reading or hearing, a multitude of cultures and people. The Gospel of Mark is clearly aimed at a Roman gentile audience; it starts with the newsworthy and popularly known story of John the Baptist, provides Aramaic-to-Latin translations for the Romans, and eliminates ponderous details of Jewish law and genealogy.[38] The Gospel of Luke, addressed to "Theophilus," meets the needs of the Greek-speaking populations of Judea, Greece, and Asia Minor and seems to fulfill the peculiarly Greek need for exacting detail and a minimum of theological loose ends. The writer of Luke explicitly claims that since he has been present for all that occurred, he is best suited to give a full accounting of the activities of the Christ. In addition, one need only look to the parables and words of John the Baptist, Christ, the disciples, and razor-tongued Paul for decidedly effective rhetorical strategies for dealing with Romans, Jews, Greek gnostics, Christian heretics, votaries of the pagan pantheon, and other subjects of the Roman Empire. Many, including John the Baptist's acerbic dismissal of claims to hereditary greatness, made it into common nineteenth-century sermons.[39] In addition, these very effective orators and writers depended rather heavily on the older Jewish scholarly, oratorical, and literary tradition that had already been finely worked and crafted over centuries and continued to underpin Christianity in Douglass's era.

The works of the early church fathers, like St. Augustine, so essential to theological study, were unabashedly classical in content. St. Augustine's *Confessions* and *City of God* are highly dependant upon Plato, Virgil, Ovid, Lucretius, and other classical masters; and Augustine was both trained in the classics and a professor of the same at Milan, the center of power in the late Western Roman Empire. Any clerical study through the nineteenth century was therefore doubly classical. Moreover, the concentration of the most important secular and religious oratory in the Greco-Roman world suggests that for Western civilization there is something inherently classical about oratory. Speaking from the podium or the pulpit, the orator is classical in tradition and training, in spirit and in truth. The pieties of the noble citizen and the ardent saint are familial if not sibling virtues. Whether the image of the senator or the Savior is evoked is a matter of oratorical intent, inflection, and modulation—shifts that Douglass was known to execute and manipulate with ease.

While African American clergy were often barred from extensive theological study at white seminaries, the nineteenth century saw a significant body of mainline Protestant black clergy emerge with formal and informal theological training that included the classics. Richard Allen broke from the Methodist Church in 1787 and established the A.M.E. Church. Absalom Jones and others who left the Methodist Church with Allen affiliated with the Episcopal Church in 1794. With slow progress and determined opposition from some white church officials, blacks were trained in Episcopalian and other seminaries. The Presbyterians had, as Wilson J. Moses notes, "early opened the doors of their seminaries to Africans, and they maintained a reputation for intellectual elitism."[40] They also opened the doors of New York's Presbyterian Oneida Institute, which included access to classical curriculum, to African Americans. The autobiographical accounts, other literary productions, educational trajectories, and political activities of many leaders and scholars emerging from the ecclesiastical tradition demonstrate that they were acutely aware of both the lessons and accomplishments of such literary forerunners as Phillis Wheatley and the value of the classics. The classical tradition that inspired Wheatley also guided the development of scholars like A.M.E. bishop Daniel Alexander Payne, founder of Wilberforce College and a friend of Episcopal priest Alexander Crummell. Wheatley's example of deploying her classical education to comment on issues of racial and revolutionary politics directly inspired other scholars. Clergyman and historian James W. C. Pennington, who married Douglass and Anna Murray, credited her in his autobiography, *The Fugitive Blacksmith*.[41]

The classics appear to have been significant to African American scholars as a pathway for personal, political, and racial advantage. Pennington, a noted scholar of classical languages and German, received an honorary doctorate from the prestigious German university at Heidelburg for his accomplishments.[42] In his autobiography, he summarized a part of his remediation after he escaped from slavery, recalling that he "had mastered the preliminary branches of English education, and was engaged in studying logic, rhetoric, and the Greek Testament, without a master."[43] A.M.E. Bishop Daniel Alexander Payne, who graduated from the Lutheran Seminary at Gettysburg, Pennsylvania, noted that in his education "[t]he chief books used for reading were monographs of the histories of Greece, Rome, and England; while the 'Columbian Orator' was the book used for training in the art of speaking," and "I said to myself, 'If [Rev. John] Brown [of Haddington, Scotland] learned Latin, Greek and Hebrew without a living teacher, why can't I?'"[44] After learning the classics and the humanities, he spent much time teaching them at a school he opened in Charleston, South Carolina, in 1829.[45] It was to Payne that Frederick Douglass helped dedicate a memorial in 1894, a white marble classical column eighteen feet in height.[46]

Episcopal clergyman Alexander Crummell's "ordinary degree" at the University of Cambridge was built on a series of examinations, which included a significant classical component. The first mini-examination of March 31–April 1, 1851, included Euclid, Books I and II; Plato's *Apology* and *Crito*; Horace's *Ars Poetica*; the Greek Gospel of St. Mark; Tacitus (complete with ancient history, geography, and Latin language); Sophocles's *Electra*; the Greek Acts of the Apostles; and the Greek first Epistle to the Corinthians. Crummell is one example of how classical instruction left its mark on the political thinking of African American scholarly clergy, contributing to their understanding of the race question and the strategies for confronting American slavery, racism, and the resulting African American cultural degradation. Thanks in part to his training at Cambridge, Alexander Crummell took a part of his view on slavery from Aristotle, a fact that produced no end of controversy. In *Politics*, Aristotle argued that a form of natural slavery existed because there were humans with reduced faculties of reason that made them most fit for the role of slaves. Slavery worked best for society when it comprised those who were naturally suited to serve. Crummell did not deny that intellectual and social inferiority fit men for slavery, but he argued that the inferiority was not natural. Rather, the degradation of man was a result of slavery. According to Crummell, if one could "raise them [enslaved blacks] to light and culture and manhood," the end was certain: "slavery could not even exist."[47] Crummell also formed some of his understanding of African Americans' condition from the Roman historians. He compared Tacitus's and Cicero's descriptions of the German barbarians to the nineteenth-century state of blacks. His interest in the work of Tacitus was rooted in the "simple but ingenious testimony he bears to the primitive virtue of the German tribes, pagan though they were, and which have proven the historic basis of their eminence and unfailing grandeur." He also believed that the German example suggested that "people simple, untrained and unadorned have been robust and virtuous; have bred brave and truthful men and chaste and beauteous women. . . .

And these excellencies have . . . made them immortal."[48] To Crummell, African Americans held the same promise, and in later years, he also ascribed these characteristics to West African tribes. Like others, he attempted to mobilize and deploy the classics in ways that would aid and transform African Americans, even to the extent of classicizing the African American population. Crummell's European educational experience demonstrates one particularly crucial point about African American scholars and clergy of the era, a matter that explains their attachment to the classics even as a steadily democratizing educational system moved to a less esoteric curriculum. Put simply, African Americans were not all committed democrats. After finishing his degree at Cambridge, Crummell despaired of returning to America: "My hopes are not bright ones even for white men and their children in America; controlled as you are by an unscrupulous and boisterous Democracy, which neither fears God, nor regards man; and by a demagogic priesthood, who devote their best energies in maintaining the sanctity of slavery, and the infallibility of the state."[49]

A.M.E. Zion Bishop Christopher Rush, who befriended Douglass, made sure to link the young A.M.E. Zion Church and common ecclesiastical language to the ancient world, especially the early Christianity of Roman North Africa.[50] His account of the philosophical and historical roots of African Methodist theology immediately builds on the intellectual and theological foundations laid by St. Augustine and other early church fathers. Rush's career also helps illustrate the role of the clergy in African American education and cultural development. Rush laid the cornerstone of the Yorkville A.M.E. Church in 1853 in Seneca Village, the first major community of free black property owners in Manhattan, which was later destroyed to build Central Park. One of the stories about the settlement is that it was named after Lucius Annaes Seneca, whose works were read by blacks of the area. Rush's Phoenix Society, begun in New York in 1883, was one of the most impressive African American organizations of the time. The Phoenix Society was largely made up of African American men, but it did have a number of white members. The society set the goal of being a core cultural outlet for blacks in New York City and "promot[ing] the improvement of the coloured people in morals, literature, and the mechanical arts."[51] After meeting the qualifications of good moral character, payment of dues and board approval, men could join the society. As Dorothy Porter illustrates, the Phoenix Society had a prominent multiracial membership, and the 1835 constitution and bylaws listed the following as officers: Rev. Christopher Rush, president; Rev. Theodore S. Wright, first vice president; Thomas L. Jennings, second vice president; Rev. Peter Williams, corresponding secretary; and Arthur Tappan, treasurer. Other board members included David Ruggles, William Hamilton, Charles B. Ray, Dr. John Brown, and Samuel E. Cornish. The society grew rapidly as did its ambitions. Porter writes,

> The Phoenix Society attempted large projects . . . $10,000 for the purpose of erecting a public edifice to be appropriated to the use of a library, reading room, museum or exhibition room, hall, etc., where colored youth and others might enjoy the benefit of such courses of lectures and other instruction on morals, literature and the mechanic arts, as are enjoyed by the white community. The Ward Societies were inaugurated . . . to . . . make a registry of every colored person, ascertaining his age, sex, occupation and his ability to read or write. They were to induce the old and young to become members of the society. Adults were to be urged to attend school and were to be impressed with the importance of sending their children to school regularly and punctually. Furthermore, each Ward group was organized to maintain a circulating library for the use of the people of color at a moderate fee, to organize lyceums to serve the advantages of public speaking and to promote lectures on science. Finally and characteristically, they were to form moral reform societies and to seek young men of "good moral character" as members whom they could expect to assist ultimately in getting a good liberal education.[52]

It is important to note that the moral and intellectual instruction became quite formalized, with lectures by clergy on "morals, scientific, and historical subjects" and the creation of an evening school for adults with a biracial faculty. This was followed by the creation of a high school targeted at youth.[53]

Like Rush, Daniel Alexander Payne pressed his love of classical education and hope for cultural progress by pressing for high educational standards in the A.M.E. Church and by surreptitiously purchasing Wilberforce College when it appeared that the denomination would not approve. In 1843, Payne and his compatriots rejected a man's ordination on educational grounds, which prompted an angry churchman to "demand violently whether one must read Greek, Hebrew, and Latin before he could be ordained." Later, Payne did press through a rigorous educational program for ministerial aspirants.[54] Payne and the rest of this elite group of clergy seized upon the classics, including Roman Christianity, as a way of arguing for the humanity and rights of blacks, improving their intellect and virtue, and resisting the leveling tendencies of the masses and larger democracy.

Daniel Payne shuddered that it was all too common for some preachers to advertise their ignorance as proof that they were of the people and to reject higher education. They would "introduce their sermons by declaring that they had 'not rubbed their heads against college walls' at which time the people would cry 'Amen!' they had 'never studied Latin or Greek,' at which the people would exclaim 'Glory to God!' they had never studied Hebrew,' at which all would shout."[55]

It was into this national and racial environment of politics, faith, and education that the young Frederick Douglass escaped, and it was into the company of these black clergy that he fell. Douglass's route from slavery into this world was circuitous but certain. He reveals a part of his preparation for his oratorical debut at Nantucket in the 1845 *Narrative of the Life of Frederick Douglass* and *My Bondage and My Freedom*. Of particular resonance for Douglass was a caustic encounter he witnessed between his mother and another slave woman who had abused him. From this basic conflict, he first learned to appreciate the power of rhetoric to effect decisive and immediate change. In the *Narrative*, Douglass was careful not to reveal anything more telling than this or his celebrated struggle for basic literacy. Douglass had much early training in the plantation life of his family and fellow slaves. He was exposed to the ancient oral tradition of storytelling and moral exhortation, folk tales, and secular and religious morality tales. The tradition emphasized the importance of sound in rhyme, imitation, tone, striking image, and metaphor. Such focus is also central to the formation of classical rhetoric and oratory.[56] According to the ancients, an audience is moved to immediate vocal and subsequent virtuous response by the skill of an orator's delivery, and both Douglass and Lampe illustrate that the slave culture's lessons placed similar emphasis on generating responses from auditors. This plantation academy was likely the early education of Douglass's youth, classical perhaps only in its implications but suggesting by similarity the ancient tradition of educating youth through the oral exercise.[57] Moreover it recalls the Socratic assertion that the greatest form of education is gymnastic for the body but lyric for the soul (lyric poetry, intellectual debate). Educative as well were the everyday examples of rhetorical combat, effectively demonstrated by Douglass's mother and the rest of the plantation community.

Douglass's narratives also describe his move with the Auld family to Baltimore, but they do not speak descriptively of the environment of the city at the time. Here too, Douglass found oratorical and political training. Twenty thousand free blacks lived in Baltimore during the 1830s, and they outnumbered slaves five to one. Their 687 registered households made up

15 percent of the households in the city during Douglass's time there.[58] Churches, schools, and voluntary associations helped form this community, and Douglass was involved in the black society of the city. Churches and schools were not only committed to their obvious missions but were also frontline social and outreach organizations that helped newly arrived blacks adjust to urban and black community life. Free black churches introduced Douglass to Methodism, an affiliation that continued and metamorphosed over his lifetime. According to *The Life and Times of Frederick Douglass*, students of the Bethel A.M.E. Church Sunday school encouraged Douglass to attend a new Sunday school at a nearby Methodist Episcopal church.[59] This is notable because the Sunday school ventures in urban black communities, including Baltimore, were far from limited scripture lessons; they were deployed and driven by ambitious, educated clergy. "Education exemplified the larger struggle of the city's blacks to advance through the strategy of separation," notes Frank Towers. "City government required African Americans to pay school taxes but barred them from attending public schools. In response, African Americans fostered independent schools affiliated with black churches and funded by blacks."[60] The Bethel A.M.E. Church established an aggressive, independent educational program and seeded programs in other black Methodist churches, including the Dallas Street M.E. Church that Douglass attended. By the 1850s, Bethel's own program showcased a formidable library of more than one thousand titles. The Sunday school tutored one hundred students and included a classical curriculum as well as instruction in scripture and Christian doctrine. Baltimore also had a branch of Christopher Rush's Phoenix Society by 1835. The spread of Sunday or "Sabbath School" instruction eventually necessitated the creation of the Colored Sabbath School Union of Baltimore to support "mental, moral, and religious" growth for the 2,665 (one in six) black youth under twenty who were attending Sabbath Schools in Baltimore by 1859.[61]

Where the Sabbath Schools were insufficient, other opportunities existed for private education. Baltimore's citizenry contained enough educated blacks and rare accommodating whites to support a number of private schools that offered instruction in English, arithmetic, music, and what was broadly referred to as natural philosophy—ranging from Socrates and Aristotle to basic natural science. Lyceums also flourished in Baltimore as educational outlets for advanced youth and adults. According to Frank Towers, the Galbreth Lyceum was a prime example of African Americans' educational success and struggle to attain autonomy from whites. Founded in 1855 in honor of Reverend George Galbreth, an early Baltimore African

Methodist Episcopal clergyman, the Lyceum was one of many lecture societies run by city blacks in the middle of the century. Patrons built a library and published the *Lyceum Observer,* one of the first black newspapers in the South. The Lyceum sponsored lectures, readings, and debates. Douglass was the only slave member of a secret debating association, the East Baltimore Mental Improvement Society (of which his future wife, Anna Murray, was a member). This little group consisted of six free blacks and the enslaved Douglass, and they routinely discussed and debated issues related to religion and the state of blacks in the nation. The society was a direct forerunner of the more public Galbreth Lyceum.[62] Douglass would have had access to Baltimore's black libraries, as well as to similar Sabbath School and improvement society libraries in the cities to which he eventually escaped—New York, Philadelphia, and New Bedford.[63]

In addition to his Mental Improvement Society and Sabbath School study, Douglass collected fifty cents from shining shoes and purchased a copy of Caleb Bingham's *The Columbian Orator* (first published in 1797). The book was designed to "inspire the pupil with the ardor of eloquence and the love of virtue."[64] Those who have studied Douglass at even undergraduate levels are familiar with "Master Tommy's copybook" and Sophia Auld's tutorial, but fewer have carefully examined the effect of Douglass's encounter with the formidable rhetorical tool, *The Columbian Orator.*[65] It is, however, the largely Ciceronian style among others, streamlined and made suitable for the new republic by Caleb Bingham, that the gifted Douglass encounters in the *Orator.* If "Master Tommy's copybook" of the 1845 *Narrative* provides the pivotal educational moment for Douglass's childhood, then Douglass's encounter with *The Columbian Orator* is the educational colophon of his oratorical life. The importance of the text to Douglass's development is prodigious, as he reminds his readers in *My Bondage and My Freedom.* Douglass credits the text, saying that it added "much to my limited stock of language" and gave "tongue to many interesting thoughts, which had recently flashed through my soul, and died away for want of utterance."[66] *The Columbian Orator* helped refine Douglass's rhetorical gifts as oratory and narrative assumed prominence in America.

David W. Blight's bicentennial edition of *The Columbian Orator* (1997) opens with "The Peculiar Dialogue Between Caleb Bingham and Frederick Douglass," which illustrates how studying American oratory necessarily and inextricably interweaves figures such as Douglass and Bingham and implicates the classical oratorical tradition in the development of many other American orators. As Blight points out, the *Orator* armed the young Douglass with the same rhetorical weaponry as his white playmates and other readers such as Stephen Douglas and Abraham Lincoln. Moreover, combined with his religious conversion, the book allowed him to fuse classical lessons and *virtus* with Christian liberation and virtue. Reflecting on his religious relationship with drayman and spiritual mentor Charles Lawson, Douglass commented, "I could teach him *the letter,* but he could teach me *the spirit.*"[67] This combination of letter and spirit would figure prominently in Douglass's future. One of the fundamental purposes of Bingham's text was to teach readers how to speak to an audience with both classical force and the comfort of common discourse. What Douglass found in the text was a primer on oratory, comprising "Pronunciation," "Gesture," and "Rules for Voice and Gesture Together," supported by the rhetorical theory and examples of Demosthenes, Cicero, Quintilian, Julius Caesar, and others. Bingham's rhetorical sections are specific in their recommendations, and they direct the reader to the appropriate classical authors for further study. Immediately, in the section on "Pronunciation," Bingham directs the reader to Cicero's *De Oratore* and the appropriate speaking character, Lucius Licinius Crassus (140–91 B.C.), who meditates on Latin pronunciation and is given as the model of an exceptional orator. Bingham's paraphrase of the parts of oratory corresponds to Cicero's texts, with pages on gesture, harmonious cadence, emphasis, and voice control, for instance, offering us insight on some of Douglass's preparation. Bingham draws inspiration from this portion of *De Oratore:*

> On all these emotions a proper gesture ought to attend; not the gesture of the stage, expressive of mere words, but one showing the whole force and meaning of a passage, not by gesticulation, but by emphatic delivery, by a strong and manly exertion of the lungs, not imitated from the theatre and the players, but rather from the camp [military camp] and the palaestra [academy of rhetoric].[68]

Cicero continues to lecture on the action of the hands, eyes, and other limbs (even the stamping of feet), and he provides instructions on the use of wit to disarm audiences and enemies.[69] Notably, Cicero argues that the use of the body should project manliness and that the action of the orator should not mimic the theatre but the [military] camp and rhetorical academies. Classical masters used the theatre to illustrate only the rudiments of oratory; they quickly removed students from the questionable influence of actors.

Bingham provided a heroic style of oratory that was important to Douglass's development. Oratory was the weaponry of classical virtue and truth, as scholars have frequently noted.[70] It was a way of both encouraging in others and gaining for oneself virtue. In addition to classical masters, Bingham offered aspiring orators like Douglass a tremendous number of generals, political leaders, and religious leaders as models. He sampled liberally from the words of historic generals and such contemporary successors as George Washington, who by the time of Douglass's emergence had been both elevated to the level of classical hero in America and rendered in the form of classical sculpture by Horatio Greenough and Antonio Canova, among others.[71] While critics such as Benjamin Franklin might have worried about the emasculating effects of classical education on the young men of the republic, it is clear that Caleb Bingham designed his text both to create the characteristics of martial manliness and heroism in his readers and to help them project those virtues through their oratory. The *Orator* operated as compendium of speeches, arrayed without respect to chronology and emphasizing issues of liberty, governance, religion, and education, among others. Of the eighty-four entries in the text, fourteen are speeches from the classical era or include significant classical allusions. Seven of the first eighteen orations are of classical origin or allusion. And a number of themes are visible, many of which appear in Douglass's speeches and writings. Bingham's introduction and the first oration, "Oration on Eloquence," lay out Cicero's recommendations and their advantages, but they would have been only the first of many speeches to demonstrate for Douglass the symbiosis between Judeo-Christian religion and the classics. Bingham includes "the Hebrews" as having excellence in oratory, as well as the Romans and Greeks, and the first oration on the excellence of Cicero and Demosthenes is by the English theologian William Perkins, read at a 1794 Harvard commencement. George Washington's first speech in Congress follows on the heels of Perkins's prayer that "Columbia always have more than one Demosthenes, to support the cause of freedom, and to thunder terror in the ears of every transatlantic Philip [of Macedon]. May more Ciceronian eloquence be ready to plead for injured innocence, and suffering virtue."[72] Perkins also utters a prayerful warning against "quicksands of vice, which have ever proved the bane of empire" and expresses hope that America can avoid them until the "last trump" sounds.[73]

After a speech by Roman general Publius Emilius, encouraging armchair generals to serve the state with their virtue and swords instead of empty, critical words, Douglass would have encountered an "Exhortation on Temperance in Pleasure" by English divine and University of Edinburgh professor of rhetoric Hugh Blair (author of the popular *Lectures on Rhetoric*). In addition to the mixing of classics, military speech, and Christianity,

Douglass's popular themes of decadent luxury and greed and the degenerate progeny of virtuous fathers also appear in Marcus Porcius Cato's speech in the Roman Senate after the Catiline conspiracy. Speeches by Gaius Cassius (conspirator against Julius Caesar) are included, as well as Cicero's oration against Catiline and Socrates's defense before Athens. Also present is the epilogue to Joseph Addison's influential play *Cato*, which directly links America to Rome, announcing that "[y]ou see mankind the same in every age: / Heroic fortitude, tyrannic rage, / Boundless ambition, patriotic truth, / And hoary treason, and untainted youth." Roman Caesar has given way to a British Caesar, and the Roman Senate that armed a Cato has its republican analog in America. "Our senate too the same bold deed have done, / And for a Cato, arm'd a Washington."[74] Central to the body of poems are many addressing liberty and slavery, including the drama "Slaves in Barbary," "Oration on the Manumission of Slaves," and the much-noted "Dialogue Between a Master and Slave":

> Humane! Does it deserve that appellation to keep your fellow men in forced subjugation, deprived of all exercise of their free will, liable to all the injuries that your own caprice, or the brutality of your overseers, may heap on them, and devoted, soul and body, only to your pleasure and emolument? Can gratitude take place between creatures in such a state, and the tyrant who holds them in it? Look at these limbs; are they not those of a man? Think that I have the spirit of a man too.[75]

In even a cursory reading of the *Orator*, Douglass would have encountered these powerful directives to oratory, manliness, and self-worth in their paraphrased forms. If we attribute to Douglass the curiosity and enthusiasm of even an average scholar, we can imagine that he acquired and perused the primary texts from which Bingham drew his models and theory. His early access to Bethel A.M.E.'s and Dallas Street M.E.'s growing Sabbath School libraries and the East Baltimore Mental Improvement Society's texts would have provided Douglass with tremendous opportunities to encounter these classical sources. Moreover, Douglass would have had access to a number of personal libraries upon his escape: his friendships with Christopher Rush, Nathan Johnson, and David Ruggles would have given him access to texts from the classics to Shakespeare to the most notable nineteenth-century productions. Douglass lore celebrates Nathan Johnson as the source of Douglass's name, plucking it from Sir Walter Scott's "The Lady of the Lake." Ruggles befriended Douglass early; it was in Ruggles's house that he first sought refuge in New York. It was also in his home that J. W. C. Pennington married Douglass to Anna Murray. Publisher, abolitionist, and board member of Christopher Rush's Phoenix Society, Ruggles might well have been the first African American book collector and book dealer. In addition to selling books, he operated his own private library of varied texts and rented them for a monthly fee. Given his affiliation with the Phoenix Society, it is a reasonable assumption that his collection included at least the most commonplace classical texts. James M. Gregory's account of Douglass's leisure reading leaves us with little room to doubt that he perused these classical texts during his later oratorical period and into his last years.

The rhetorical and historical tools of *The Columbian Orator* and its classical sources would have armed Douglass with potent weapons to critique and deconstruct the logic of American slavery and assail the romantic pretense of classical republicanism and virtue advanced by the American South.[76] In Douglass's earliest known and recorded speeches, from 1841 until 1846, direct classical references appear to be nonexistent (although in New York in 1842 he does get into a nasty oratorical exchange with a former slave named Julius Caesar).[77] However, the effect of the classical rhetoric as presented by Bingham is remarkably visible; the opening speeches of Douglass's abolitionist career deploy a number of the Ciceronian strategies recommended by Bingham.

The first of Douglass's speeches that reporters recorded in his own words, a lecture delivered in Lynn, Massachusetts, in October 1841, employs recognizable elements of oratory emphasized in both *The Columbian Orator* and the primary rhetorical writings of Cicero. Douglass begins his Lynn speech with an apparently nervous confession: "I feel greatly embarrassed when I attempt to address an audience of white people. I am not used to speak to them, and it makes me tremble when I do so, because I have always looked up to them with fear."[78] Genuine or not, Douglass's professed hesitation to speak to a white audience is telling. Gregory Lampe aptly notes that the gesture demonstrated "respect for his white audience."[79] But, the move also followed Bingham's advice to execute a series of introductory statements that establish respect for the audience, compose the orator, and focus the attention of the audience on the orator. Douglass appears to have pragmatically infused or further informed his application of Bingham with the racial character of the era. His deference to the audience is an act of particular caution, given the unpredictability of white sentiment. Nonetheless, this humble introduction also seems deployed in part to prepare for the execution of one of Cicero's other primary instructions, repeated in part in Bingham. Cicero's exhortation to the orator in *On the Parts of Oratory* includes the advice that rhetors should offer an audience their "merits or worth or virtue of some kind, particularly generosity, sense of duty, justice, and good faith."[80] In *On Invention,* he also proposes that orators openly address issues raised against their virtue. Moreover, they should call attention to the hardships and misfortunes they endured, the circumstances of their deliverance, or how they triumphed in order to assure audiences of their virtue and ability to persevere.[81]

The main charge against Douglass's virtue was grounded in racists' doubts about black intelligence. Most whites believed that African Americans could neither attain and demonstrate significant levels of intelligence nor transcend appetitive desires and demonstrate virtue. As Douglass frequently noted, abolitionists had lamented not being able to find a former slave to tell his narrative of slavery. Many escaped slaves could not span the huge educational and oratorical chasm between the field and the forum, but even abolitionists were guilty of assuming that if they did find a slave who could tell his story, the intellectual argument against slavery was still best left to white men.[82] Douglass's opening volley of rhetoric strikes these issues and opponents. His rhetorical eloquence quickly moves him from deferential beginnings to a direct recitation of his virtue as a speaker and his unquestionable experience and expertise. He establishes authority as the orator through testimony:

> My friends, I have come to tell you something about slavery—what I *know* of it, as I have *felt* it. When I came North, I was astonished to find that the abolitionists knew so much about it, that they were acquainted with its deadly effects as well as if they had lived in its midst. But though they can give you its history—though they can depict its horrors, they cannot speak as I can from *experience.* They cannot refer you to a back covered with scars, as I can; for I have felt these wounds; I have suffered under the lash without the power of resisting. Yes, my blood has sprung out as the lash embedded itself in my flesh.[83]

Very quickly Douglass establishes his authority over both the white audience he has previously admitted being hesitant to address and even the abolitionists for whom he has undertaken a trial lectureship. He is clearly no apprentice lecturer at the end of the first paragraph. Moreover, he takes the opportunity to establish his intellectual credentials by revealing how he has not only perused the political oratory of John Quincy Adams, whose own intellectual power in the classics and elsewhere was well known but also introduced congressional oratory to other slaves:

I well remember getting possession of a speech by John Quincy Adams, made in Congress about slavery and freedom, and reading it to my fellow slaves. Oh! What joy and gladness it produced to know that so great, so good a man was pleading for us, and further, to know that there was a large and growing class of people in the north called abolitionists, who were moving for our freedom.[84]

Douglass follows this by initiating the attack on slavery with a technique not at all alien to Bingham or the ancients. Douglass continues to establish his virtue by offering an account of his owner's vice and punctuating it with provocative examples of violence. By launching into a highly detailed description of his former master's activities, he generates images of cruelty that powerfully illustrate his own suffering and invites the listener to compare the virtue and manhood of the master and the slave.[85] As Bingham argues, the ancients insisted that the orator should be a good man, one who would take up the cause he espoused and with sincerity win hearts: "[In drama] Anger and resentment, at the appearance of cruelty, concern and solicitude for distressed virtue, rise in our breasts; and tears are extorted from us for oppressed innocence." Therefore, the earnest arguments of a man who has demonstrated himself to be heroic or virtuous will surely produce the same effects with images of cruelty.[86] Douglass speaks of his blood springing out from the embedded lash, and the whipped and scarred slave quite quickly begins to add to the canvas of images:

I have seen this pious class leader cross and tie the hands of one of his young female slaves [Douglass's cousin Henny] and lash her on the bare skin and justify the deed by the quotation from the Bible, "he who knoweth his master's will and doeth it not, shall be beaten with many stripes."[87]

The graphic violence in Douglass's earliest recorded speech is just the first example of an increasing gallery of violent images that will illustrate his oratorical and narrative projects. This suggests that however influential the *Orator* might have been on its own, it was not the sole secular influence on Douglass's oratory. The tendency in eighteenth-century literature had been toward graphic, insider tales of intrigue in politics and society.[88] Douglass's audience and readership were already primed for inside stories from the heights, depths, and hidden recesses of the American slaveholding republic. In addition to their general readiness, the American population was just that, American, and descriptions of Douglass's speeches in particular suggest that his productions contained qualities of emotion, revelation, and theatrical manipulation that made the man and his story more provocative, coarse, and democratically accessible than recommended by the purely classical rhetorical directives of republican and imperial Rome (which encourage virtuous temperance in oratory even as they demand forcefulness). Douglass employed some elements of the theatre and the streets as well as the military camp and *palaestra*.

To traditional oratory, Douglass added a brutal realism that included the physical details of American slavery's torture and sexual abuse. Beatings, whippings, and slaves' bloody submission, especially of women, regularly punctuate Douglass's speeches and narrative projects. Douglass details a well-known secondary exploitation of blacks, and many scholars note that black cultural resistance to slavery's sexual exploitation and its destructive impact on black family structure was significant, from slaves' strategies of marriage and reproduction to remarkable attempts at family reunification.[89] However, Douglass's accounts of the abuse exist in graphic detail neither suggested nor required by classical masters of oratory; and, as Deborah McDowell writes, "[O]ne can easily argue that, with perhaps the exception of his mother and grandmother, slave women operate almost totally as physical bodies, as sexual victims."[90] These scenes, in oratory and narrative, rhetorically pierce the veil of mere nineteenth-century and Victorian social propriety to reach and address actual questions of virtue.

These provocative and extra-classical additions still take their effect through traditional means. Pronunciation and emphasis, central to Bingham's text, are clearly at play in Douglass's Lynn, Massachusetts, speech. The text of his speech from the *Pennsylvania Freeman* italicizes for emphasis "feel" and "experience" in his opening sentences. Later, Douglass informs the audience that "many slaves *know* that they have a right to their freedom" and that slaves can bear the whip "without a murmur, compared to the idea of *separation*" from their families. Bingham lingers on the effect of pronunciation, delivery, and gesture to emphasize the words that should strike at the heart of a listener. Echoing Socrates, he argues that "[t]he influence of sounds either to raise or allay our passions, is evident from music."[91] After Douglass creates his own poignant picture of the state of slaves and piques the audience's emotions, he offers the solution to the horrors—emancipation—declaring:

> Emancipation, my friends, is that cure for slavery and its evils. It alone will give to the south peace and quietness. It will blot out the insults we have borne, will heal the wounds we have endured, and are even now

groaning under, will pacify the resentment which would kindle to a blaze were it not for your exertions, and, though it may never unite the many kindred and dear friends which slavery has torn asunder, it will be received with gratitude and a forgiving spirit.[92]

Douglass goes on to remind the crowd of the images of slavery: emancipation is what the slave wants to free him from the lash, keep him with his friends, and end the "agony of a mother when parting from her children." Concluding, Douglass reminds the audience of his sad but heroic journey and that prejudice "hangs around [his] neck like a heavy weight." As this first speech illustrates, Douglass is clearly a bit more prepared than he and others were willing to admit at the time, and the composition of his speeches throughout his three-month trial period exhibited a knowledgeable deployment of rhetorical technique.

As Douglass became more acclimated to the abolitionist circuit, he frequently turned his attention to proslavery and Southern-sympathizing politicians. The most prominent political trio of the era—Henry Clay, John C. Calhoun, and Daniel Webster—would prove to be some of his favorite targets for direct and oblique assaults. At this point in his career, Douglass was eager to denounce slavery and turn the issue of virtue against slavery's supporters. His attacks centered on implying or demonstrating that his opponents lacked virtue, a tactic strongly recommended in *The Columbian Orator* and its foundation texts. Read as classical *virtus*, virtue was intimately related to manliness, heroic qualities, and *pietas*. Douglass focused his attacks on virtue in terms of morality and manliness and true religious and civic piety. By 1844, Douglass had begun to argue that the Constitution was a proslavery document that had compromised the highest ideals of the republic to preserve slavery. Moreover, corrupt politicians from the North and the South conspired to circumvent the ideal of liberty and preserve a tacit national political commitment to slavery while feigning civic and religious piety. To illustrate the political strength of the proslavery forces in Washington, Douglass targeted the famous and visible political alliances protecting the institution. In "No Union With Slaveholders," a May 28, 1844, speech, Douglass assails the North for its accommodating proslavery politicians:

> I am astonished at the existence of any desire on the part of pious and religious men, to be in union with slaveholders. What is their character? Are they so very pious and religious? Oh, yes! they're *very pious;* and the North knows how to suit them, when there's to be a nomination, with a style of piety that will unite perfectly with their own.

> The South brings forward for your President, Henry Clay, and the North stands ready with the vice-President—the Rev. Mr. Frelinghuysen![93]

Douglass's attack is not simply a sarcastic criticism of southern piety. He also launches a thinly veiled assault on their masculinity and virtue. He suggests a curious marriage between the great political men of the two regions:

> [O]f course I did not mean any harm to Mr. Frelinghuysen; I was only illustrating the nature and character of the Union, by this match that they have made between the piety of the North, and the Slavery of the South. I meant no harm to Henry Clay. They have married Henry to Frelinghuysen, (tremendous applause,) and it's a type of the National Union; but I am astonished that Freemen do not forbid the banns.[94]

This odd and sarcastic suggestion of a same-sex marriage elicits a favorable response from the audience—humor that Douglass eventually became wary of—and it also introduces a considerable move toward claiming a lack of masculinity or virtue in his opposition, effectively feminizing them. Douglass proceeds to decry northern senators who bore infamous insults on the floor of the legislative body:

> There are your great men in Congress—look at them! Your Choate, and your Bates! Do they rise to say a word about your business that they're sent there to do—they're bullied down, and obliged to sit and hear Massachusetts scoffed at and insulted! They had to sit and listen; and so are all the North bullied down by them. And you consent to be their kidnappers! their putters down of insurrections![95]

Not only are northern politicians cast as the females of political marriages, they are also bullied and shown to be impotent in the Senate. Moreover, Douglass directly attacks the southern political structure, deconstructing southern honor and suggesting the degradation of the North at the hands of dishonorable men:

> Who can fix the brand of murderer—thief—adulterer, on the brow of the man that you associate with, and salute as *honorable?* The *Honorable* Henry Clay! the *honorable* John C. Calhoun! And those ministers who come to the North with the price of blood on their hands—how shall moral principle be diffused among the people on the subject of slavery, while they are hailed as *Reverend!*[96]

In early speeches, indirect classical references are the only textual evidence of classical influence, but they can be significant. We might compare Douglass's assault on corrupt leaders with Cato the Younger's (96–46 B.C.E.) speech on the Catiline conspiracy, given before the Roman Senate and reproduced in *The Columbian Orator*:

> At such time, in such a state, some talk to us of lenity and compassion. It is long that we have lost the right name of things. The Commonwealth is in this deplorable situation, only because we call bestowing other people's estates, liberality, and audaciousness in perpetuating crimes, courage.
>
> Let such men, since they will have it so, and if it becomes the established mode, value themselves upon their liberality at the expense of the allies of the empire, and of their lenity to the robbers of the public treasury; but let them not make a largess of our blood; and, to spare a small number of vile wretches, expose all good men to destruction.[97]

Douglass remembers Cato's speech and employs the tactic of exposing dangerous misnomers, in this case of vice named virtue. In Douglass's attack, complacent citizens of the republic are content to allow murderers, thieves, and adulterers to be named "honorable" and "reverend," in order to avoid conflict, just as Cato argued that traitors, criminals and looters of the public treasury were called "liberal" and "courageous."

When politicians were not Douglass's targets, the church and ministers often took their places. Another of Douglass's early speeches was also one of his most memorable. He gave his famous "Slaveholder's Sermon," in which he skewered and mocked the Christianity of southern slaveholders and ministers, many times over his oratorical career and as early in trial period as a November 4, 1841, address at Hingham, Massachusetts. In this and other lectures, Douglass emphasized a mimicry and satire in word and gesture that captivated, provoked, and unsettled audiences, and he also employed a variety of techniques from *reductio ad absurdum* to complex parody:

> Oh! if you wish to be happy in time, happy in eternity, you must be obedient to your masters; their interest is yours; God made one portion of men to do the working, and another to do the thinking; how good God is! Now you have no trouble or anxiety; but ah! you can't imagine how perplexing it is to your masters and mistresses to have so much thinking to do in your behalf! You cannot appreciate your blessings; you know not how happy a thing it is for you that you were born of that portion of

the human family which has the working instead of the thinking to do! Oh! how grateful and obedient you ought to be to your masters! How beautiful are the arrangements of Providence! Look at your hard, horny hands—see how nicely they are adapted to the labor you have to perform! Look at our delicate fingers, so exactly fitted for our station, and see how manifest it is that God designed us to be the thinkers, and you to be the workers—Oh! the wisdom of God.[98]

The speech brings together the recognizable cadence of the sermon with the jarring extra-scriptural content of the message. Moreover, the speech signifies on a number of issues. "Their interest is yours" is a likely double entendre on the self-interest served in securing economic gain from stolen labor and feigned brotherly love. The division of the body of man into workers and thinkers corrupts both the vision of the body of Christ and the ideals of democracy. Moreover, the physical comparison of hard hands and "delicate fingers" suggests the actual weakness of the slaveholding class. This combination of greed, corrupted civic and religious piety, and physical weakness contrasts sharply with both classical and Christian visions of virtue.

We have to consider the complexity of the style Douglass brought to such speeches, especially those touching on morality in religion, as a remarkable synthesis of oratorical styles, the conviction and force of the pulpit, the rhetorical preparation of the classics and Bingham, and the plantation academy all creating a stinging delivery, tone, gesture, and sound. James Monroe, an abolitionist who heard the "Slaveholders Sermon" on numerous occasions, described it as

a brilliant example of irony, parody, caricature, and *reductio ad absurdum*, all combined. It abounded in phrases which, though innocent in the original preacher, when delivered by Mr. Douglass with suggestive tone and emphasis to a Northern audience, became irresistibly ludicrous. . . . To do him justice . . . you must imagine his marvelous power of imitation and characterization—the holy tone of the preacher—the pious snuffle—the upturned eye—the funny affectation of profound wisdom . . . and the tearful sympathy with which the speaker dwelt upon the helpless condition of his hearers in case they should cease to be the property of slaveholding masters.[99]

Monroe perceived Douglass's skill at combining rhetorical forms, but in the Hingham speech Douglass also attacks the racism of the church as part of a continuum of American racism from region to region, not a peculiar occurrence limited to the South. He illustrates the racism of the Church in New Bedford and skewers the northern revival as well:

> Another young lady fell into a trance—when she awoke, she declared she had been to Heaven; her friends were all anxious to know what and whom she had seen there; so she told the whole story. But there was one good old lady whose curiosity went beyond that of all the others—and she inquired of the girl that had the vision, if she saw any black folks in Heaven? After some hesitation, the reply was *"Oh! I didn't go into the kitchen!"*[100]

It is notable that Douglass deploys the rhetorical mimicry described by the ancients to assail his foes. It is also remarkable that he employs, as a matter of mimicry, other oratorical styles. However, it is all too easy to look at the "Slaveholder's Sermon" as a sideshow, a humorous use of popular Christian homiletics to drive home a more classical point of virtue. Or one can imagine that Christianity itself is part of the joke. It is also easy to imagine that Douglass arrived at his "Slaveholder's Sermon" and his oratorical prowess predominantly through *The Columbian Orator* and Cicero. One needs only to assume that no African American source could contribute substantive formal intellectual or oratorical training. Ultimately, this is no more accurate than the assumption that Douglass was created by W. L. Garrison. What Douglass seems to accomplish is a multiracial and cross-cultural rhetoric, well in advance of what contemporary American rhetorical study recognized in the late twentieth and twenty-first centuries—synthesized from the rhetorics of the plantation, pulpit, classical palaestra, and antebellum political world—over which he gained mastery and even the skill of exquisite mimicry. And, within this potent rhetorical cocktail, there are elements not necessarily part of any canon of rhetoric. In *Reclaiming Rhetorica*, contributor Drema R. Lipscomb examines the rhetoric of Sojourner Truth and also explores the fallacy of the continuing classical tradition of rhetoric, seemingly given empire without end and presenting "nineteenth-century American rhetoric as a classical tradition derived primarily from ancient Greek and Roman sources. This tradition is also depicted as a continuous thread, surviving without a break from ancient to contemporary times."[101] In the same volume, Andrea Lunsford argues that the discipline of rhetoric has been largely male "not because women were not practicing rhetoric . . . but because the tradition has never recognized the forms, strategies, and goals used by many women as 'rhetorical.'"[102] However, this tendency is not merely to read rhetoric as male and classical but to read it as *white,* male, and classical. That line of white descent marginalizes all other rhetoric from ethnic populations. The rich, multilayered rhetoric of Douglass that was so inexplicably effective consisted of an experience with and mastery of multiple, multicultural, and multiracial rhetorical forms that were not commonly experienced together by average or even highly educated rhetors. Moreover, neither the caustic give-and-go or mimicry of slaves on the plantation nor African American homiletics would have been recognized as a suitable partner, much less a mimetic vehicle for the classical oratorical tradition. Yet it is this combination of forms, a combination that hybridized the classical tradition, which yielded Douglass.

Douglass's narratives suggest that he gained significant knowledge and oratorical training from the African American religious community. Scholars have unearthed Douglass's position as an A.M.E. Zion exhorter, which helps satisfy superficial questions about how he acquired the general manner and sermonic cadence of Christian ministers of the era and was able to press home the parody. However, this approach to his religious experiences—asking how he acquired his religious cadence rather than what he acquired from the intellectual tradition of African American Christianity—generally operates on the premise that all Douglass could get would be a style and not a substantive theological, philosophical, intellectual, or oratorical stance. Ultimately, it suggests that Douglass imported substance into the African American Christian homiletics, bringing his *Columbian Orator* with him down the center aisle of the A.M.E. Zion Church. However, it is equally likely that many congregations had not only been baptized with the classics but also had countless suppers of them in their semisecular social clubs, self-improvements societies, and lyceums in cities throughout the Northeast and West.

The call and response of the black sermonic tradition (which demanded that the orator be intimately involved with the auditors) as well as its heavily dramatic elements of imagery and illustration would have continued beyond the plantation and into the urban church tradition of Douglass's Baltimore. Douglass was able to hear in Baltimore some of the influential black ministers of the day: the Reverends Edward Waters, Nathaniel Charles Peck, and Lewis G. Wells. Douglass notes Wells as having been the first black man he ever saw give a lecture from a written manuscript. Douglass's narratives also repeatedly indicated his great respect and heartfelt debt to a number of ministers, including Christopher Rush. Especially among black Methodists, there was already an active movement among clergy such as

Rush, Payne, and Pennington to align black homiletics and clerical training with the most exacting classical standards. The black churches had their own tradition of oratory that had learned to use the tricks, strategies, and lessons of the Old and New Testament writers, early church fathers, and the plantation academy to achieve oratorical power over their black Christian auditors. In short, they were no amateurs.

By 1820 the A.M.E. Zion Church had begun to codify oratorical rules for its ministers and exhorters, an ongoing process that periodically enriched and expanded the guidelines. Reverend William Serrington, whom Douglass called a man of "high intelligence," recruited him to become an exhorter (Christopher Rush added some encouragement as well), which in the church licensed him yearly to preach to the local congregation and to do so often. That local congregation would have been remarkably heterogenous. From 1838 until 1841, Douglass experienced a culturally diverse New Bedford that comprised Native Americans, Europeans, Africans, Asians, and Polynesians.

Douglass would have gotten considerable oratorical and political training as an exhorter in this environment, not the least of which would have come from his active speaking schedule, the many important abolitionist and religious speakers hosted by his and other churches, and particular traditions of the A.M.E. Zion Church. Douglass heard Jehiel C. Beman, Dempsy Kennedy, John P. Thompson, Leven Smith, and Christopher Rush, whom Douglass counted as among the greatest speakers he had ever heard. Moreover, Douglass attributed part of his success to those men.[103] The *Doctrines and Discipline of the African Methodist Episcopal Zion Church* gave significant general instruction on the art of preaching. The rules were wide-ranging, from punctuality to the use of gestures, and appropriate tone and accessibility of language. The sermons were to "appeal to the intellect (the mind), the emotion (the feeling), and the volition (the will)" of the auditors, with the intent to persuade a listener to embrace Christ. A simplicity, force, and clarity were demanded, attributes that would "suit the comprehension of the uninformed." These rules and directions were seriously applied and enforced by the church, and the Reverend Douglass would have been a faithful practitioner of the guidelines.[104] He could not have missed their similarity to the instructions found in *The Columbian Orator*:

> To instruct, to persuade, to please; these are its [oratory's] objects. To scatter the clouds of ignorance and error from the atmosphere of reason; to remove the film of prejudice from the mental eye; and thus to irradiate

the benighted mind with the cheering beams of truth. . . . An Alexander and a Cesar [sic] could conquer a world; but to overcome the passions, to subdue the wills, and to command at pleasure the inclinations of men, can be effected only by the all-powerful charm of enrapturing eloquence.[105]

With this classically inflected African Methodist oratorical tradition and training, Douglass would have approached the pseudo-Christianity and sermons of slaveholding and proslavery Maryland and southern ministers with both the eye of the secular statesman-orator and the A.M.E. Zion orator—both roles related through a classical forefather but the latter descending also from the African American experience in exclusion, oppression, and servitude. The southern ministers and congregations would be caught on double prongs of parody and denunciation, those of the secular forum and the religious pulpit. Whether lifted from Cato or John the Baptist, the attack would be directly upon those sons who claimed or used the sacred words of the fathers or the Father as perverse excuses to do evil that their virtuous fathers and divine Father would have condemned.[106] It is a theme that Douglass used often, including in his oration "What to the Slave is the Fourth of July?"

It is directly from this African Methodist oratorical environment that the young Douglass emerged to astonish the Garrisonian abolitionists. As Douglass became active in the diverse and vibrant New Bedford community, it was no wonder that he found himself in the path of a solicitor for the abolitionist paper *The Liberator.* According to the several accounts in the *Narrative, Life and Times of Frederick Douglass,* and *My Bondage and My Freedom,* Douglass eventually became a reader of the paper. The periodical sharpened his understanding of the abolitionist movement and led him to hear William Lloyd Garrison. Douglass became a participant in the New Bedford abolitionist movement, eventually taking up the role of a regular speaker and leader. In the three-month trial period with the Garrisonians and afterward, the effect of Douglass's rhetorical armament was visible in the responses of crowds and reporters as well. Moreover, those who knew the rhetorical techniques and recognized their signals openly reacted with astonished enthusiasm. After the Hingham speech, the *Hingham Patriot* said of Douglass that he was "very fluent in the use of language" and comparable to "men who have spent all their days over books."[107] Nathaniel P. Rogers, editor of the *Herald of Freedom,* a paper in Concord, New Hampshire, declared that Douglass was nearly unmatched in speech: "It is not declamation—but oratory, power of debate. He watches the tide of discussion with the eye of a veteran, and dashes into it at once with all the tact of the forum or the bar. He has wit, sarcasm, pathos—all that first-rate men show in their master efforts."[108]

Rogers's declaration of Douglass's rhetorical power pinpoints some of the more intriguing reflections of reporters and witnesses to Douglass's speeches. He notes that more than mere declamation, the audience is treated to true oratorical skill. The master effort that Douglass matches with first-rate men evokes the virtuoso performance that Wheatley longed for, the demonstration of talent that would elevate any poet to the ranks of Virgil or Homer or Terence. The comments of Douglass's auditors suggest that to some Americans, he is reaching these heights. The goal of classical oratory is to produce virtue within the speaker and the listener: the soul affected by oratorical eloquence recognizes virtue, which, in turn, can itself "irradiate the benighted mind with the cheering beams of truth."[109]

The chronicle of remarks persuasively demonstrates that audiences perceived Douglass to be intrinsically virtuous. Moreover, the commentary on his eloquence and virtue is intimately entwined with vocal assertions of his innate masculinity and heroism, which reach their apex with classical heroic and even divine comparisons. Those who knew the elements of classical training that distinguished educated men clearly recognized the technical aspects of Douglass's oratorical skill, and those who did not certainly imagined Douglass as a spectacle of near-miraculous masculinity. Perceptions of Douglass's manhood and virtue became very much part of the orator, just as Bingham and ancients from Cicero to Quintilian suggested would result from successful oratory. In a quite literal sense, Douglass's body became intimately entangled with the discourses of black liberation and virtue.

In Milbury, Massachusetts, the *National Anti-Slavery Standard*, described Douglass as follows: "The fugitive, who produced such an interest at Nantucket, again called forth pity and horror at his story. He is shrewd and discriminating, and his deportment is graceful and manly."[110] He was also called "eloquent and thrilling" in his speech. A Middlesex County, Massachusetts, bill advertising an abolition meeting declared, "[T]he colored man speaks with great power and pathos. He states his own history and the workings of slavery upon his own mind with great eloquence."[111] According to John Blassingame, the adjectives "bold," "manly," "striking," "massive," "colossal," and "majestic" were commonly used to describe him, and he was said to convey in features "repressed rage," "self-control," "dignity," and "unyielding firmness." Moreover, an American diplomat to Haiti described him as a "tall and manly form of physical grace and vitality," whose "physical equipment left little to be desired."[112] The phallic undertones of these and other lines suggest in no small sense that Douglass's masculinity, both phenotypic and oratorical, played a central part in the seduction of American and European audiences. In these and other accounts, Douglass was described with many variations on handsome and was widely held to have regal characteristics. As a piece in the *Sacramento Bee* declared:

> There was no emasculation in the speeches of Douglass: no effeminacy. They broke in upon his auditors. . . . Men who looked at him, who listened to him, knew that his heart, his soul, his manhood, his conscience, every fibre of his [being] were pulsating in the burning words he flung forth. They knew he was honest and sincere; therefore he commanded respect, attention, admiration, even though he frequently evoked bitter opposition.[113]

And when auditors and commentators looked for superlative terms to sum up Douglass's remarkable blackness, heroic form, and virtuous voice, they selected descriptions that were increasingly inflected with classical allusions, including comparisons to the Roman slave-rebel Spartacus.[114] The *Herald of Freedom* account of Douglass's November 11, 1841, speech in Providence, Rhode Island, prominently cast Douglass as a figure of heroic proportions:

> The fugitive Douglass was up when we entered. This is an extraordinary man. He was cut for a hero. . . . A commanding person, over six feet, we should say, in height, and of most manly proportions. His head would strike a phrenologist amid a sea of them in Exeter Hall, and his voice would ring like a trumpet in the field.[115]

Still others chose specific classical heroes to compare to Douglass's heroic form:

> As this Douglas[s] stood there in manly attitude, with erect form, and glistening eye, and deep-toned voice, telling us that he had been secretly devising means to effect his release from bondage, we could not help of thinking of Spartacus, the Gladiator; . . . A man of his shrewdness, and his power both intellectually and physically, must be poor stuff . . . to make a slave of.[116]

Meanwhile, Elizabeth Cady Stanton wrote that Douglass "stood . . . like an African prince, conscious of his dignity and power, grand in his physical proportions, majestic in his wrath" and had audiences "magnetized with his eloquence, laughing and crying by turns with his rapid flights from pathos to humor. All other speakers seemed tame after Douglass.[117]

The power Douglass demonstrated to Stanton was soon to affect far more people, largely because by 1844 it was clearly evident that larger portions of Douglass's life story were bound for publication. As Blassingame notes, Douglass's speeches continued to reach new heights of oratorical power, and by the February 11, 1844, speech that unveiled significant elements of his life story, the meetings were among the best the abolitionists had attended. Nathaniel Rogers, from whose report the account of the speech is taken, declared that after Douglass's description of his family and life on the plantation, he "ought not to have been followed at all," adding,

> After getting though this [the narrative elements] . . . and giving I suspect, no token to the audience of what was coming—though I discerned, at times, symptoms of a brewing storm—he closed his slave narrative, and gradually let out the enraged humanity that was laboring in him, in indignant and terrible speech. It was not what you could describe as oratory or eloquence. It was sterner—darker—deeper than these. It was the volcanic outbreak of human nature long pent up in slavery and at last bursting its imprisonment. It was the storm of insurrection—and I could not but think, as he stalked to and fro on the platform, roused up like the Numidian Lion—how that terrible voice of his would ring through the pine glades of the south on the day of her visitation—calling the insurgents to battle and striking terror to the hearts of the dismayed and despairing mastery. He reminded me of Toussaint among the plantations of Haiti. There was great oratory in his speech—but more of dignity and earnestness than what we call eloquence. He was not a speaker—performing. He was an insurgent slave taking hold on the right of speech, and charging on his tyrants the bondage of his race. One of our Editors ventured to cross his path by a rash remark. He better have run upon a Lion. It was fearful, but magnificent, to see how magnanimously and lion like the royal fellow tore him to pieces, and left his untouched fragments scattered around him.[118]

We should not take it lightly that the terms "Numidian" or "Numidian Lion" were used to describe Douglass. "Numidia" is the archaic term for the area occupied today by Tunisia and parts of Algeria. Moreover, it was the area's Roman provincial name, and countless specimens of its native lions were shipped to gladiatorial contests and circuses. Numidia was the region where a young Jugurtha united the tribes and rose against Rome, as well as the province where the Roman client king Juba II received the hand of Cleopatra Selene, daughter of Antony and Cleopatra, by Octavian after the conquest of Ptolemaic Egypt. The Numidian lion has literary, political, and religious currency.[119] As early as the seventeenth century, poet and courtier Sir John Denham penned, "As a Numidian lion, when first caught, endures the toil that holds him." The King of Morocco gave one to President Andrew Jackson as a gift. According to Brewer's *Dictionary of Phrase and Fable*, the lion had an obscure religious significance to the story of the Messiah:

> Lion and the True Prince (*The*). *The lion will not touch the true prince* (1 *Henry IV.,* ii. 4). This is a religious superstition; the "true prince," strictly peaking, being the Messiah, who is called "the Lion of the tribe of Judah." Loosely it is applied to any prince of blood royal, supposed at one time to be hedged around with a sort of divinity.
> "Fetch the Numidian lion I brought over;
> If she be sprung from royal blood, the lion
> Will do her reverence, else he'll tear her."
> *Beaumont and Fletcher: The Mad Lover.*[120]

The provocative imagery of Douglass as the formidable Numidian Lion, the vaguely apocalyptic Christ of the Revelation—coming to judge the unrighteous, or a Jupiter who "hurled the thunderbolts of Truth against this spiritual wickedness in high places, and against gilded villainy and ecclesiastical wrongdoing" illustrates how far Douglass's continually developing oratorical technique, physical power, and sheer force of argument had elevated him.[121] Still, the instructions of Bingham and the classical masters are visible in this description—the volcanic eruption of virtue, not just rhetoric: the storming voice, visible earnestness, and finally, a regal, heroic bearing of the *palaestra* and not the performance stage. At rhetorical war against slavery he was an *agathos,* free to visit full power on his enemies and exceed Victorian limitations of propriety. At the same time, in three short years after his Nantucket speech, Douglass had become the epitome of black humanity and the Aeneas of his race: virtuous, pious, and heroic to the threshold of demigodhood. Revelation, heroic transformation, and resurrection are no less suggested by Douglass, who says that the lecture period with the Garrison organization "was literally the opening upon me of a new Heaven and a new earth—the whole world had for me a new face and life itself a new meaning. I saw myself a new man, and a new and happy future for my downtrodden and enslaved fellow countrymen."[122]

The image of resurrection offers us a host of possibilities, both Christian and classical. The Christ image is immediately before us, the Messiah who seeks to have the cup removed but is simply faced with crucifixion and resurrection or the collapse of universal order. There is also the model of pious Aeneas, survivor of burning Troy, with likely death and slavery for his family behind him or a geographic and political wilderness and the gods' promise of a new and better life ahead of him. He has no real choice but to forge ahead, despite his lingering desire to find less difficult pathways. Speaking of the *Narrative*, Rafia Zafar argues that because he was, as an African American, outside the realm of humanity, Douglass had no choice but to write his way into a heroic position or a position of power. He could aim for a superlative example like that of Benjamin Bannecker, but, ultimately, he had to write himself as a spiritual descendant of the founding fathers, especially Benjamin Franklin, and into American humanity. "Douglass's appropriation of the memoir of the self-made man," writes Zafar, "must be understood from the vantage point of the 'socially dead' seizing upon literate means as an act of resurrection, if not birth."[123]

Zafar is likely too reserved in his analysis, for it is clear from the words of Douglass's auditors that they reached further back than Franklin for their descriptions. They reached beyond the founding fathers for the classical models they and their Puritan ancestors, like Cotton Mather, used to define virtue.[124] Douglass would have needed to write himself according to those classical specifications, eventually fashioning himself in the mode of the classical figures that inspired the Founders. He would have to be not just an heir of Franklin but of Spartacus, Cicero, Cato, or any number of heroes of field and forum. Moreover, after achieving resurrection or birth from the power of his narrative and oratory, Douglass seems to perceive a necessary change in the nature and goals of his work: he wants to assume power and create change, not just seize control of his body or tell his story. Douglass argues early on that he was uncomfortable just telling his story and looked for ways to contextualize and denounce slavery. The development of his oratory suggests that he looked for more and more complex and substantial methods, examples, and images to uncover and denounce evil. He was particularly worried through the 1840s about becoming something of an abolitionist narrative-comedy act. The laughter he generated in the "Slaveholders' Sermon" and "No Union with Slaveholders" came at a cost:

> One of the hardest things I had to learn when I was fairly under way as
> a public speaker was to stop telling so many funny stories. I could keep
> my audience in a roar of laughter—and they liked to laugh, and showed

disappointment when I was not amusing—but I was convinced that I was in danger of becoming something of a clown, and that I must guard against it.[125]

Moreover, by the time he emerged from the Garrisonian period of his oratory, he not only desired to speak more profoundly about slavery but also had to respond to the oratorical needs of a changing audience. By 1854, Douglass had received his first call to speak before a lyceum audience, and invitations increasingly poured in from literary societies, ceremonial committees, universities, and other lyceums. Douglass was also called on for eulogies and memorials of various types. These audiences and subjects exceeded the sufficiency of his narrative and required that he read, research, and critically examine a variety of books, pamphlets, histories, academic disciplines, and public issues. These more formal oratorical occasions also changed both the class structure of his audiences and his relationship with them. He was paid, sometimes handsomely, for his words, and he was well aware of the freedom and power his more secure finances provided him. His new vocation as a formal speaker was one

> full of advantages mentally and pecuniarily. When in the employment of the American Anti-Slavery Society my salary was about four hundred and fifty dollars a year, and I felt I was well paid for my services; but I could now make from fifty to a hundred dollars a night, and have the satisfaction, too, that I was in some small measure helping to lift my race into consideration.[126]

He later argued that "Aristotle and Pericles are all right; get all that, too; but get money besides, and plenty of it."[127] Ironically, it was by using classical figures like Aristotle and Pericles that Douglass was able to fully become a financially sound, intellectually independent, self-made man.

It is also worth remembering that 1856 also marked the beginning of Douglass's relationship with Ottilie Assing, the German and half-Jewish journalist and writer who is now believed to have been his companion and mistress. They were certainly intellectual partners and companions in spirit. Assing had begun to report on the slavery issue early in her time in the United States, sending columns back to *Morgenblatt für gebildete Leser*. She also visited James W. C. Pennington's congregation and developed a cordial relationship with his family, even teaching his son German.[128] After she translated Pennington's *The Fugitive Blacksmith* for her German readership, she began *My Bondage and My Freedom*, becoming enthralled by Douglass. In 1853, she traveled to Rochester to meet him. Soon they developed a complex relationship that ranged from Assing's translation of *My Bondage and My Freedom* to a lengthy affair. She wrote of introducing Douglass to German texts in translation, and they read other European literature and philosophy together.[129] Douglass emerged from slavery in the midst of the Transcendentalist era, and whatever classical works he had already encountered were likely tinged by the German Romanticism that also energized the Transcendentalist movement. Assing, who spent twenty-two summers in the Douglass home, became the German tutor to the youngest daughter, Annie, who eventually attended a German school in Rochester and excelled in German reading and composition. We know that sometime during the first three years of his pairing with Ottilie Assing, with whom he enjoyed sharing music, philosophy, and the classics, he also learned to read and write German.[130] He had acquired these skills by 1859, when he fled to Europe after John Brown's raid on Harpers Ferry. He would have certainly perused the Transcendental and Romantic writers with Assing, if not before, and perhaps even in German. Karl Marx too was among Assing's favorites. Interestingly, while traveling in Rome she also commented on their classical explorations.[131] Ultimately, his travels, writing, reading, and companionship with Assing encouraged him to think of himself as citizen of the world, above and beyond the racial and cultural limitations of the United States.[132]

Given this broadening view of himself, it is no great surprise to see how Douglass, who had no choice but to write himself into existence and into new and more lucrative audiences, would write himself as a larger-than-life figure, not just heroically as the true son of the founding fathers but also as the Spartacus, even the Aeneas or Moses, of his race and be hailed as one with Christian and classical virtue. He had created a romantic, heroic, superlatively pious, even gnostic space outside the confines of the traditional church.[133] He had written and spoken himself into a prototypical American, the disciple of the founding fathers' ideals, and the real heir to Benjamin Franklin. He was a self-made man, the image of the classical hero, the ancient voice of the orator, the minister in the pulpit, and statesman of his race. Zafar also argues that "[m]anifestly, Douglass means for us to think of him as an American individual as much as he paints himself as a synecdochic Afro-American."[134] Henry Louis Gates Jr. notes how thorough was his success:

> In, 1866, in an essay entitled "What's to Be Done with the Negroes," George Fitzhugh makes a remark *en passant* that helps us understand the

sheer presence that Douglass had, by that time, come to have in American letters as the metaphorical sign of the intellectual potential of the African-American. "We are not perfectionists, like the northern people," Fitzhugh writes, "and should not expect or *try* to make Solomons or even Frederick Douglasses of the Negroes."[135]

What Douglass did with his oratorical power—his image as manly Spartacus, Numidian lion, pious leader, transformed or resurrected heroic man, and stately orator—is easily as provocative as the evolving images. From this position just shy of Solomon, both superlative African and superlative American, Douglass attacked his enemies with refined fury. Douglass's prototypical written speech, the famous "The Claims of the Negro, Ethnologically Considered" (1854), assailed the idea of black inferiority where it was particularly dangerous and problematic: at the level of "scientific" or "academic" racism. The dam of public opinion that held back opposition to slavery was partly constructed of academic defenses of slavery and ivy-clad theories of black inferiority. Douglass spent months researching and writing the speech after consulting with the president of the University of Rochester and Professor Henry Wayland. The speech at Western Reserve College was the first keynote address at a major university by an African American. The Philozetian and Phi Delta literary societies at Western Reserve invited Douglass; and three thousand people, more than the number in attendance at the actual graduation ceremony, sat through his two-hour speech. Douglass opened by declaring it to be an honor to speak to the august assembly, and he also wasted no time snatching a laurel for his brow:

> It is a new chapter in my humble experience. The usual course, at such times, I believe, is to call to the platform men of age and distinction, eminent for eloquence, mental ability, and scholarly attainments—men whose high culture, severe training, great experience, large observation, and peculiar aptitude for teaching qualify them to instruct even the already well-instructed, and to impart a glow, a luster, to the broad theatre of active life.[136]

Of course, Douglass immediately declares himself unfit for the task, but the list reads like a declaration of his merits and an argument for admission to an exclusive society. Oddly enough, the dash following "attainments" in his description also seems to mark the very gap he hopes to close in the speech: between the society of old hereditary power, class distinction, and scholarly achievement and his punning and ironic "severe training," "large observation," and "peculiar aptitude for teaching" that characterize his harrowing and heroic journey up from slavery.[137]

Douglass first suggests that the graduates before him must take a stand on the issue of the Negro, for a "neutral scholar is an ignoble man." While claiming that his analysis will not be scientific, he proceeds with an analysis of the major and minor claims against the humanity and character of the Negro. The opening claim is that the Negro is not a man. Interestingly enough, Douglass's defense is to argue from the basis of oratorical eloquence; one need not equal Henry Clay, Daniel Webster, or John C. Calhoun in eloquence, logic, and intelligence to be recognized as a man. Yet, Douglass is clearly offering himself in comparison to these men, whom he has frequently denounced and abused and will continue to attack around the country. Continuing, Douglass frequently paraphrases scholars known to the audience, refers to the New Testament, and then arrives at the ethnological claims of the Negro.

Douglass's first argument is the centrality of Egypt to Western civilization, foreshadowing the lengthy argument of Martin Bernal 133 years later, and he notes the ancient Egyptians' mechanical and architectural skill. He points out that Greece and Rome obtained their civilization from Egypt, reminds his auditors that the fact is not disputed by scholars, but notes that Egypt is in Africa. Furthermore, Douglass argues, the scholarly research on Egypt betrays an active attempt to reduce if not eliminate the Negro from the story of the ancient world. Douglass points to Samuel G. Morton's observation in his *Crania Americana* that the Copts, Egyptians, and Nubians possess African features and ancestry but argues that Morton's mighty struggle to claim that the inhabitants of Egypt were not in any way "real Negroes" (even against the opinions of some of his colleagues) suggests how prejudice masquerades as scholarship.

Douglass next seeks to establish the resemblance of the Egyptians to Negroes and employs first French and English scholars and then, as a coup, Herodotus. Quoting ethnologist James Cowles Pritchard, Douglass declares, "'Herodotus traveled in Egypt. . . . After mentioning a tradition, that the people of Colchis were a colony from Egypt, Herodotus says, that 'there was one fact strongly in favor of this opinion—the Colchans were *black* in complexion and *woolly* haired.'"[138]

Douglass goes on to argue that the Oracle at Dodona was alleged to have been established by a female captive of the Thebaid, who was said to have been black because she was Egyptian. To this Douglass adds yet another classical source, Aeschylus, to buttress the claim that the ancient

Egyptians were known to be black. After briefly discussing the vast period of history involved and disavowing any claim to expertise, Douglass boldly claims that "it may be safely affirmed, that a strong affinity and direct relationship may be claimed by the negro race, to THAT GRANDEST OF ALL THE NATIONS OF ANTIQUITY, THE BUILDERS OF THE PYRAMIDS."[139]

The speech continues with a discussion of the languages of North Africa and Ethiopia, during which Douglass uses the linguistic resources of the Classical Museum of the British Association (1846) and the *Transactions* of the Philological Society to argue that Semitic and North African languages are within the same linguistic family.[140] For evidence that strong civilizations, ancient and modern, benefited from diversity, Douglass turned to his classically educated friend, doctor, fellow author, and University of Glasgow graduate James McCune Smith, who had written an article on the subject.[141]

"The Claims of the Negro Ethnologically Considered" differs from earlier speeches in at least four substantial ways and heralds significant changes in Douglass and his oratory. First, Douglass clearly adheres to some of the formulae and commonplaces of *The Columbian Orator* and his old style: he creates rapport with the audience by expressing his lack of fitness for the task, and he attempts to provide the audience with some evidence of his own virtue. But he is forced to move beyond his plantation story not only to establish his own virtue but also to contend with issues of race beyond the plantation and slaveholding. His narrative is absent except in an obscure and ironic form in the opening statement, and he accomplishes his own elevation by demonstrating his ability to comprehend and deploy virtues other than strength or personal experience, not his ability to defeat Edward Covey. Moreover, in the speech Douglass cannot stand in for his entire race against a world of slaveholders; yet he can be its statesman or champion by moving out of the plantation and even abolitionist world to wield Herodotus or Aeschylus at pivotal moments in international scholarly and political arenas. His racial task is, quite literally, "distinguishing himself from the apes" in the scholarly arena rather than the barnyard battlefield.[142] Personally, Douglass is forced to close the gap between himself and his new audience by acquiring the knowledge to which his gritty bootstrapping gave him access and demonstrate the new acquisition and ascension in his oratory. The slave might well have been made man, as his *Narrative* asserted, but to create further change, the man needed to become a scholar and a statesman.

Furthermore, the standards of virtue and the signs of power change in the speech. It is not simply an oratorical shift for a paying or elite audience that causes Douglass to trade the virtue of physical victory against Covey for the virtue of scholarly or classical knowledge. Virtue becomes a more complex, composite concept for Douglass—intellectual, political, spiritual, and physical. By writing himself into the position of scholar, statesman, classical hero, race warrior, representative man, clergyman, and descendant of the founding fathers, he is faced with understanding and exercising multiple virtues or synthesizing something to encompass them all. Although Douglass could earlier have depended on the virtue exhibited by physical power, self-liberation, personal experience, and A.M.E. Zion training and authority, at some point he had to discern and study other honored virtues, understand them, embrace them, embody them, and exude them in oratory. Despite his exhorting status Douglass was not visibly tethered to the doctrine and demands of the established church; neither was he formally a scholar nor a warrior nor a statesman.[143] But in pursuit of new audiences and new influence or power, he developed the ability to recognize virtue outside his own narrative and religious experience. Moreover, he became skilled at expressing core virtue in terms suited to diverse audiences or roles. Pursuing the question of black humanity into academe, acquiring the imprimatur of the scholar, and critiquing the damage racism does to objective, scientific, virtuous scholarship are examples. Finally, in this speech the classics ceased to be merely the oratorical superstructure for Douglass's arguments: the classics became the argument. The classics emerged in the speech with individual value, power, and authority. Douglass clearly recognized that Herodotus and Aeschylus had authority sufficient to undermine the scholarship of contemporary white ethnologists and scientists, and he deployed them for that purpose. It would not be the last time he used the power of the classics for intellectual and oratorical advantage. Once the transformation from abolitionist speaker to national orator occurred, Douglass had both a more complicated position as an orator and improved tools and weapons to use in his ongoing struggle against slavery. However, it would be inaccurate to say that Douglass abandoned his old style in the face of the change. Reports from journalists and other auditors confirm that he moved between carefully prepared remarks and extemporaneous, sometimes fully original, speeches. He learned to adjust his oratory to the occasion, but as the data about classical references suggest, he increasingly found uses for the classics in his oratory. Proslavery and southern-sympathizing politicians were some of his most frequent targets, and classical references appeared often in his attacks.

When Douglass broke from the Garrisonians and acquired independent finances, a new audience, and a new set of oratorical and intellectual tools, his oratorical and political styles grew more confrontational. Douglass even undertook the task of redefining, rewriting, and unequivocally enunciating the attributes of the exceptional man, the variety of man who in any race would provide the foundation of civilization. Clearly, it was to the labor and invention of men that he attributed the rise of civilization and to indolence and vice and slavery that he attributed its decline. Douglass suggested that by observing the acts and fates of the great civilizations of the past his auditors could build better men and a better civilization. Douglass employed the classics to exemplify greatness, practicality (in work or education), or manly virtue. Conversely, Douglass also deployed the classics to illuminate decadence, emasculation, degeneracy, injustice, or depravity.[144]

In an 1857 speech, "The Significance of Emancipation in the West Indies," Douglass warns that Greek civilization passed away "in a trance of artistic beauty, and architectural splendor."[145] According to Douglass, the cultural defense against such ostentation and pageantry is for great men to concern themselves largely with invention and creating economic capital. Such creations are enduring and useful to civilization. Douglass lists men who are inventors or mechanical creators and therefore benefactors of the world. As he understands it, there is no danger that those who contribute directly to the world's comfort and general prosperity will ever be forgotten or despised by history. Douglass goes on to list Arkwright, Watt, Fulton, Franklin, Morse, and Daguerre. The great men of civilization are those who produce something valuable for civilization. Slaveholders, who produce nothing and steal others' labor, rank below even the creators of the most esoteric cultural artifacts. The fall of the great, ancient civilizations suggests as well that some greater spiritual or virtuous goal must be present in the practical, creative man if his creation or contribution is to have lasting value or meaning:

> "Men do not live by bread alone," said the great Redeemer. What is true of individual men, is also true of societies, and nations of men. Nations are not held in their spheres, and perpetuated in health by cunning machinery. Railroads, steamships, electric wires, tons of gold and silver, and precious stones cannot save them. A nation may perish in the midst of them all, or in the absence of them all. The true life principle is not in them. Egypt died in the sight of all her imposing wealth and her everlasting Pyramids. The polished stone is there, but Egypt is gone.[146]

In "The Trials and Triumphs of Self-Made Men," an address delivered in England in 1860 and in some variation many times afterward, Douglass links the development of self-made men in a nation to honest labor. But Douglass does not argue that the self-made man is sufficiently virtuous if the labor is honest. According to Douglass, self-made men are not invulnerable men and perhaps not even the "best made men." In the acquisition of admirable and practical qualities, Douglass notes that they may as easily develop or acquire a negative quality: "[S]uch men are generally very egotistical." One of the principal dangers of this egotism is that

> they too often display a want of respect for the means by which other men have risen above the level of the race. They are too free in disparagement of schools they never attended, and colleges, of which they are ignorant. In this they assume a place that does not become them; for whatever may be their merits they are generally but relative merits—they are out-siders. They may pass judgment upon the best means of self education, but they may not lay down the law as to the best means of educating others. There never was yet a man who had educated himself who could not, by the same exertion and application and determined perseverance, have been better educated by the help of the ordinary instructions.[147]

Douglass's caveat about the self-made man resonates strongly with his oratorical and intellectual experience at Western Reserve College. Apparently there are lessons that the self-made man must learn beyond ambition and honest labor. Ignoring the wisdom of the ages is not part of Douglass's direction to the self-made man, and a series of virtues—scholarly, professional, civic, and moral—must make up his character. The result of their absence can be seen in the ruins of classical civilizations.

Douglass brings his criticisms to bear on the South in countless speeches, but he increasingly focuses on southern claims to the legacy of Greek and Roman republican virtue. In "Revolutions Never Go Backward" (1861) and "Fighting the Rebels With One Hand" (1862), Douglass warns that the South has abandoned intellectual, moral, and civic virtue, content to forego honest labor for stolen slave labor. Moreover, they have ignored the examples of history. He declares that "Egypt, Palestine, Greece and Rome had their warnings of impending collapse" and failed to heed them.[148] As the "best friend of his country," Douglass insists in "Revolutions Never Go Backward" that the seeds of the Civil War's destruction and tumult were sown not by the hardworking people of the South but by a class corrupted by opulence and privilege, "who are permitted to live by stealing" rather than by the manly virtue of hard work.[149] Having already discredited the political triumvirate carrying the banner of the South, Douglass extends his attack to declare that "[w]e owe it to the existence of a set of respectable robbers and murderers who work their fellow men like beasts of burden, and keep back their wages by fraud."[150] By the end of the address, Douglass has characterized the rebels of the South as a mob intoxicated with not only the liquor of decadence but also the first blood of battle. This illicit bacchanal is merely an aperitif to whet an appetite for destruction. Douglass drives home his point with a classical analogy, arguing that the South has played assassin to the nation, with the old Union dead like Caesar and the action at Fort Sumter the blow of Brutus.[151] "The first proclamation of Mr. Lincoln was received with derision at the South," he points out. "It is said that the cabinet of Jeff. Davis read it amid roars of laughter. They were intoxicated with their victory at Charleston." For Douglass, the appropriate summation is in the words of Euripides: "Whom the Gods would destroy, they first make mad." Douglass continues to deploy classical allusions, using the madness of Nero to explicate the South's attack on the Union: "Nero fiddled while Rome was on fire and men have danced over the jaws of an earthquake. But those who have been merry in the morning have wept and howled in the evening."[152] Legend holds that the mad Nero ordered large sections of Rome to be burned so that he could rebuild the city to his own designs and enlarge his own palace without the expense of imperial land purchases. It is also held that Nero watched the devastation from the Tower of Maecenas, no less, and played his original composition, "The Sack of Troy."[153] This willingness to overturn the state and betray the *patria*, the homeland, is particularly resonant if we remember the slaveholder's bedrock commitment to servitude against all. One slaveholder revealed the extent of this devotion as he committed himself to the traitorous southern cause. To preserve African slavery "he would even undo the [American] Revolution: 'Should a dissolution of the Union ever take place, we could place ourselves under the protection of Great Britain, she guaranteeing us our slaves.'"[154]

This primary betrayal of *patria* opens on to a wider disintegration of masculine virtue. When Douglass compares the rebels of the American South to mad Nero, the allusion paints southerners with the broad brush of the worst classical vices. Accusations against Nero, in particular, go far beyond burning Rome to all manner of predilections and desires traditionally held to have been vice, from sadism to masochism to homosexuality. With his own superlative virtue solidly established, Douglass can argue with authority that the crimes of the South encompass a wide range of moral disintegration. Douglass saddles the South with the infamous vices of the Roman imperial age, so discomfiting to Americans, instead of the manly virtues of its republican golden age.

Douglass's classical attack on the South amplifies the graphic details of his written and spoken narrative. The beatings described in the 1845 *Narrative* and his early speeches were widely known by the beginning of the Civil War, and the images would have rushed back into readers' and auditors' minds with the advent of the classical allusions. Douglass's Aunt Hester is stripped and beaten for running away to meet her slave paramour, and Douglass declines to elaborate on the rather obvious issue at hand, saying only, "Why master was so careful of her, may safely be left to conjecture."[155] Although Douglass does not directly address sexual slavery in the episode, he does inform readers that his aunt could easily match beauty against most black and white women of the area. Douglass's own battle against Covey's attempt to bind and whip him—"Mr. Covey seemed to think he had me, and could do what he pleased . . ."—offers an additional suggestion about the kind of control some masters wished to exercise. Scholars have illustrated the disturbingly voyeuristic quality of Douglass's scenes of masters beating women slaves, but the intersection in Douglass's work of white masters' desires for exclusive access to and control over both male and female slaves' bodies and the conjured image of Roman imperial decadence also expertly signifies on the South's celebrated rhetorical and cultural pretenses of emulating a classical republic or the virtues of the ancient world. Douglass's classical assault also brings him into direct conflict with some of the founding fathers. Thomas Jefferson insisted that American slavery was superior to its Roman predecessor because it did not countenance capricious violence and torture. Jefferson pointed to Cato, who restricted reproduction among slaves and sold off his old and diseased slaves along with "everything else become useless." According to Jefferson, one would not find an American counterpart to Vedius Pollio, who "in the presence of Augustus, would have given a slave as food for his fish, for having broken a glass."[156] In oratory and narrative, Douglass easily demonstrates that the murder of slaves was commonplace, and his accounts of sexual and physical violence suggest that the American republic inherited both the virtues and vices of the ancient world.

Douglass's use of the classics to critique and recast the politics of race and abolition and address issues of virtue in the United States illustrates the effectiveness of classical rhetorical tradition both as a single tool and when used with other traditions to amplify argument. It also demonstrates the particular power of the classics to generate images of humanity and virtue that destabilized both entrenched, racist perceptions of blacks as intrinsically inferior, lesser forms of humanity and the foundations of American slavery.

However, there were costs to the discursive dependence on virtue and masculinity in the battle for abolition. The discourse of hyper-masculinity —oratorical supremacy, heroic qualities, civic and religious *virtus* and *pietas,* self-made manhood, leonine ferocity—demands that both orator and the auditor increasingly distance themselves from the feminine as they pursue higher *virtus* and power.[157] Douglass's storied search for his father, the gradual narrative loss of his mother, his name change from matrilineal Bailey to Douglass, his seizure of rhetorical control from abolitionists, and so on all demonstrate how the course of classical, masculine, heroic virtue requires the orator to remove all diminutions of manhood. The diminutive—servant, apprentice, son, boy—must give way to master, teacher, father, or self-made man. There is a distinct acquisition of power related to this narrative and oratory of conquest—purposeful, if not from the beginning, then in the unfolding. As a subordinate turned conqueror, then orator, and finally leader, Douglass's kinship is not only with the ancient orators and proponents of republican virtue but also with those generals, orators, and emperors who transformed the ancient republic into empire. We might remember the first of these is none other than Julius Caesar.[158] Moreover, as the methods of telling and the messengers change, a *renaming* takes place that has classical resonance. As conquering Scipio becomes *Africanus* and adopted Octavian becomes *Caesar Augustus,* so does Frederick Augustus Washington Bailey slip the yoke of his given name and become Frederick Douglass.

This process of renaming and making men, heroes, statesmen, or rulers does not occur without a characteristic unseating of previous power. Aggression is often a hallmark of masculinity, and the aggression unleashed by Douglass's ascendance is important to any analysis of his work. Douglass disrupts, unseats, and seizes power in his relationship with his enslaver. He tells his story of slavery and freedom directly, provocatively, and repeatedly; and he eventually defies even the abolitionist leaders who brought him to public light.

Moreover, in telling his story, Douglass very powerfully abandons the process of entreaty, exceptional self-deprecation, and enshrouded protest that one finds in earlier writers like Phillis Wheatley. Wheatley introduced the tradition of "protest through excessive compliance" as a way of alluding to or illuminating contradictions and hypocrisy in American and Christian society, and she used the language and classical training of the elite to code and shield her work.[159] Douglass took the podium to directly address, cajole, chastise and accuse his American and European audiences, even when it meant criticizing abolitionists or breaking from their ranks and philosophical stance.

Near the end of his life, Douglass appears to engage in an active campaign to seize a specific legacy and name for himself. His later speeches and activities seem partly orchestrated to burnish his life and accomplishments and canonize his position as a heroic man. He associates himself with the most essential, powerful, and defining elements of ancient civilization: the Egyptian, Greek, and Roman past and their descendant states and cultures. The Grand Tour of Europe was standard for persons of wealth or high standing; and Douglass made a tour of Britain, France, Italy, Greece, and Egypt with his new wife, Helen Pitts. What is particularly remarkable about this journey is Douglass's extensive oratory and publications on the subject of his trip. Douglass made it quite clear to his audiences (the Metropolitan A.M.E. Church in Washington, D.C., unknown for the second lecture, and broadly in newspapers and his 1892 *The Life and Times of Frederick Douglass*) that he was received by the best classes and notables of Western nations and that he was intimately aware of the politics and histories of those nations. Moreover, Douglass took special care to indicate that he knew the intimate histories and importance of the classical sites he visited.

Central to Douglass's account is his insistence on providing his personal assessments and reflections on the nations, historic sites, and important figures he encountered. He justifies the expense of travel and the practical and prudent question of "[w]ill it pay" to travel with what he calls the natural inclination of man to wander from home. Adapting Joseph Addison's *Cato* (so important to the eighteenth century's classicization of the American Revolution and American *pietas*), he argues, "No pent up Utica contracts our powers, or limits our habitation to any part of the globe."[160] He also roots his travel in self-improvement and the Bible: "There is no denying that there is some connection between knowledge and traveling, though everyone may not find it. The Sacred Writings tell us that in the latter days men shall go to and fro in the earth and knowledge shall increase."[161] Should any doubt remain about the advisability of travel, he offers us Ralph Waldo Emerson's travels as an example.[162] Douglass also picks up the themes of his earlier "The Claims of the Negro Ethnologically Considered," declaring in the lecture to the A.M.E. congregation that he went to Egypt to settle questions about its ancient past:

> I went to Egypt partly to discover the truth, so far as the truth can be discovered by seeing the present population, as to what kind of people were the ancient Egyptians. I had read in ethnological works that the people who built the Pyramids were of the white race, and had heard it affirmed on the other hand, that they were veritable Negroes. I should have been glad to have found the first statement entirely contradicted, and the latter one entirely confirmed, for though a great ancestry does not prove greatness in their descendants, it does imply the possibility of greatness,

and I wanted this confirmation for the benefit of the colored people of this country in their contest against popular prejudice.[163]

Douglass pronounces the Copts as proof that the ancient Egyptians were neither black nor white in their common American form, but it is notable that he is still seeking to find tools for contending with contemporary racism in the ancient world. Moreover, when he does pick up his lecture on his travels from France to Italy, Greece, and Egypt, he makes an interesting declaration that characterizes the function of his trip. He proposes that it is what an individual intellect makes of the sights and experiences of the Western world that is of interest and note. The Grand Tour was in many ways a final examination or virtuoso performance of the cultivated man. "In account with the philosophical suggestion," Douglass writes, "that much of the interest felt in the objects that surround us in the world, is due to the lights and shadows in which we view them, I shall give you more of my thoughts of things [I saw] than details and descriptions of the things themselves."[164]

Recounting his travels from Paris to Rome, he notes that the ground between the cities is thought-provoking because it is the cradle of Western Europe and the civilization that crossed the Atlantic and was "brought to the shores of America;—where some think it will reach its highest development and perfection—a pretension to which I have not the least objection, and shall rejoice in its fulfillment." After this endorsement of the West, Douglass notes that the same land is the field of "heroic endeavor" that determined, with the helmet, shield, and spear of the West against the sling and arrow of the barbarian, the course of civilization.[165] On the heels of that statement, he weaves Africans into the ancient world:

> One does not need to be very learned in the science of ethnology or archaeology to discover [during his travels] here, [in the men, the manners and the customs prevailing]—something of Egypt and Africa, as well as Greek and Roman influence.
>
> As we move eastward and southward between the two great cities, black hair, black eyes, full lips and dark complexions increase. You see the South and the East in the style of dress; in the gay colors, the startling jewelry and the free and easy outdoor life of the people.[166]

Douglass goes on to make comparisons between the Europeans and blacks, noting the customs, habits, and characteristics generally assigned to blacks that are present in Europeans. He argues that these are signs of the influence of Africa on Europe and the "kinship of nations." When his chronicle of travel arrives at Rome, he showcases his familiarity with the city and his studied opinions of its historic places and citizens. In the Forum, he meditates on the fiery rhetoric of Cicero and his orations against Catiline and Antony. He notes the Palatine Hill and the baths of Titus, Diocletian, and Caracalla; he follows this with accounts of the Temple of the Vestal Virgins, the Capitoline Hill, the Arch of Titus, and the Column of Trajan. He balances his assessment that the Roman world is the foundation of Western civilization with the sobering assertion that "the lap of pleasure, the pursuit of ease and luxury, are death to manly *courage, energy, will*, and *enterprise*."[167]

His account of his journey to Egypt displays the same tendency to perform his familiarity and affinity for the ancient world and connect that world with African Americans, both to benefit his race and his own stature. He looks to the inhabitants of Egypt and admits, "I said to myself, you fellows are at least in your disposition, half brothers to the negro."[168] He meditates on the Christian and Jewish historic and religious experiences in Egypt, invoking Moses and Joseph, and regales the reader with his ascent to the top of the highest pyramid (of Cheops). At this point, Douglass provides the reader with a stunning image of himself in a moment of figurative conquest. He is the great orator, leader, and thinker, beyond all his race and most Americans and astride the pyramid of Cheops, "above the world below." He contemplates his position in the sky, a moment oddly like an Assumption, musing that "[t]aking the view altogether—the character of the surroundings; the great unexplained and inexplicable Sphinx; the Pyramids and other wonders of Sakkara; the winding river and valley of the Nile; the silent, solemn and measureless desert; the seats of ancient Memphis and Heliopolis . . . stir in the man who beholds it for the first time, thoughts and feelings never thought and felt before."[169]

The pensive and venerable Douglass that James M. Gregory records, the seasoned orator and statesman poring over the great works of the Roman era and pondering the chronicle of his own words, should not be a surprise to the judicious reader of Douglass's life and works. It is in the classical image and the classical model of civic success that Douglass seeks his own laurels. He hopes to be immortalized by his race and nation for his works, as were the great orators and statesmen of the ancient world. He seeks his own apotheosis into the pantheon of honored fathers of the American republic that he averred would finish and improve the work begun by those Western founders with his own deeds and works printed, bound, and continually read—proof that the slave was most assuredly a man and something more.

CHAPTER THREE
SINE QUA NON
THE VOICE OF ANNA JULIA COOPER

The podium of the 1893 World Congress of Representative Women in Chicago held a formidable array of African American women. After bitter complaints from prominent black women that the Columbian Exposition's women's exhibit exemplified the exclusive and racist nature of the event, organizers invited Anna Julia Cooper, Fannie Barrier Williams, Frances Jackson Coppin, Sarah Woodson Early, and Hallie Quinn Brown to address the exposition's visitors.[1] However, the presence of the women was much more an extension of the theme of the exotic at the event than a sincere attempt at racial inclusion.[2] Beyond the main section of the exposition, on the periphery of which was the women's pavilion, stood the exhibits for the Asian, Middle Eastern, and African races. Shirley Wilson Logan notes, "[T]he board [of the exposition] presented these women as anomalies to the received and accepted views of blacks at the time."[3] Equally interesting and disturbing, Logan continues, is the role exposition organizers asked the renowned orator Frederick Douglass to play:

> In the tradition of authentication prominent in nineteenth-century slave narrative introductions, Douglass was prevailed upon to speak after Francis Coppin's discussion of [Fannie] Williams' speech, as if to validate what the women had said. He was the only man allowed to make

remarks after the opening session of the General Congress. Douglass, exhibiting his well-honed rhetorical charm, expressed excitement at hearing "refined, educated colored ladies addressing—and addressing successfully—one of the most intelligent white audiences that I ever looked upon."[4]

Douglass's position as intermediary and authenticator for the accomplished, educated women on the podium is telling, since his subjection to white authenticators was precisely the kind of indignity he sought to avoid and escape. It is also intriguing and telling that the orators could be vouched for (to the satisfaction of white auditors) by a black man. Moreover, in terms of formal training alone, the women were generally better educated than Douglass. Williams attended the Collegiate Institute of Brockport, New York; the New England Conservatory of Music; and the School of Fine Arts in Washington, D.C. Hallie Q. Brown attained a B.A. degree at Wilberforce and was a professor of elocution there. Coppin was an Oberlin graduate, as was Early. Cooper, Harper, and Early were classically educated; and many among the orators, especially Cooper, were fully capable of rhetorically challenging Douglass at the podium.[5] That their oratory required his validation further illustrates the diminished position black women held in late-nineteenth-century America. Women were not generally imagined to possess virtue that was not tied to virginity, matrimony, or motherhood, and their capacity for reason and intelligence was in doubt. They were certainly not imagined to possess the manly, heroic, and civic virtues traditionally addressed and engendered by classical or contemporary orators.

Frederick Douglass's own masculinist rhetoric of virtue, manliness, and heroism had helped reduce the voices and roles of black women to rhetorical and narrative background material. In his narrative and others, such as James W. C. Pennington's, women served as objects of perpetual suffering, whose physical abuse and violated sexual virtue gave evidence of white depravity and called black men to the defense of vulnerable women. Narratives of exceptional, virtuous, and heroic escaped male slaves proliferated in this period. Douglass's many iterations of his struggle were joined by those of Pennington, William Wells Brown, Henry Bibb, Henry Box Brown, Josiah Henson, and countless others. Americans since Emerson had embraced the idea of representative men, and in the postbellum era, they directed questions about how to contend with the "district of Nature" that included blacks and the "Negro Problem" to representative black men like Douglass.[6]

The many nineteenth-century narratives that described black males acquiring manhood, education, religious transformation, and freedom did little to improve the prevailing stereotypes of black women's moral depravity, intellectual deficiency, and spiritual benightedness. Black women's discussions of physical and sexual violence, though deployed to assail slaveholders' virtue, were often double-edged. As Harriet Jacobs's much-noted narrative predicament in *Incidents in the Life of a Slave Girl* (1861) illustrates, frank discussions of sexuality and sexual abuse could further reduce their position in relation to white, Victorian standards of feminine virtue and culture. African American women were beset by a multitude of problems. The mythology of depravity and benightedness distanced them from their white, Victorian counterparts and thus helped exclude them from larger discussions of women's rights. Moreover, the same mythology encouraged white men's predation and abuse of black women, while encouraging black men to look to Victorian womanhood as the exemplar of feminine beauty and virtue.[7]

After Douglass's death in 1895, the well-established role of representative black leader remained, and his ultimate successor, Booker T. Washington, established a school and school of thought that helped define Reconstruction and Gilded Age racial politics and compounded the problem with which Anna Julia Cooper and other black women were already contending. Washington's Tuskegee philosophy of industrial education, domestic purity, economic self-sufficiency, and political neutrality, which was launched nationally in his 1895 speech at the Cotton States Exposition in Atlanta, has been thoroughly explored by such scholars as Louis Harlan.[8] Washington's strategy of ameliorating white anger by encouraging black submission on issues of educational, political, and social equality created a variety of additional problems for African Americans, who were already witnessing a substantial retrenchment by racist southerners, morally and militarily exhausted northern citizens, and opportunistic politicians and industrialists who desired economic growth, prosperity, and potential American imperial expansion more than social equality. Voting rights and political, educational, and economic advances made in the wake of the Civil War were quickly disappearing. Many whites were unnerved by the prospect of a black population with comprehensive educations, economic aspirations, and political ambitions. For that reason, they embraced Washington's political and educational plans. This alliance of white retrenchment and black accommodation seemed destined to doom future generations of African American men to peonage, disenfranchisement, and inferior education—and African American women to all this, plus domestic servitude.

Many African American writers and intellectuals recoiled at Washington's power, his revisionist stance on slavery, and his hostility to higher education and sociopolitical advancement. As William L. Andrews notes, a series of novels emerged in response to Pauline Hopkins's call for authors to "faithfully portray the inmost thoughts and feelings of the Negro with all the fire and romance which lie dormant in our history."[9] Authors such as Hopkins, Frances E. W. Harper, and Emma Dunham Kelley linked a revisionist project of correcting the stereotype of black women with the larger project of racial uplift.[10] Although these novels run straight into the (s)mothering arms of domesticity and embrace Victorian standards of culture and gender, they also employ references to the classics as they explore questions of cultural uplift and morality. In Frances E. W. Harper's *Iola Leroy*, the character Reverend Carmicle, who marries virtuous Iola to virtuous Dr. Latimer, assesses the future of the black race in part by indicating that "[y]oung people are making recitations in Greek and Latin where it was once a crime to teach their parents to read."[11] Through Frederick Douglass, we see how in text and voice the slave is made man, but Harper and other authors produce uplift exemplars through whom we also see black women re-created. Beyond concerns of interior didactic oratory, one can identify a series of romances in which the power of classical allusion is deployed. Hopkins's *Contending Forces* showcases the character Sappho Clark, and W. E. B. Du Bois's *The Quest of the Silver Fleece* is a twist on the yarn of Jason and the Golden Fleece.

In addition to these reactions and the uplift movement spearheaded by socially active black "club women," scholarly organizations also emerged that would challenge the anti-intellectual and accommodationist forces deployed by Washington.[12] The American Negro Academy, of which Cooper and Du Bois were members, strove to promote literary and scholarly productions among blacks, encourage youth to pursue higher culture, respond to attacks on African American culture, intellect, and rights, and publish annual papers on items of particular scholarly and cultural importance to African Americans.

Two particularly powerful literary responses to Gilded Age retrenchment, Washingtonian submission, and the marginalization of women emerged near the turn of the twentieth century. Anna Julia Cooper's *A Voice from the South* (1892) and W. E. B. Du Bois's *The Souls of Black Folk* (1903) offered complementary plans for African American cultural, education, and political advancement that challenged racist retrenchment and the philosophy of racial submission. Both texts relied heavily on classical references and allusions to Western cultural and intellectual descendants of the classics, but Cooper's text used these tools to critique the historical position of women in the West. Moreover, she relied on the literary, political, and religious history of Western culture as tools to create an alternative model of gender and virtue in America and address the plight of southern black women.

Anna Julia Cooper's provocative text has drawn considerable attention from women scholars, in particular. They have been rightly impressed by her character and accomplishments: her literary productions; her enviable academic achievements (including her 1925 doctorate from the University of Paris); her unflinching ethics in the face of the cutthroat political attacks emanating from the Tuskegee Machine and Washington, D.C., on liberal education for blacks; and her broad campaign for women's social, political, and educational elevation. However, a number of those scholars have regularly lamented in Cooper what they see as a reading of nineteenth-century womanhood that too easily accepts period gender stereotypes and conventions, particularly the cult of true womanhood. Mary Helen Washington, Karen Baker-Fletcher, and Ann duCille all express reservations, questioning Cooper's apparent comfort in deploying women primarily in nurturing roles and using other domestic conventions of the period. They also point to images of "privileged" women in *A Voice from the South* and to a "Christian [and Western] ethnocentrism" that duCille argues may make Cooper complicit in marginalizing Asians and non-Christians.[13] Ann duCille also notes that

> while [she] had a finely honed sense of the imperialist impulse and its power to colonize the female mind and body, she never quite managed to fully extricate her own mind from the tenets of true womanhood, as she proclaimed the purity and chastity—but most emphatically not the submission and domesticity—of black women.[14]

Recent critical attention to Cooper has been mixed, both in opinion and in rigor. Vivian May bluntly confronts the various criticisms and evaluations of Cooper, even taking great care to map out the dangerous waters of biographical criticism on one hand and, on the other, to use biographical details to enhance our understanding of this complex scholar. She also defends Cooper's rich language and intellectual depth against those who have argued that she was duped by or complicit in dominant discourse. Still, May faults Cooper because her true activist and radical credentials are obscured when she "employs Eurocentric or erudite modes of writing, stereotypes other ethnic groups, or draws a distinction between her life and the everyday lives of most black women."[15] Refreshingly, May recognizes that Cooper's scholarly training did not blind her to the racist uses to which similar training had been put, and Cooper routinely challenged narrow, racist, colonialist, and imperialist politics, policy, and intellectual assertions.[16] While May does an admirable job interrogating the practice of narrowly measuring Cooper's "activism" in ways that discount her intellectual activism, it is perhaps more important that she also reminds us how very committed Cooper actually was to both grassroots community action and more national or international causes. Unfortunately, May does not overtly challenge the idea that the classics and Cooper's exquisite inquiries into the interplay of Western secular and Christian cultural intellectual elements and race are part of a "Eurocentric" mode in which solidly activist blacks would have no interest or stake. At no point does May reveal a familiarity with the classics or the nature of the African American experience with them, and they remain a shadowy part of Cooper's allegedly elitist erudition. The underlying assumption remains that the classical world could not possibly be a world of the colored or a world for the colored.

Less careful commentary on Cooper is common even in contemporary works by authors who ostensibly have as their project a thorough recovery and recounting of African American accomplishment. Stephanie Evans's *Black Women in the Ivory Tower, 1850–1954: An Intellectual History* (2007) demonstrates the dangers of seeing merely the ivory tower of white intellectual activity and not fully recognizing the ebony column of African American scholarly activity. Evans spends five pages looking into the development of higher education in the United States, discounting the classical content of early institutions as an "American (white) aristocratic lens" through which black scholars in the classical curriculum were forced to look. Although she notes the Latin content of the curricula of the schools, she ignores Latin beyond the first mention, choosing to focus on a Greek study as a whitewash of Africa.[17] While Oprah Winfrey gets a mention in the text, the major commentators on classical education in America do not. As I, along with a number of others, have demonstrated, the influence of Rome and the Latin tradition on American thought cannot be denied. In the African American intellectual tradition, it is the Roman voice, in the example of Maecenas and African Terence, that speaks first in Phillis Wheatley's work, and it is the cosmopolitan and multiethnic Rome that is a key element in recoloring the classics. But it is easy to see how Evans misses this, because black scholars who contend with the classical world rank relatively low in her analysis. She quotes Cooper's "The Higher Education of Women" on the intellectually invigorating qualities of Socrates,

Virgil, Homer, Sappho, Dante, and Milton, but sums up her energetic defense of the classics as a "musing."[18] Following up her point with selections from Du Bois's *The Souls of Black Folk*, Evans dismisses his expression of kinship with Shakespeare, Balzac, Dumas, Aristotle, and Aurelius with the deflating comment that "[b]oth authors mastered the Romantic language prevalent among the college-bred class in the early twentieth century and made the case for African-American intellectual capacity."[19] She mentions Mary Church Terrell's classical study but only in the context of presumptions about its unfitness for women's study. In no place does the content and application of the classics appear in the text, but the classics are uncritically presumed to be the ornaments, musings, or mere foppishness of an elite, "college-bred" class. In this, the text fails as the intellectual history it aims to be.

Charles Lemert, in the introduction to his and Esme Bhan's recent edition of Cooper's work, provides an evenhanded but ultimately apologetic reading of Cooper. How we understand Cooper, he suggests, comes down to how seriously we take her critique of the traditional gender roles and expectations in *A Voice From the South*. Lemert points to Claudia Tate and others to suggest that Cooper is engaged in using the language of true womanhood to conduct "strategic transformations of the true womanhood doctrine."[20] In *Domestic Allegories of Political Desire*, Tate suggests that Cooper maps out a black Victorian womanhood distinguishable from the standard Victorian mode.[21] Contemporaries such as Julia Ringwood Costin and Ella Wright Pleasant insisted that women should be of pleasant disposition, obviously feminine, and in no way masculinized by demonstrating an interest in politics, championing social reform, or exhibiting the "vicious" desire for publicity. They should "know naught of women's rights and universal suffrage" and should leave all professional activity to men. According to Costin, women writers were immodest and in danger of polluting the population with their writings: "Only an utter lack of femininity could make it possible for a woman to stand before the world and proclaim its vice."[22] Tate argues that Cooper was one of the women whose work feminized discussions about African American citizenship but called for an end to exceptionally feminizing women. She favored a fully active female citizenry, encouraged and understood the need for women's employment, and championed equal education while arguing that women possessed inherent characteristics of sympathy and virtue that made them exceptional soldiers for social reform.[23]

Lemert also reminds critics of Cooper's powerful ability to rhetorically trap readers and auditors and points to her most ardent defender, Hazel

Carby, who argues that "Cooper developed a complex analysis of social, political, and economic forces as being either distinctly masculine or feminine in their orientation and consequences. She saw the intimate link between internal and external colonization, between domestic racial oppression and imperialism."[24] She was both an opponent of patriarchal power and a true critic of the true womanhood convention. Lemert's argument is compelling, and considerable evidence exists that Cooper was not committed to "true womanhood," at least not as the concept is generally understood. It is apparent even in this richer critical environment that the nature of Cooper's scholarly training and the intellectual foundation it provided her has been largely disregarded.[25] In her thoughtful work, Ann duCille does not elaborate on the impact of Cooper's Greek and Latin classical training on her critique of domestic conventions, even though women's societal roles, intelligence, and virtue are regularly discussed by some of the most familiar classical writers, including Homer (*Iliad* and *Odyssey*), Plato (*Republic*), Aristotle (*Politics*), Virgil (*Aeneid*), and Ovid (*Metamorphoses* and *Ars Amatoria*). Although Lemert mentions Cooper's teaching the classics, humanities, mathematics, and sciences, even he does not pursue her educational interests any further. The classics may not be standard materials in the architecture of feminist critiques of the nineteenth-century womanhood ideal nor in contemporary literary criticism; but the classics, particularly those of Cooper's early college education, are a central column in the structure of her education, career, and scholarly work. They are, therefore, essential to critiques of her life and work. The context for both Cooper's attack on the degradation of women and her insistence on the culpability of black and white men in that degradation is a vast metanarrative of the classical Western literary and cultural tradition. In *A Voice From the South,* Cooper grounds her analysis of the predicament of southern African American women and the entire South in a reading of Western civilization and expansion from the end of Rome into the chivalric period of the Middle Ages, through the Carolingian and Italian Renaissances, and into the modern era.

It is a mistake to ignore Cooper's tremendous investment in the classical and descendant tradition of the West when we examine her writing and her understanding of the gender politics of the Victorian era. That she was demonstrably committed to the classics and classical education, both as a scholar and a teacher, should immediately alert us to the likely centrality of this strain in her thought and work. Her own classical education dates from her early youth, entails advanced university study, grows to include modern Western languages and history, and results in such professional triumphs as her translation of *Le Pelerinage du Charlemagne* and her doctoral work at the Sorbonne on the failures of the French Revolution. By ignoring Cooper's classical background, scholars have lost a significant tool for discerning the aims and intent of Cooper's writing, especially as it relates to her ideas about gender. They have failed to ask why Cooper would deploy classical allusions, texts, and figures in a book declared to be a plea for the colored girls of the South. Nor have they asked what role the classics could have possibly played in redefining the role of women, black women in particular, in the late nineteenth century. They might easily have asked how the classics, so heavily masculine in language and focus, could have done anything but reinforce Victorian ideas of virginity, marriage, and domesticity as the proving ground of virtue for women. Moreover, a woman undertook considerable risks in employing the classics, risks that were particularly evident in the context of the Victorian sense of female virtue as tied largely to virginity, motherhood, and domestic expertise. For generations men had argued that classically educated women polluted the reason necessary to good government with rogue passion and fancy. Moreover, they were also believed to be masculinized by the intellectual tools of oratory, history, and political thought. "A woman of great classical learning," writes Caroline Winterer, "risked becoming dangerously unfeminine, what authors variously called *virilis femina, une homasse* (man-woman), a virago."[26]

Ultimately, the scholarly research done on Cooper is significantly impoverished without a thorough examination of her classical background and use of the classics in *A Voice from the South*. The question of whether she was committed to domesticity and true womanhood or was actually a vanguard feminist cannot be answered without knowing what role the classics played in her work. Her memorable and terribly overused claim— "Only the BLACK WOMAN can say 'when and where I enter, in the quiet, undisputed dignity of my womanhood, without violence and without suing or special patronage, then and there the whole *Negro race enters with me'*"—can be read either as a significantly underestimated declaration of an empowered, classically educated womanhood or a pretty, Victorian affirmation of the uplift era's pure, black, domestic goddess. The appropriate reading depends on whether Cooper deployed the classics to operate as a liberating or restricting tradition for women. If Lemert is correct that Cooper can rhetorically trap readers, then from what source did she derive this rhetorical power? If Cooper is rightly criticized for possessing a Christian and Western ethnocentrism that permeates her writing, then what is its nature and source? If Cooper's apologists are correct that she strategically transforms the ideal of true womanhood, then will her curricular choice to teach the classics to boys and girls, her deployment of Sappho, Aspasia, and other classical and later Western women, and her critique of Achilles and the idea of virtue help explain how she effected the transformation in her own writing and teaching?

A Voice From the South was a collection of essays likely composed between 1886 and 1892, and a number of these essays were given as speeches before and after the formal publication as a book. Cooper spoke to mixed audiences, as well as audiences of black male clergy in the Episcopal Church, to whom she emphasized the black church's interest in preserving and improving women to advance Christianity and broader cultural virtue. She employed a number of forms in the book: allegory, autobiography, history, poetry, literary criticism, and oratory. Looking at Cooper's language as a result of the classical rhetorical training she received at St. Augustine's and Oberlin reveals new complexity in her work.

Cooper's rhetorical training is of particular importance when we observe that she (along with many of those women at the podium at the Chicago Exposition) helped reintroduce black women's voices and texts to a largely male-dominated (black and white) discussion of political, spiritual, and intellectual concerns that had seen precious little activity from black women, except for Phillis Wheatley and the limited work of Anne Plato, Maria Stewart, and Sojourner Truth. The serious reintroduction of oratory during the Woman's Era has a traditional classical resonance, with Cooper taking on the role of the orator, the traditionally masculine figure who addresses virtue but also generates virtue in the audience. Moreover, Cooper's use of her personal narrative and experiences infuses the text and oratory with Ciceronian flair of the variety noted in *On Invention* and *On the Parts of Oratory*. Like male orators (Frederick Douglass, for instance), Cooper not only exhorts readers and auditors of both genders to virtues of bold but gentle heroism, courtesy, intellectual accomplishment, classical and Christian *pietas*, and elements of high culture but also offers personal trials as evidence of her exceptional character and worthiness as an exemplar.

When Cooper emphasized the obstacles to her classical education or spoke of affronts she suffered in Great Britain (reversing the black oratorical celebration of British racial tolerance that Douglass had made a near tradition), the rhetorical moments resonated on a number of levels. Like Wheatley and Douglass, Cooper allows the audience to ponder the dissonance between the obvious virtue of the writer or orator and the traditions of racial intolerance that bedevil her. Cooper also employs the language of her audiences, whether the polite requirements of genteel society or the language of black male audiences. Polite, self-effacing phrases such as "I confess," "I would beg," "so far as I am informed," "now please understand me," and so forth may operate as concession to convention (and Cooper's critics argue as much).[27] However, that metalanguage, as conventional and accommodating as it is, can just as easily be direct strategizing born of Cooper's classical training. Again, Cicero's directions on oratory, with which Cooper was undoubtedly familiar, patently encourage such overtures to an audience to cultivate good will. They are meant, literally and figuratively, to disarm hostile audiences; and we should remember that these instructions were intended for male speakers on political, diplomatic, and religious battlefields. This strategy also demonstrates an important flexibility in her speaking and writing, what Elizabeth Alexander calls creating "an African-American, female, demonstrably thinking self from whatever intellectual material was at hand."[28]

Voice not only capitalizes on Cooper's own experience but also on her variety of voices. As Alexander points out, Cooper "moves easily into her remembered slave dialect of those 'troubled souls' at the same time that she is fluent in elegant standard written English."[29] Reflecting Ciceronian principles, Cooper can, as an orator, appear to be like the people she addresses and both authentically represent and play to their local sensibilities. Moreover, she can assume oratorical positions across the socioeconomic and educational spectrum with ease. Douglass's great success with synthesizing and applying a versatile oratorical style and manipulating a multiplicity of rhetorical weapons should make Cooper's versatility all the more understandable and expected. Douglass eventually developed the oratorical versatility to address university audiences, abolitionist meetings, women's organizations, and religious congregations across Europe and America while maintaining the position of authentic representative and voice of the enslaved, largely unschooled black masses. Cooper also cultivated this remarkable versatility, which added to her oratorical power, but she possessed as well scholarly tools that exceeded Douglass's more meager formal training. Cooper was an accomplished linguist, fluent in her native English, but also in Latin and French. She used those linguistic tools at opportune moments to deconstruct racist assaults on prominent figures like Paul Robeson, who was accused of uncontrollably lapsing and infusing his role in *Othello* with "black" dialect. Dismantling the usual white representations of black speech in "The Negro's Dialect," Cooper illustrated how the facts of the evolution of language from Latin to Romance language, to Old, Middle, and varieties of American English rendered the sounds of white reporters' created dialects virtually impossible and patently ridiculous.[30]

Although Cooper uses oratory and other forms to address political and racial issues, she employs the narrative to place herself firmly and quite visibly *in* the discourse. This is certainly necessary, if only because Cooper could ill afford to cede intellectual space, the opportunity for voice, or rhetorical weapons when engaged in what would turn out to be a struggle for both intellectual and professional freedom. While Cooper, wrote African American women into the discourse of politics and culture she also gained some power by making herself an exemplar for women. Unlike the majority of male writers in the classical and later Western tradition, even such contemporaries as Frederick Douglass, J. W. C. Pennington, Alexander Crummell, and others, she offers many other women as examples. As she writes and speaks of Ovid and Tacitus, she also writes and speaks of the Spartan women, Amazons, Penelope, Andromache, Lucretia, and Sappho. In *A Voice from the South,* Cooper employs classical women as direct exemplars, no longer limiting the exemplary figures to males but intentionally making them female.

Cooper's provocative writing, her presence as a woman writer, and her classical references underscore some of the major cultural and educational changes of her time. In particular, late-nineteenth-century American education reflected the tensions and transformations of the period. The era after the Civil War was America's first truly modern period, and any historical treatment of the age establishes the major themes of the time. The nation experienced massive immigration from Central and Southern Europe (and to a lesser extent, Asia, and that is only rivaled by late-twentieth- and twenty-first-century immigration), industrialization and urbanization throughout the Northeast and parts of the Midwest and South, and a growing commercial and industrial ethos that increasingly privileged marketable skills over liberal education. Political corruption and shaky business schemes proliferated, and the political machine emerged as a regular fixture of American local and national politics. This was the era Mark Twain labeled "The Gilded Age," a moniker that reflected the materialistic shell of wealth that hid the moral and political decay of the republic.

As Caroline Winterer notes, colleges and universities reflected the shift in cultural priorities in a number of ways. First, the number and nature of the institutions changed. The 1862 Morill Land Grant Act guaranteed that new monies would flow from states to support old institutions. Moreover, it funded new colleges that emphasized the sciences, engineering, and agriculture, and appealed to a new constituency that was considerably more diverse than previously seen in American education.[31] Women increasingly entered college, and their number rose from 21 percent of the college population in 1870 to 40 percent in 1910. Although these percentages are for a relatively elite population of Americans in general, women increasingly became part of that elite band.[32] A number of major new colleges emerged between 1865 and 1892, including Vassar (1865), Cornell (1868), Wellesley (1875), Smith (1875), Bryn Mawr (1884), Stanford (1885), and the University of Chicago (1892).

The standard B.A. also had to compete with the new B.S. and a variety of new degrees that allowed students to eliminate one or both of the classical languages. The classical languages were no longer required for freshmen at Harvard after 1883, and in the first year of the new requirements 77 percent studied Latin and 64 percent studied Greek. Those numbers dropped to approximately 33 percent and 16 percent by 1900. At Yale in 1886, approximately 33 percent of students' time was devoted to the ancient languages. In 1899, it only took up 20 percent, with Greek study nearly disappearing; entrance requirements around the nation began to shed Greek as a prerequisite.[33] In the high schools, the population of students enrolled increased as education democratized. With this enrollment surge, the study of Latin increased for a short while. Despite a lingering patina of elite preparation that the classical languages provided, Latin eventually declined in high school education, and with the exception of private high schools that regularly fed into colleges and seminaries (which actually saw an increase in Greek for some time), Greek was practically extinct by 1910.[34]

Industrialists, anticlassicists, and some university professors disparaged the classics, stressing that the education of a modern age needed to reflect utility and scientific study. Scholasticism and the classical tradition were replaced slowly by both laboratory or workshop education and the notion that scientific research ennobled and intellectually disciplined the mind far more than the study of ancient, dead civilizations. Classicists and classical study did not crumble before the assaults of industrialists, turncoat professors, and scientists. While they embraced the notion that the classics were materially useless, they argued nonetheless that the classics enriched civilization, tamed men, and produced culture. Caroline Winterer notes the novelty of this approach:

["Culture"] sprang up at the same historical moment that science and utility also gained a foothold in the curriculum, for culture and utility formed rhetorical bookends, straddling two poles of Victorian educational thought. At one end utility advertised the modern university's alliance with progress and science, while at the other end culture signaled higher education's age-old ties to broadly gauged learning and civic preparation. The word *cultured* appeared in American writing at this time to describe something that one could *be*, marking the apotheosis of the self-transformative possibilities of classicism and liberal learning. The end product of self-culture was to *be cultured*.[35]

It is noteworthy that the classicists of this era—exemplified by Basil Lanneau Gildersleeve, William Watson Goodwin, Henry Simmons Frieze, and William Sanders Scarborough among the elder scholars and Thomas Day Seymour, William Gardner Hale, and John Henry Wright among the younger ones—many of whom allied themselves to a broader group of academics in what would eventually be called the "humanities," became the first group of American classicists to produce memorable works in their fields and gain national, if not international prominence.[36] This is not to say that classicists did not abhor some of the productions of the newer fields, such as the social sciences; educational psychology was a favorite target. Nonetheless, the humanities—literature, languages, philosophy, and history—also rejected the supremacy of usefulness and were in some cases close cousins to the classics. This move inadvertently opened the study of the classics to women and began to address one of the most onerous gender-related problems of the classics, the question of whether feminine virtue could be derived from the classics and be a virtue that could be shared equally by men and women. Winterer notes:

> [The shift from pure classics to the humanities] helped to erode the highly masculine world of classicism, opening its ranks both ideologically and numerically to women. Culture as earthly self-perfection was a goal toward which both sexes could strive, and indeed women by the late nineteenth century were often perceived as being more open to cultivation than men because of their ostensibly softer, gentler natures. With high culture now defined as the opposite of business and industry, it also became a province for feminine values removed from the masculine sphere of the market. Culture was antimaterialism, antiaggression, antiexploitation.[37]

As a result, a culture of art, music, and the classics that was increasingly abandoned by men going out to conquer the commercial sphere owed its very existence to their wealthy wives and daughters and independent scholarly women, who "became the female Medici to the museums, libraries, and symphonies of the Gilded Age."[38] In addition to the feminization of the classics and high culture, many remaining academic classicists, such as Confederate apologist Basil Gildersleeve of the Johns Hopkins University and the University of Virginia, attempted to keep the classics part of a broader literary knowledge for the culture at large while encouraging some specialized study in the classics.[39]

Anna Julia Cooper's education suggests that the feminization of the classics took more than a woman's mere appearance at the doorway of a classroom. Acquiring a classical education was a hard-fought struggle for her as a woman, and blackness only toughened the fight.[40] Cooper began her educational career standing on a chair to reach the blackboard at St. Augustine's Normal and Collegiate Institute in Raleigh, North Carolina. For a yearly stipend of one hundred dollars, the young scholar served as a remedial preceptor for older students at the institution. St. Augustine's was itself younger than the diminutive and precocious teacher, but it was from this unlikely source that Cooper got her first taste of the classics. Formed in 1867 by the Protestant Episcopal Church and housed in an old military barracks in 1868, St. Augustine's mission was to prepare men and women to teach the African Americans of the South and also create a body of men for the ministry. Decades of official denial of education to African Americans, codified in an 1831 North Carolina law, had left the black population in dire need of basic education for all ages. That the young Cooper, literate and therefore advanced in comparison to many of her substantially older peers, was called on to teach. St. Augustine's curriculum reflected a substantial investment in the dissemination of Latin and Greek classics, something not uncommon in white schools but remarkable in a Reconstruction-era training school faced with educating an almost universally illiterate population of former slaves. In her biography of Cooper, Leona Gabel argues that the focus on classical education served a profound need peculiar to the freedmen: "Psychologically, freedom for the average emancipated slave meant a life-style as remote as possible from the one he had known. For the more intelligent, ambitious freedman, it meant becoming a teacher or a preacher or achieving a college degree, goals to which literacy was the key."[41]

The classics helped train the students for these fields and offered potential access to a better life, one significantly distant from the travail of slavery. Cooper's education at St. Augustine's reflected this classical bent, but her gender created some difficulties. Although her doting principal included her in many of the classes for male theology students and even invited her into the first Greek class formed at the school, Cooper lamented that a woman had to "fight her way against positive discouragements to the higher education."[42] Especially rare for women was the chance to pursue courses of training that cultivated the philosophical and intellectual virtues deemed desirable in men, particularly the classics so integral to the creation of the theological and scholarly class. In an era during which "the three R's, a little music and a good deal of dancing, a first rate dressmaker and a bottle of magnolia balm [were] quite generally enough to render charming any woman possessed of tact and the capacity for worshipping masculinity," Cooper's intention to attend college was received even by her beloved principal with "incredulity and dismay."[43] Shocking though her course of study might have been, the educational foundation provided by St. Augustine's launched Cooper's scholarly journey and introduced her to the classics. Cooper continued her studies at Oberlin College, which, among its other progressive tendencies, demonstrated a penchant for educating African American students. Cooper's letter to Oberlin's president requesting admission and demonstrating financial need reveals the comprehensive classical education she had drawn from her North Carolina school:

> I completed the course at St. Augustine's . . . which included besides the English branches & Latin: Caesar, seven books; Virgil's *Aeneid,* six books; Sallust's *Catiline* and *Jugurtha;* and a few orations of Cicero;— Greek: White's first lessons; Goodwin's Greek Reader, containing selections from Xenophon, Plato, Herodotus and Thucydides; and five or six books of the *Iliad;*—Mathematics: Algebra and Geometry entire.[44]

The young Cooper entered Oberlin as a sophomore, having already been a teacher, and "earnestly desir[ing] to take an advanced classical course in some superior Northern college."[45] The Oberlin curriculum fed her intellectual appetite with classics, mathematics, sciences, philosophy, modern literature, languages, history, and a noted conservatory. College also introduced Cooper to Mary Church Terrell, future author of *A Colored Woman in a White World,* who eventually taught Latin with Cooper in Washington, D.C. Cooper earned the A.B. from Oberlin in 1884 and the M.A. in mathematics in 1887. She taught modern languages at Wilberforce University and mathematics, Latin, and German at St. Augustine between degrees.

Cooper's classical curriculum reveals how her vision of the West developed and what fueled her particular concern for the virtuous education of women and men against indolence, rashness, narrowness, and cruelty. The seven books of Caesar's *Gallic Wars* that she read at St. Augustine's would have taken Cooper on a long journey with the ambitious general, through the conquest of Gaul and into Britannia. The texts would have been laden with Caesar's clear military genius and equally clear lessons in how to entice readers and exercise clever politics and self-promotion. Virgil's

Aeneid tempers the glorious image of Roman conquest with Aeneas's contemplative, none-too-certain journey from conquered and enslaved Troy to tempting Africa, dangerous Italy, and the founding of noble Rome. Civic virtue and the building of culture and law are as important in *The Aeneid* as force of arms. Fulfilling prophecy, honoring vows, piously following the gods' plans and personal destiny, making alliances, and planning for the *pax romana* are key to Aeneas's journey, but Virgil also seems not entirely convinced that Rome has honored its mythic past.[46] Also central to the narrative are the education, virtue, and destiny of Ascanius, Aeneas's son and the first Iülus (or Julius) of the Roman world. By reading Sallust at St. Augustine's, Cooper would have noted that Sallust, a follower of Caesar, provided in his *Catiline* and *Jugurtha* a vision of the great man as a maker of history. However, Sallust also praised the purity of virtue and hard work of the early Romans, decried the laziness, corruption, and violence of contemporary Romans, and included commentary on the oppression of the people by the aristocracy. He elevated such men as Gaius Marius as true champions of the people against those like Lucius Cornelius Sulla, who used and enshrined violence as a political tool against rivals and the people. Catiline was for him, as for Cicero and Cato, an example of the corrupt new Roman, who valued power over virtue and sought out other people's desires to create loyalty to him. In *Jugurtha*, Sallust argues that young Romans view that past only with jealousy:

> But in these degenerate days, on the contrary, who is there that does not vie with his ancestors in riches and extravagance rather than in uprightness and diligence? Even the "new men," who in former times always relied upon worth to outdo the nobles, now make their way to power and distinction by intrigue and open fraud rather than by noble practices; just as if a praetorship a consulship, or anything else of the kind were distinguished and illustrious in and of itself and were not valued according to the merit of those who live up to it. But in giving expression to my sorrow and indignation at the morals of our country I have spoken too freely and wandered too far from my subject. To this I now return.[47]

Jugurtha, the story of the Numidian king's rebellion against Rome, was exemplary to Sallust because Jugurtha was not only intelligent, athletic, and a hunter but also capable of resisting luxury and idleness, which were his birthright to enjoy even as the commoner son of a royal concubine. Equally poignant to Sallust, at least in the Roman version of the Numidian uprising, was that the ambitious Jugurtha had been warned by an avuncular general Scipio Africanus to take the slow, virtuous, and safe path to power. However, he eschewed virtue and resorted to murder, bribery, and war to seize Numidia. Important also was the rise of Gaius Marius, reformer of the Roman army and man of the people, who chastised the empire and the patrician class of Romans for abusing the plebian population.

The orations from Cicero that Cooper read likely included some of the most popular of the era: *Pro Archia Poeta* (a defense of Aulus Licinius Archias), *De Officiis* (On Duties), *De Oratore* (On the Parts of Oratory), or *In Catilinam* (Against Catiline). *Pro Archia Poeta* celebrates the value of literature and literary scholars to society and defends Greek Archias against Roman xenophobia. *On Duties* provides one of the most comprehensive examinations of republican Roman virtue, touching on the philosophical core of Roman citizenship and civic duty as an expression of highest humanity. *De Oratore* examines the core components of successful oratory, and is one of the foundations for the lessons in *The Columbian Orator*. The issues of the Catiline Conspiracy, addressed by Sallust, were argued before the Senate by Cicero and Cato and were a foundational element of Addison's *Cato*. The Xenophon of Cooper's study is almost certainly the *Anabasis* and perhaps part of the four books in the *Memorabilia of Socrates,* in which Xenophon defends the life and work of his teacher, Socrates. The *Anabasis*'s chronicle of a Greco-Persian military expedition, treachery, and the Greek army's long retreat through hostile territory is one of the first Greek texts to discuss the Persian Empire, its decadence, and the overall flaws of the East. It also offers particular insight on both manliness in hopeless situations and questions of virtue in circumstances of unconventional warfare. Xenophon's other works also included treatises on hunting and the conduct of the ideal cavalry officer. While Plato's works were widely known and studied, *The Republic* alone would have provided Cooper with impetus to contemplate the virtue of the citizen and the state, as well as to imagine an equal education for women and men like that of *The Republic*'s guardians.

Herodotus and Thucydides clearly provided Cooper with an appreciation of the cultural value and political use of history. Herodotus's *History* also presented her with a vision of Africa and Africans fundamentally different from that generally held by even educated whites in Cooper's era. They, of course, imagined Africa to be a wasteland populated by quasihumans devoid of not only the intellectual and technological elements of civilization but also the Christian religious and secular civic virtues of civilization. Africa and Africans ultimately existed outside human history per se. Herodotus's chronicle included blacks in the classical world and mythology and extolled their cultural virtues as progenitors of Greek civilization, which was enough to help inspire Martin Bernal to look more closely at the relationship between Greece and Africa. This vision of blackness predated the white racist, black nationalist, and Ethiopianist doctrines of Cooper's era and provided a classical component to Cooper's uplift vision, one not beholden to traditional African American, Victorian, or Christian cultural politics. Each of these modes placed significant, ultimately race-inflected limitations on the relationship between the Ancient and European West and Africa—a problem undermining some contemporary analyses.

Thucydides's *History of the Peloponnesian War,* which was likely the text Cooper read at St. Augustine's, is a history of the military demise of the Athenian Empire and is notable for its tendency to attribute historical events to the workings of humans, not the gods or fate or anything supernatural. In addition, Thucydides gives some indication that the Athenian Empire was doomed (despite the glorious principles of Periclean democracy so widely celebrated in the West) because it came to believe that those in power have no need to contend with justice, compassion in war, or the will of the gods. We should remember that the virtuous use of power is central to *A Voice from the South.* Homer's *Iliad* brought Cooper face to face with the eternal questions of individual virtue, Achilles's rage, the nature of human suffering, and the relative virtues and vices of Greece and the Troad. The Homeric saga no doubt antagonized Cooper with its treatment of women, and she eventually used the failures of Achilles as an example of why African Americans needed to reconsider and redefine virtue.

Among the many observations one can make about Cooper's education, three broad ones seem particularly valuable in evaluating the effect of the classics on her work. First, she was armed with a classical education that privileged virtuous ambition and cautioned against luxury, greed, and injustice, which destroy the virtues and power of individuals and empires. Moreover, it despised tyranny and taught that merit should win one the rule over others. Notably, democracy is not the preferred form of rule; nor does this intellectual tradition embrace any notion of a broad equality of men. Second, she did not imbibe the contemporary ideas of race or gender. She possessed a historical sense of blackness that was informed at least in part by Herodotus and likely by Terence and other figures of antiquity. Doubtless, Cooper was familiar with the North African roots of her alma mater's namesake, St. Augustine, and both would have been aware of the centrality of Roman Africa to the politics of the empire. Cooper clearly came to understand women's intellectual and political possibilities in terms of the classical women who helped her to describe women's ambition and attainment as traditional and with glorious precedent. Sappho, Aspasia, the Amazons, and others appear frequently in *A Voice from the South*.[48] Cooper described women as powerful and full of potential, and she recommended equal education for women. She specifically rejected the nineteenth and early twentieth centuries' veneration of Sophocles's character Antigone, who does not appear among her heroines. Ordinarily, Antigone's independent, provocative, and passionate actions to interfere in the world of men would have been seen as uncharacteristic and unseemly for the Victorian woman, but because they ended safely and predictably with her death, she was a favorite tragic woman of the era.[49]

Finally, the classics work in conjunction with Cooper's conventional but intellectualized Episcopalian Christianity, giving her a tool to reshape the meaning of Christianity in her text. The orthodox Anglican liturgy and doctrine celebrated in Washington, D.C., offered Cooper a rational, stable, knowable framework to critique and use in her work.

In 1887, the newly minted graduate Anna Julia Cooper moved to Washington, D.C., and began a thirteen-year tenure as a teacher of Latin at what was then the Preparatory High School for Colored Youth (later M Street School and Dunbar High School). The school had claimed as principals Mary Jane Patterson, Richard T. Greener (first African American A.B. graduate of Harvard), and Francis L. Cardozo. Cooper's move to Washington introduced her to African Americans like Charlotte Forten Grimke and Dr. Francis K. Grimke and placed her in a relatively cosmopolitan atmosphere. The city possessed a considerable educational, cultural, and economic variety in the black population, giving rise to a class structure so intricate and exclusive that Booker T. Washington suggested that it was unfit for any African Americans who wished to commit themselves to the improvement of their race. This proved exceptionally untrue of Anna Julia Cooper, whose *A Voice From the South: By a Black Woman of the South* emerged in 1892.

Cooper's *Voice* is remarkable because she deploys the classics not just in terms of allusions, history, or lessons drawn from antiquity but also because the author embarks on a substantial reinterpretation of the classical transmission of empire and learning from Rome to the postclassical West. She critiques the historic foundations of Western concepts of civilization, gender, virtue, and Christianity. In her broad investigation of Western history, she reconsiders the sources of secular and Christian ideas of womanhood, investigates the sources and validity of secular and Christian ideas of feminine and masculine virtue, and ultimately reinterprets virtue, gender, and education. Cooper's text interpolates the prevailing discourse of virtue, manliness, and exemplariness with its opening lines. The prologue after the heading *Soprano Obligato*, "Our Raison d'Être," immediately employs a classical allusion. Cooper compares the South to the Sphinx of ancient Egypt, noting that "she inspires vociferous disputation, but herself takes little part in the noisy controversy."[50] According to Cooper, who vacillates between the metaphors of the Sphinx and music, the Negro has been the muffled chord in the Sphinx-like South, and the black woman has been the most silent note in the chord—the most silent and mysterious Sphinx, locked within blackness and southernness.[51] The nature and race of the Egyptian Sphinx have been key since Cooper's era in attempts to determine the nature and race of the earliest Egyptians, but the Theban Sphinx has also been part of a celebrated classical myth of which Cooper would have been aware: Travelers to ancient Thebes might well encounter the deadly creature, who allowed them in and out of the city only if they correctly answered a riddle.[52] Failing to solve the riddle brought destruction. Cooper implies that the most silent and most potentially deadly Sphinx is the black woman, and leaving her riddle unanswered is cultural suicide for African Americans and America at large. It also strikes an Ethiopianist chord in that, both literally and figuratively, the West will have to look back to Africa to secure its future.

Moving from the opening to the chapter "Womanhood: A Vital Element in the Regeneration and Progress of a Race," Cooper adopts the judicial forum as a metaphor for the black experience in America. She argues that the "trial" of the African American has been shoddily conducted, largely because ignorance and racism have obscured the facts in evidence but also because the witness of the black woman has been tampered with:

> Attorneys for the plaintiff and attorneys for the defendant, with bungling *gaucherie* have analyzed and dissected, theorized and synthesized with sublime ignorance or pathetic misapprehension of counsel from the black client. One important witness has not yet been heard from. The summing up of the evidence deposed, and the charge to the jury have been made—but no word from the black woman.[53]

The legal nomenclature for the metaphors is Western and American: The adversarial system, witnesses, and evidentiary references are recognizable. It is also interesting to observe that the claims Cooper makes against the conduct of the attorneys reflect violations of well-known and basic duties to the client and to the court and of competency that were widely held as essential to the practice of the law and eventually codified into canons in the American Bar Association's 1907 Code of Ethics. The duties to the client and court and for competency exist even now in various state conduct rules for attorneys and the Model Rules of Professional Conduct. But, some of these legal elements are also classical, recalling the orations her university education and adult study would have made second nature. Her arrangement is not unlike Cicero defending Archias the poet, or trying Catiline before the Senate, or Cato arguing against Catiline. The trial is perhaps the most recognized forum for oratory, and it is the place where Demosthenes reached his height and Cicero shone. Cooper launches her oration *pro femina afra* in the first pages of *A Voice from the South*. When she begins to argue for her black female client, she starts with neither the modern state of the race nor the words of other prominent black and white "clients" and "counsel" of the era. Rather, she begins with a bit of legal history and precedent—the Christian, Feudal, and classical roots of the ideal of womanhood. Within three pages she reaches the classical era and the Roman historian Tacitus, who recounts the Germanic barbarians' treatment of women.

Cooper argues that abusing and devaluing women is non-Western and non-Christian.[54] Roman culture venerated the hearth, the home, the family, and the good wives who formed the foundation of the Roman family. Tax breaks and monetary concessions flowed to mothers who produced large numbers of children. Even the barbarians of the age valued their women, according to Tacitus, who noted the "tender regard for woman entertained by these rugged barbarians before they left their northern homes to overrun Europe."[55] So, to Cooper, devaluing women is beyond barbaric; she argues that the vice is Oriental and Islamic. The barbarian hordes who overran Rome were in some ways culturally superior to the Asians or Muslims of her era. Against classical and Western Christian womanhood, Cooper compares the fate of women in what she depicts as cruel and barbaric Asian and Islamic cultures.[56] The contemporary example of the Ottomans provides a broad entrée into questions of civilization, gender roles, theology, and virtue. The Ottoman Empire and, by extension, the whole of the East, was doomed to being the "Sick Man of Europe" because "[t]he harem here, and—'dust to dust' hereafter . . . was the hope, the inspiration, the *summum bonum* of the Eastern woman."[57] Using the open door of the era's East-West conflict, Cooper approaches her core argument against the abuse and disregard shown to women in America. No civilization can thrive without a rich appreciation for women; the treatment of women dictates the richness of a nation's culture. Destroying women's rights also destroys masculinity and reason:

[Muslim men's] minds were not the normal outgrowth of a healthy trunk. They seemed rather ephemeral excrescencies which shoot far out with all the vigor and promise, apparently, of strong branches; but soon alas fall into decay and ugliness because there is no soundness in the root, no life-giving sap, permeating, strengthening and perpetuating the whole. There is a worm at the core! The home-life is impure! And when we look for fruit, like apples of Sodom, it crumbles within our grasp into dust and ashes.

It is pleasing to turn from this effete and immobile civilization to a society still fresh and vigorous, whose seed is in itself, and whose very name is synonymous with all that is progressive, elevating and inspiring, viz., the European bud and the American flower of modern civilization.[58]

Cooper's floral imagery of buds, blooms, and roots calls to mind Phillis Wheatley's warning to students of the University at Cambridge to guard their souls, which are "blooming plants," against the evils that could destroy their virtue.[59] Moreover, Martha Nussbaum's investigation of goodness in the classical world, *The Fragility of Goodness* (1986, 2001), echoes this idea of humans, their virtue, and the overall human good as delicate flora susceptible to the blight of vice and error. Helene Foley translates *The Odyssey*'s celebration of wise, loyal Penelope with the language of abundant plant and animal life:

Lady, no mortal man on the endless earth would have cause to find fault with you; your fame goes up into the wide heaven, as of some king who, as a blameless man and god-fearing, and ruling as lord over many powerful people, upholds the way of good government, and the black earth yields him barley and wheat, his trees are heavy with fruit, his sheep-flocks continue to bear young, the sea gives him fish, because of his good leadership, and his people prosper under him.[60]

As Richard Waswo points out in *From Virgil to Vietnam: The Founding Legend of Western Civilization* (1997), one of the most enduring themes of the transmission of empire and learning is literal and figurative cultivation—both *cultus* or culture in the people and the transformation of the wilderness into blooming and fruiting crops.[61] The imagery of growing flora pervades the discourse of civilization, and in that long line of descent, the bud-and-flower metaphor Cooper uses to describe Anglo-American civilization strongly suggests the transmission of empire, culture, and learning. With American education experiencing both a growth in women students and a feminization of the classics and the humanities, Cooper sculpts a theory of civilization that recognizes the supremacy of being cultured, the centrality of women to culture, and the importance of nurturing and protecting women to secure civilization and culture, if not empire. Cooper's rhetorical move makes the abuse of women a non-Western, non-Christian, and fundamentally uncivilized characteristic that is hostile to masculinity and reason. This allows her to subvert the traditional philosophy of gender, which had traditionally held that women's fancy and emotion were dangerous to masculine reason and virtue, and assume the mantle of cultural, historical, and religious orthodoxy. It also creates a provocative, orientalist division between benighted Muslim Africans of the weak East and the Christian Africa and African Americans who are coworkers in culture with the rest of the post-Roman West—a friendly gesture toward Episcopalian and other missionary and colonization projects in West Africa undertaken by such clergy as her friend Alexander Crummell.[62]

After having described love for women as the virtue of even the barbarians outside Rome, outlined what she sees as the failure of misogynistic Islamic culture, and ascertained the key to culture, Cooper embarks on a new telling of the story of the West: a tale of how the West escaped barbarism, how it evolved its sense of virtue, how that understanding of virtue changed, how the change altered and damaged the relationship between men and women, and how America must act to save and enrich its postbellum civilization by correcting, improving, and renewing the valuable but imperfect Western empire themselves. If Ottoman Turkey was doomed because it despised women, then the West was blessed with health and great potential because the religious and cultural foundation of Christianity compelled Western men to honor women. Returning to that original relationship would improve the West, and Cooper describes both the path back to that ideal and how the West first strayed from it. Improvising on the Christian theological themes of the time, Cooper revises the notion of fallen womanhood and New Testament redemption. She argues that women have a special relationship with Christianity, since in his terrestrial life and ministry, Christ lifted the fallen woman to equality with man, "refusing to countenance the shameless and equally guilty monsters who were gloating over her fall."[63] By both this act of grace toward women and by turning to women in times of persecution and even in death, Christ establishes

> a rule and guide for the estimation of woman as an equal, as a helper, as a friend, and as a sacred charge to be sheltered and cared for with a brother's love and sympathy, lessons which nineteen centuries' gigantic

strides in knowledge, arts, and sciences, in social and ethical principles have not been able to probe to their depth or to exhaust in practice.[64]

The gentle and transforming qualities of women, celebrated by the empire and validated by Christ, characterize not only the Christian woman but also the church. Cooper argues, again playing within the bounds of orthodoxy, that this feminized church represents the bride and helpmeet of Christ. This womanly church is the force that turns the disastrous fall of the Roman Empire into an epic tale of how the West civilizes the barbarian hordes into the new Rome, which is the modern church. Cooper argues that the survival of the church from the fifth century onward came from the union of barbaric and Christian forces in the rubble of fallen Rome. The first stage of this transformation is not an intellectual change, and critics are no doubt troubled by Cooper's decision to describe the church as a woman who entices and manipulates the barbarian by dazzling him with religious pomp, the display of church finery, and the mysteries of Christian ritual.[65] But, Cooper also argues that men diminish the Christian rebirth of the West when male clergy depart from the theological example provided by Christ and begin to see women as a threat to culture and faith. They embrace and encourage a misreading of the relationship between men and women that rivals the errors she sees in her orientalized Asian and Islamic cultures:

> The Church as an organization committed a double offense against woman in the Middle Ages. Making of marriage a sacrament and at the same time insisting on the celibacy of the clergy and other religious orders, she gave an inferior if not an impure character to the marriage relation, especially fitted to reflect discredit on woman.[66]

More disturbing and corrupt, according to Cooper, was that the male clergy of the church, having made marriage a sacrament and celibacy the rule for themselves and female religious orders, promptly began violating the boundaries of both and burdening women with the inevitable social and practical problems. Including a bawdy quip by Chaucer, she underscores the seriousness of this move to the overall status of women.[67]

The church gave its imprimatur to the idea of sex as an impure act, helped create and advance the mythologies of women as creatures of appetite and sources of corruption for men, and reduced them to forbidden objects of desire—tolerably possessed only within marriage. We have considerable scholarly evidence about what these developments meant for the ideas of female virtue, the female body, and women as property.

Cooper's reading of the early church in the Middle Ages quickly evolves into a critique of the popular conception of female virtue. She strongly suggests that the transmission of culture from the fallen classical world to the reborn West rapidly became an imperialist project with women as the newly annexed and colonized territory. Cooper argues that, although gradual smoothing and calming of the rough and violent barbarian hordes made it possible to transform the coarse affection for women into chivalry, that victory was itself reduced by men to a "respect for the elect few among whom they expect[ed] to consort."[68]

Incomplete and compromised though they would become after their successes, the church and the chivalric tradition blunted the sharp edges of barbarism. According to Cooper, the early feminine (and perhaps feminizing) church, carried the forgiving, constructive, and civilizing message of Christ, and by manipulating the politics of the invaders' cultures, molded the barbarians from the fall of the old Roman Empire until the coming of the Holy Roman Empire, triumphing in the ascension of Charlemagne. Cooper's *Le Pelerinage de Charlemagne,* a translation in modern French during her graduate studies at Columbia University, also resonates strongly as an indication of her attachment to the Carolingian Renaissance as an example of America's potential to make Reconstruction an intellectual, racial, and spiritual renaissance.[69] "The result was she [the church] carried her point," according to Cooper. "Once more Rome laid her ambitious hand on temporal power, and allied with Charlemagne, aspired to rule the world through a civilization dominated by Christianity and permeated by the traditions and instincts of those sturdy barbarians."[70] In *The Idea of the Renaissance,* William Kerrigan and Gordon Braden provide a concise but descriptive sketch of the project of barbarian and Christian alliance that Cooper addresses:

> Reconquered in the sixth century, Italy is technically reintegrated into the old empire for two indecisive centuries; but the Byzantine exarchate at Ravenna is ended for good by the Lombards in 751, and the Roman Popes turn to the Franks for protection. After a half-century, it is their momentous joint idea—with some scholarly prompting—to secure this alliance as something more than tribal politics. In 800, the Frankish king is invested at Rome with the putatively greater dignity of emperor of the newly reproclaimed western empire.[71]

Kerrigan and Braden also elect skepticism over outright derision for the Holy Roman Empire (which has inspired laughter on more than one occasion). Similarly, despite its faults, Cooper suggests that Charlemagne's program of *Renouatio Romanii Imperii* (or some similar kind of renaissance) is the appropriate goal for America. His motto contains the hope for the former slaves and owners of her age. Ideal Christian womanhood and the chivalric tradition represent the two "ennobling forces" of Western womanhood that Cooper insists can again transform the people.

In the spirit of this great tradition of rebirth, and believing that women will carry in the household gods to the renewed civilization, Cooper makes her plea for her clients, the "colored girls of the South," who among women will be the civilizing, regenerating influence for the largely coarse manhood emerging from Reconstruction. These modern barbarian masses of freed slaves, defeated Southerners, and materialistic Gilded Age men—as rugged and forbidding as any Vandal or Visigoth and stalking through the rubble of the old southern empire—can still be refined by women. Cooper continues to argue that this civilizing influence is the truest and best *summum bonum* of a culture's women. Women's position "determines the vital elements of its regeneration and progress," and motherhood is by extension a holy and essential cultural project that should have the protection of civilization. The *sine qua non* of the American nation is the elevation of women in full recognition of their temporal ability to civilize the savage urges of mankind and their divine task of preparing young minds as fertile ground for the growth of Christianity. Superficially, this assertion seems supremely domestic and thoroughly orthodox for the era. However, Cooper begins to redefine the very lessons of civilization that must be taught, the goal of teaching, and the nature of the women who will bear that responsibility. She also connects the work of educating the masses to the larger contribution the Negro has to make to civilization. While this nineteenth-century ideal of racial characteristics and contribution may be unsettling to the contemporary scholar, within the context of the era and in the absence of a national and global environment conducive to globalist or multiculturalist thinking, it is not unusual:

> That the Negro has his niche in the infinite purposes of the Eternal, no one who has studied the history of the last fifty years in America will deny. That much depends on his own right comprehension of his responsibility and rising to the demands of the hour, it will be good for him to see; and how best to use his present so that the structure of the future shall be stronger and higher and brighter and nobler and holier than that of the past is a question to be decided each day by every one of us.[72]

Cooper sums up the African American racial project as one of being *cultured*—what she describes as being stronger, higher, brighter, nobler, and holier—rather then becoming property owners or masters of trades or commercial successes. That question of how to be stronger, higher, brighter, nobler, and holier can be answered by the womanhood of the race, the "fundamental agency under God" for the uplift of African Americans. Scholarly and spiritual learning, both of which build the intellectual virtues of wisdom and insight, make up part of the answer to this question, and Cooper grounds the creation of these virtues in Christianity and the classics. For Cooper this question of virtue is one of internal perfection, not martial might or physical power, a sentiment that echoes the scholarly spirit of her era. Cooper reengineers gender and virtue, noting that "weaknesses and malformations" have to be weeded out with all other degenerate elements of "a manhood and womanhood impoverished and debased by two centuries and more of compression and degradation."[73] In "The Higher Education of Women," Cooper revises the inherently masculine character of classical virtue, suggesting that virtue exists outside specific gender; moreover, the fullest articulation of manhood and womanhood depends on the proper integration of qualities traditionally presumed to be sex-linked:

> [B]oth [presumed masculine and feminine traits] are needed to be worked into the training of children, in order that our boys may supplement their virility by tenderness and sensibility, and our girls may round out their gentleness by strength and self-reliance. That, as both are alike necessary in giving symmetry to the individual, so a nation or a race will not degenerate into mere emotionalism on the one hand or bullyism on the other, if dominated by either exclusively; lastly, and most emphatically, that the feminine factor can have its proper effect only through women's development and education so that she may fitly and intelligently stamp her force on the forces of her day, and add her modicum to the riches of the world's thought.[74]

Perhaps because many of those, even in her own intellectual and cultural milieu, whom she might have chosen as models and examples, would have been largely circumscribed by domestic conventions of marriage, family, nineteenth-century patriarchy, and Christian orthodoxy (even as they championed a general educational and cultural uplift for their race), Cooper looked beyond her contemporaries for examples of masculine and feminine virtue, manliness, and heroism that were more easily and freely adapted to her purposes.[75] The lessons of the classical heroes, orators, and rulers provided possibilities to repair and refine manhood and womanhood, which had been damaged and altered by immoderate masculinity, martial aims, patriarchal ambitions, and the neglect and subordination of gentler, feminine-coded qualities to masculinity. Immoderate feeling, violent masculinity, and rage had a classical exemplar in Homer's Achilles, and Cooper saw Achilles (as well as other heroes) as a fine example to exploit: "The vulnerable point, [is] not in the heel, but at the heart of the young Achilles; and here must the defenses be strengthened and the watch redoubled."[76] The hearts of the young Achilles, the young Aeneas, the young Ascanius, and the stories of the hearts of the archetypal youth, heroes, and ideals of the West became the intellectual and moral examples and training ground for the hearts of Cooper's ideal men and women.[77]

The life of Achilles is not new ground for African American writers: Phillis Wheatley looked to the friendship between Patroclus and Achilles as a virtuous example in "To Maecenas." But, for Cooper, Achilles provided an excellent context for reimagining masculine virtue and its relationship to womanhood. Greek superhero though he might be, Achilles remains as problematic a figure as he is heroic. The primary passion of Achilles is rage, and even if one can argue that his anger at Agamemnon is justified, that seething rage borders on the inhuman and the barbaric. It threatens both his Greek brethren and Trojan foes by turning an *agathos* into a creature devoid of virtue and reason and ruled by passion. Contemporary scholars are quick to point out that Homer's poem raises a significant question about the origin of human suffering, which is perhaps a product of the fickleness of the gods and men's own reckless ambition and unrestrained passion.[78] The *Iliad* opens with Achilles raging against Agamemnon and proceeds to his infamous sulking in his tent. That uncontrolled rage wastes legions of Trojans, including Hector, but it eventually costs Achilles his life when his one weakness is exposed. His explosive fury of life burns out quickly and leaves the hero to endure the endless, shadowy life of the afterworld. This is the end of the unrefined man, and Cooper also notes some contemporary men as examples of this unharnessed genius and potential running wild: "Byron, like a rocket, shot his way upward with scorn and repulsion, flamed out in wild, explosive, brilliant excesses and disappeared in darkness made all the more palpable."[79]

Achilles disappears into the shadowy afterlife, but at least in literature he is able to tell Odysseus and readers how meaningless his brilliant excesses have been.[80] Key to Achilles's story and fate is that the women in his life are problematic divinities, mere trinkets to be won as the booty of war, or objects to be quarreled over for honor and sex. Thetis plunges him into Styx for protection, but afterward she only pleads his case or answers his whining complaints. The great hero is truly without guidance, even though his mother is a goddess. The heart of Achilles is as weak as his heel, and it is the heart of an Achilles that Cooper believes women can educate in true virtue. Regenerating and educating the hearts of men is the great missionary project for the black woman "who stands mute and wondering at the Herculean task devolving upon her."[81] Cooper's focus on the regenerating and transforming qualities of women and the potential reshaping of Achilles is interesting. She subtly rejects much of the philosophy and martial, manly discourse of virtue so prominent in the influential oratorical tradition and in the male slave narrative tradition so regularly used by major representative black men such as Frederick Douglass. Cooper describes the transformation from uncontrolled, unrefined manhood to masculinity refined for the good of the *community* in classical terms, but this transformation has activist potential for the local community of African Americans. Cooper offers an alternative to the making of masculinity and virtue, rather than adhere to the lessons of the military camp and the *palaestra* or even the fields of slavery. Virtue, manliness, and heroism remain central goals, but they are redefined in terms of the most productive relationship between men and women. Moreover, virtue also includes a commitment to securing advances for civilization and building and regenerating culture. In place of the wrathful, arrogant, vain, or weak Achilles, Agamemnon, Paris, or Menelaus, who waste their lives and wreck their civilization pursuing martial virtue and fighting over Briseis, Chryseis, and Helen of Troy as trophies for the palace and bedroom, Cooper envisions men of a richer, more refined masculinity. These men will recognize the regenerative influence of women and aid and protect the yet unreconstructed women struggling to acquire the voice, culture, and refinement that will unlock their regenerative powers. While not limited to traditional roles of protecting women, these are men who "let their interest and gallantry extend outside the circle of aesthetic appreciation; men who can be a father, a brother, a friend to every weak, struggling unshielded girl."[82]

Cooper's call for virility to be tempered by tenderness and sensibility and aimed toward building culture echoes elements of both the morally virtuous man of Aristotle's *Nichomachean Ethics,* the Ciceronian man of duty in *On Duties,* and the Virgilian Aeneas, the hero who goes cold with fear and comforts, feeds, and serves his men. Aeneas loves his son, weeps for his wife, longs for a real relationship with his mother, and hesitates in his drive toward conquest. Even at the end of *The Aeneid,* Aeneas pauses in his rage to attempt to spare Turnus, his enemy. Cooper is certain of the kind of *pax Americana* that will be lasting—one born out of leadership exemplified by Aeneas:

There are two kinds of peace in this world. The one produced by suppression, which is the passivity of death; the other brought about by a proper adjustment of living, acting forces. A nation or an individual may be at peace because all opponents have been killed or crushed; or, a nation as well as individual may have found the secret of true harmony in the determination to live and let live.[83]

Not surprisingly, *The Aeneid* is among the texts Cooper taught her co-educational classrooms of students. Cooper found the formidable weapons against hordes of unwashed barbarians and the wayward young Achilles(es) in the classical curriculum she studied and taught. Cooper served as the principal of M Street High School in Washington, D.C., from 1901 until 1906 and as a teacher of Latin for many years after her 1910 reinstatement. Cooper's M Street program was so successful that she drew considerable attention for her curriculum, pedagogy, and success in sending students to college. Under her leadership and because of its rigorous curriculum, M Street received accreditation from the top schools in the northeast corridor, which meant students were exempt from college entrance examinations. Many went on to Ivy League educations at Harvard and other institutions. When Father Felix Klein, a professor at the Catholic Institute of Paris, indulged his curiosity about the M Street School with a surprise visit, he was surprised by the rigor of the Latin class he visited and recounted his experience in *In the Land of the Strenuous Life*:

We spent the hour on the first eleven lines of the poem; and without being aware of it I stayed to the end, deeply interested. It is not every day that one has occasion to sing the Trojan hero (the teacher strongly recommended "hero" as a translation of *virum*), or the fabled beginnings of Rome, in the society of American negroes under the direction of a woman of their own race.

My amiable guide [Cooper] . . . had been able to obtain for one of her students a scholarship at Harvard University, and this she thought, with good reason, would be a splendid encouragement for the others, and a means of increasing the number of leaders who seek to elevate her race.[84]

Cooper's classical curriculum seemed to follow a different stream of the classical tradition than was regularly navigated in her era. Cooper still encouraged virtue, *virum* (which, as Father Klein observed, Cooper maintained as "hero"), and heroism—*eximia virtus* or *animus fortis*. But she drew out their meanings from the moral lessons of the classical epics and Christianity, not simply oratory or the texts that emphasize martial manliness. Cooper's approach would seem to emphasize the best civic attributes of the heroes while critiquing their commitment to the well-being of their people. She was concerned with the flaws in the heart of Achilles and the gentle and complicated heroism of Aeneas. Moreover, in teaching *The Aeneid,* as she was doing during Father Klein's visit, she was immediately drawn into discussions of preserving, moving, and rebuilding culture and the tremendous problems of commitment, piety, determination, and flexibility that the project entails—a more than suitable subject for nineteenth-century African American youth. Quite plainly, she and her students were studying the fundamental *translatio,* from burning Troy to Rome (via Africa in *The Aeneid,* we might add), a project of building culture and transmitting knowledge.

Civic virtue, *virtus* and *pietas,* is the primary concern for men, women, and the West in *A Voice from the South,* and Cooper encourages civilization to recognize the many voices that can enrich and fertilize the blooming plants of virtue. Virtue, as Cooper's historical lesson demonstrates, is remarkably fragile, and the course of civilization can be tremendously altered by failures to protect blooming *virtus* at crucial moments. The difference between a slain Achilles and a flourishing Aeneas is the nature of the virtue they possess. In light of how Cooper reconstructs a relatively gender-neutral but heroic civic virtue, we should be careful not to assume that this image of weak women shielded by gallant men represents the culmination of Cooper's vision for women. After all, she sings the Trojan hero for Father Klein and a classroom of boys *and* girls. Although she calls for a new virtue and gallantry to shield women from abuse, she also requires that women be both central to their creation and eventually its joint holders with men. She desires that women have the access to the same education as men and the same virtues and commitment to advancing civilization. Her call to arms is social, educational, and vaguely like the call to raise a new legion of heroic women:

> Let our girls feel that we expect something more of them than that they merely look pretty and appear well in society. Teach them that there is a race with special needs which they and only they can help; that the world needs and is already asking for their trained, efficient forces. Finally, if there is an ambitious girl with pluck and brain to take the higher education, encourage her to make the most of it. Let there be the same flourish of trumpet and clapping of hands as when a boy announces his determination to enter the lists; and then . . . let money be raised

and scholarships be founded in our colleges and universities for self-
supporting, worthy young women, to offset and balance the aid that can
always be found for boys. . . . Let us then, here and now, recognize this
force and resolve to make the most of it—not the boys less, but the girls
more.[85]

Failure to complete the second step of jointly owning *virtus* and *pietas* has dire consequences for the future of the race, according to Cooper.
Rather than becoming stronger, brighter, nobler, and holier, African Americans will degenerate and succumb to the weakness, malformation, impov-
erishment, and debasement introduced into the race by slavery.[86] To build
culture, African Americans will have to judiciously manage nature and
nurture to engineer virtuous men and women. Otherwise, Cooper argues,
the unrefined African American men and women will degenerate and exhibit extreme and undesirable characteristics of their gender.

To manage the virtuous growth of the young heroes and heroines of
the race, ensure the regeneration and improvement of the race, sustain the
healthy relationship between men and women, and advance the scope and
speed of Christian conversion, Cooper argues that civilization must invest
in the proper education of women. In *Voice*'s chapter "The Higher Education of Women," Cooper argues that if the sum of women's existence is to
"be pretty, dress prettily, flirt prettily, and not be too well informed," then
all Western civilization is in grave danger.[87] Clearly, women can remain
neither the powdered, corseted, and closeted variety of refined Victorian
woman nor the ignorant, unshielded black woman of the South. Women
must be well educated and armed for the task of conquering new territory
for civilization, including barbarian men or unlettered youth. Educated
women are necessary to civilization, and despite men's reservations, the
idea is not in any sense a new one. Cooper provides numerous examples of
educated and powerful women:

[T]he higher education of women has already had a trial and should,
in the past, have produced some of these glowing effects. Sappho, the
bright, sweet singer of Lesbos, "The violet crowned, pure sweetly smiling
Sappho" as Alcaeus calls her, chanted her lyrics and poured forth her
soul nearly six centuries before Christ, in notes as full and free, as passionate and eloquent as did ever Archilochus or Anacreon.

Aspasia, that earliest queen of the drawing-room, a century later
ministered to the intellectual entertainment of Socrates and the leading
wits and philosophers of her time. Indeed, to her is attributed, by the best

critics, the authorship of one of the most noted speeches ever delivered by Pericles.[88]

Cooper continues to provide historic examples of lettered women and their productions through the Renaissance, arguing that men and civilization are best strengthened when women can intellectually engage Homer, Socrates, Virgil, Dante, or Milton.[89] Her references also suggest that women have already been behind those canonical productions and in the intellectual tradition following them. She specifically points to the Greek and Latin poetry penned by Italy's exceptionally well-educated Olympia Fulvia Morata. Chronicling her own difficulty in acquiring a classical education, Cooper insists that the key to the success of civilization is to recognize the power of the educated, Christian woman and resolve to "make the most of it."[90]

Like Ascanius, Cooper lets fly one special arrow in her defense of women's education, and it lodges in the English writer, Matthew Arnold, who had suggested that education ruined young women for marriage. Cooper called this "the most serious argument ever used against the higher education [of women]. If it interferes with marriage, classical training has a grave objection to weigh and answer."[91] Arnold's objection raised the historic fear that classical education transformed women into the *virago*. Speaking of her own education, Cooper lamented the fact that traditionally, frivolity and fashion sufficed for a woman who had the ability to worship masculinity. Cooper argued that this dearth of intellectual, spiritual, and emotional improvement was not only injurious to women but also dangerous to sexual virtue and the institution of marriage. If marriage retained its position as the *sine qua non* of women's lives *and* desirability in the marriage marketplace was determined by how successfully women advertised their ignorance, then marriage under this regime could not be wholesome for society. Moreover, Cooper suggested that women were less virtuous when uneducated, and education made them not only self-reliant but also more chaste:

> I grant you that intellectual development, with the self-reliance and capacity for earning a livelihood which it gives, renders woman less dependent on the marriage relation for physical support (which, by the way, does not always accompany it). Neither is she compelled to look to sexual love as the one sensation capable of giving tone and relish, movement and vim to the life she leads.[92]

Cooper continues with the themes of self-reliance and profound intellectual development, arguing with almost Emersonian resonance, that woman is broadened and deepened and put in greater touch with the universe by extending her intellectual horizons: "Not a bud that opens, not a dew drop, not a ray of light, not a cloud-burst or a thunderbolt, but adds to the expansiveness and zest of her soul." She can draw on and commune with Socrates, Dante, Virgil, Homer, Milton, Sappho, and others as she labors with men in the construction of civilization. However, she argues, one cannot imagine that these tremendous scholarly sources and their gifts could "destroy or diminish [women's] capacity for loving." Interestingly enough, Cooper suggests that higher education frees women from having to diminish themselves simply to enter the marriage convention: "Her standards have undoubtedly gone up. The necessity of speculating in 'chawnces' [sic] has probably shifted."[93] What Cooper suggests is that the marriage relationship will be transformed from a speculative marketplace, in which women are marketed to men and acquired by them, into a more noble partnership between women and men. Men will have to display virtues that will make them suitable partners for a body of women whom, Cooper also suggests, education will make more broadly passionate and engaging. In any case, an educated woman will not become a *virago;* rather, Cooper suggests that the marriage bond will be more passionate and profound between two well-formed companions.

When Cooper turns to the question of how education fits women for the domestic sphere, she neither attacks the nineteenth-century convention of motherhood nor spends her own words on the subject. She defers to the answer given by a Mrs. Armstrong, who responds to Grant Allen's "Plain Words on the Woman Question."[94] Armstrong suggests that higher education can only better prepare women for motherhood and the affairs of the household. It is interesting that Cooper does not explicitly assign women to this role.

Cooper is careful not to rigidly assign roles to men or women, even in terms of learning the classics. A fair and moderate supporter of both the classical and industrial programs, Cooper insists that for the good of the culture students should follow their talents:

> I believe in allowing every longing of the human soul to attain its utmost reach and grasp. But the effort must be a fizzle which seeks to hammer souls into preconstructed molds and grooves which they have never longed for and cannot be made to take comfort in. The power of appreciation is the measure of an individual's aptitudes; and if a boy hates Greek and Latin and spends all his time whittling out steamboats, it is rather foolish to try to force him into the classics.[95]

Not only does Cooper suggest that some boys are not suited to Greek and Latin, but given her call for women's education, it follows that some girls are cut out for the classics and well deserving of places held by untalented boys. The matter of native talent aside, Cooper would never admit that the acquisition of meat, bread, money, and products was a superior form of life. Here she seems to echo Emerson's *The American Scholar* and to foreshadow Du Bois's *The Souls of Black Folk:*

> It is an enormous waste of values to harness the whole man in the narrow furrow, plowing for bread. There are other hungerings in man besides the eternal all-subduing hungering of his despotic stomach. There is the hunger of the eye for beauty, the hunger of the ear for concords, the hungering of the mind for development and growth, of the soul for communion and love, for a higher, richer, fuller living—a more abundant life![96]

Cooper insisted on maintaining a classical curriculum to prepare students for higher intellectual engagements. Her program successfully educated African American students for the Ivy League as well as for technical careers. Cooper, though not visibly wedded to the notion of a Talented Tenth as was her contemporary Du Bois, certainly saw great value in the classics as an intellectual and spiritual nursery for virtue. Du Bois wrote that "[e]ducation must not just teach work—it must teach Life. The Talented Tenth of the Negro race must be made leaders of thought and missionaries of culture among their people. No others can do this work and Negro colleges must train men for it. The Negro race, like other races, is going to be saved by its exceptional men."[97] Cooper's extensive work figuratively added a much-needed "and women" to Du Bois's call to arms for heroes dedicated to the people. She pursued her cultural and educational mission with both genders in mind, and she encouraged a virtue more closely grounded in the relationship between individuals and between an exceptional individual and her people. As she cautions in *Voice,* no great, self-made men, no singular man, can represent the people. African Americans "too often mistake individuals' honor for race development and so are ready to substitute pretty accomplishments for sound sense and earnest purpose."[98] The real guide for individuals and the people was in an education in virtue and discipline that could improve and arm them all. As Cooper would have understood, the classics suggested an African American presence in the classical world and did not instruct black students that they were inherently inferior. On the contrary, the classical and humanities curricula cultivated the very qualities that had suggested otherwise to an ever-lengthening line of black scholars and leaders. It was also "a means to understanding the development of the western world and blacks' inherent rights to equality within that world."[99] Accordingly, Cooper was not alone in her educational course. The great majority of black church-supported and northern missionary schools adopted a curriculum mixing standard English instruction with a version of classical training, the humanities.[100]

What emerged from Cooper's remarkable project was a substantial expansion of the existing African American literary and intellectual project. By using the classics to articulate an intellectual position and enable a unique reading of race and gender, she provided a new way for African Americans to address each other and a broader American audience. She could encompass varied and even hostile groups of women, men, freed slaves, the white South, and the Gilded Age North in the expansive narrative of the West, and she had no need to excuse or accommodate errors and crimes in the process. Neither was she compelled to adhere to Victorian standards of white American society nor the restrictive Afro-Victorian mode and narrow Christian morality developing in the parlors of club women and the broader black middle and upper classes. Just as Phillis Wheatley shaped a poetics from a classical education that allowed her to intervene in closed, white, masculine discourse, the classically trained Cooper "use[d] much of the same language and knowledge of her intellectual 'fathers' (white) and 'brothers' (African-American)," along with her personal experience (writing in "mothers" and "sisters"). The result was a "new space" between the narrative and the political treatise.[101] Not only did the classics of Cooper's early education and lifelong study provide rhetorical strategies and historical lessons that enabled her to amplify a number of otherwise silent voices, it also provided a narrative of civilization that gave those voices and people a place in the Western story. Her sweeping historical analysis of the *translatio* and the West opened up more widely the possibility that African Americans could legitimately critique, correct, and amend the Western imperialist *translatio* and take part in the culture of the New World into which they had been thrust. Cooper's work also signaled that an African American intellectual elite could address blackness and cultural development from a nuanced and complex intellectual position not linked to the voice and will of whatever black leader arose by accident of politics and history. The classics held a body of moral and intellectual lessons that were relatively objective and practically race-neutral compared to nineteenth-century race politics. Moreover, they could be safely absorbed, pondered, used to form intellect and character, and eventually deployed to address contemporary concerns. If nothing else, there was a rich new body of allusions, narratives, historical lessons and ironies, heroes, villains, and literary possibilities for romance, criticism, political commentary, and all other incisive uses of the pen. Intriguingly, *Voice* and its classical accoutrements also suggested that there was a new arena and body of weapons with which African American women could combat their own political and cultural disadvantages, even if that required them to challenge black men. This rich addition to the genre of uplift literature provided an effective literary vehicle for discourse on the politics of blackness and a counter to Washingtonian pragmatism, aggression, and revisionist realism.

CHAPTER FOUR

QUO VADIS?

W. E. B. DU BOIS AND *THE SOULS OF BLACK FOLK*

The critical attention to Anna Julia Cooper's writing pales in comparison to the volume of scholarship that W. E. B. Du Bois's internationally renowned *The Souls of Black Folk* has produced. Du Bois has long been recognized as one of the most important African American writers and among the most influential American writers. He has been repeatedly examined and diagnosed as a black nationalist, Afrocentrist, black radical democrat, Marxist, elitist, racial romanticist, lingering Christian, agnostic, and even purveyor of the Uncle Tom stereotype. But academe has canonized *The Souls of Black Folk* without more than superficial attention to his classical education and vast array of classical allusions. The chapter "Of the Meaning of Progress" demonstrates Du Bois's use of Cicero, and "The Wings of Atalanta" boldly announces its classicism in the title. Du Bois explicitly describes his educational alternative to industrial education as being that of the pharoahs, Plato, Virgil, the *trivium,* and the *quadrivium.*[1] His analysis of the opportunities, dangers, and challenges African Americans face clearly pits the pursuit of the good life and its meaning, wisdom, and culture—the virtuous life—against the barbaric pursuit of wealth, power, and possessions.

Despite Du Bois's overt use of the classics in *The Souls of Black Folk,* especially in his core educational philosophy, few scholars have pondered the implications of the preeminent African American scholar of the twentieth century having envisioned African American education as a classical education. None have adequately addressed what lessons, virtues, strategies, or tools Du Bois intended for an education grounded in the classics to provide African Americans. The absence of the classics from scholarly discussions of Du Bois is hardly to be believed, given the sheer volume of commentary on Du Bois, the many printings of *The Souls of Black Folk,* and the relatively recent centennial of its publication. Yet, even the well-known facts that Du Bois was educated at Fisk, Harvard, and Berlin, that his first job was as a professor of classics at Wilberforce (the college surreptitiously purchased for the A.M.E. Zion Church by classically educated Bishop Daniel Alexander Payne), and that *Souls* explicitly deploys classical references, a classical education program, and Cicero for the hill folk of Tennessee have stirred precious little interest among scholars.

Among those who have worked at the edges of Du Bois's classicism, Francis Broderick's *W. E. B. Du Bois: Negro Leader in a Time of Crisis* (1959) lists Du Bois's college reading at Fisk and Harvard in some detail, including classical works.[2] He also suggests that Du Bois embraced the classics as part of a network of humanities that was a conduit of culture for African Americans. Unfortunately, he does not press further with an analysis of how the classics operated in Du Bois's literature and philosophy. Keith E. Byerman determines that Du Bois is reaching for moral truths told beautifully, but he does not identify this as an extension of the classical tradition. Du Bois's experiences with classical rhetoric and Greek and Roman epics certainly emphasized this fusion of aesthetic beauty and virtue. Byerman includes in his analysis many of the passages from *The Souls of Black Folk* that deploy classical allusions, and he points to Du Bois's suggestion that the antidote to the materialism and vulgarity of the "profane city is the sacred campus. . . . It is also a different discursive universe. It speaks the language of the *trivium* and *quadrivium,* a method that is itself classical rather than modern."[3] Byerman argues that Du Bois alters the economic meaning of "usefulness" and invests it with more noble classical goals—"to know the end and aim of life"—but Byerman invokes the passages containing classical references without fully evoking the spirit, content, and intellectual and cultural implications of those allusions, an approach that veils their meaning and eviscerates their power.[4]

Zhang Juguo, like many scholars, lists some of Du Bois's educational curriculum in his general biographical information, but he also provides a long list of classical scholars that should pique the interest of contemporary scholars: Homer, Herodotus, Plato, Demosthenes, Sophocles, Livy, Tacitus, Caesar, Cicero, Virgil, and Horace.[5] Zhang notes Booker T. Washington's objections to classical education among African Americans, but this reference never quite erupts into full-blown analysis. While the classics are clearly a subject of debate, the depths of the debate are never plumbed. Raymond Wolter's *W. E. B. Du Bois and His Rivals* (2002) examines the conflict between Du Bois and Booker T. Washington without examining either the classical educational tradition that Du Bois deployed in response to Washington or the variety of classical allusions throughout *The Souls of Black Folk*. Neither does he investigate how Du Bois's classical background and classically inflected philosophy might have contributed to his conflicts with other rivals, such as Oswald Garrison Villard, Marcus Garvey, or Walter White. The venerable Wilson J. Moses implicates Du Bois in transmitting the Christian myth and the "Uncle Tom Myth" in *Black Messiahs and Uncle Toms* (1982).[6] As recently as *Afrotopia: The Roots of African American Popular History* (1998, 2008), Moses repeats the assessment of Du Bois as a peddler of Uncle Tom mythology and sharpens the critique by asserting that he is a racial romanticist with a resistance to modernity.[7] Although *Afrotopia* is undoubtedly a complex and nuanced view of the development of Afrocentrism and a more in-depth reading of Du Bois than commonly seen, Du Bois's classicism—and the classicism of other subjects of Moses's analysis—is never examined closely. For instance, Moses discusses Du Bois's Christianity by summing it up as a part of a general American social gospel:

> I am using this term, "Arminianized Calvinism," in association with the doctrine of American perfectionism, a concept rooted in the tradition of John Winthrop's City on a Hill. American perfectionism has meant a belief that the Christian must perform responsible civic duties in order to create a "righteous empire" in the United States. By the late nineteenth century the perfectionist impulse to create the kingdom of God in America had evolved into a doctrine called the Social Gospel.[8]

Now this might be true in the main, but why should we believe that the social gospel, broadly construed, is the same for American whites and African Americans, especially those blacks steeped in classics? The civic duties Du Bois learned in his educational curricula at the very least start out as being, in substantial part, locally Ciceronian and broadly Roman, if not Greek as well. He does not trust movement Christianity or the organized

church, and his writing points toward a virtue he had imagined to be a nobler, brighter humanity built on the *trivium* and *quadrivium*. Summing up
Du Bois as a part of the general social gospel phenomenon is problematic,
especially when Moses does not give any attention to how his personal architecture of God and civic virtue are put together with some classical materials. Additionally, Moses looks at *Dusk of Dawn* (1940) in this particular
section but does not consider *The Souls of Black Folk* until sometime later
and with no attention to classical content. Although some scholars limit
their view of Du Bois to *The Souls of Black Folk* and ignore his transformation across time, it is equally problematic to look at religion and ignore Du
Bois's earlier writings. It is only by examining his view of religion from
beginning to end that we understand his development.

Moses, like many others, seems unable to fully explain Du Bois's declared disassociation from organized religion and the excesses of the black
Protestant tradition when he clearly uses symbols, stories, and elements of
Christianity throughout his work—a religious tinge that colors much of
his discussion of the morals, destiny, and civic virtues of the black population. However, it may be because scholars have not considered the fusion
of piety and civic duty that emanates from the classical tradition, which
was part of Du Bois's foundation. The primary image of God in Du Bois's
world may be that of the Judeo-Christian tradition, not of the classical pantheon, but the promise of redemption is the preservation of a civilization
with Roman virtue or Greek *eudemonia* seen in the classical world, not just
the redemption of the cross. When Du Bois fuses these two traditions, he
brings into being the kingdom of God—reshaped into a renewed civilization for America, African America, and eventually Africa—through the
pious and dutiful pursuit of knowledge and virtue and the rejection of base
self-service and personal advantage and vice. Certainly this is a cousin of
the social gospel of general discussion, but it is peculiarly Du Boisian and
part of a long line of classical fusion with African American Christianity,
from Wheatley to Du Bois.

Even when it comes to the clear influence of Germany on Du Bois, it
seems that we should be more careful. Here Moses insists that Du Bois is
caught up in the German "conception of *Kultur,* which implied the idea of
a folk spirit rising up out of the souls of the masses." He also allegedly was
influenced by the lectures of his university years and "began to adapt the
concept of *Volksgeist* (folk soul or people's spirit) to the American and the
Pan-African condition."[9] I think we cannot fault Moses on this point, for
it is undoubtedly true in part. However, we can probe further and ask why
would this be the sole or major contributor to Du Bois's ideas of culture

and the people's spirit, especially when the Roman idea of *cultus* precedes the German *Kultur* by two millennia, with the Ciceronian description of Roman citizenship representing a higher, powerful humanity also having a considerable age and pedigree of its own.

In both 1982 and 2008, Moses looked at Du Bois's assertion of the will of God and the destiny of African Americans without the lens of classicism. If nothing else, the more active or martial element in Du Bois should tip us off that something a bit more robust than New Testament Christian meekness is going on. The John Jones visible in "Of the Coming of John" teaches on the French Revolution and kills the white assailant of his sister with a tree branch. In *Dark Princess* (1928), Matthew Towns and his blue-blooded Kautilya are plotting global revolution. Uncle Tom fades and Achilles, Aeneas, Memnon, Camilla, and Penthilesea materialize when destiny and Christianity are mixed with Homer, Virgil, and Cicero. Moreover, Moses fails to view Du Bois's concern about the materialism and willingness to sell anything from the black body to black civil rights for the right price in the context of a classical view of civic virtue and duty. Here Cicero, central to Du Bois's education, is instructive.[10]

When Cornel West undertook a thorough evaluation of Du Bois in "Black Strivings in a Twilight Civilization," the monumental meeting of great minds still opened with a judgment of Du Bois as having been "shaped by the prevailing presuppositions and prejudices of modern Euro-American civilization."[11] The soaring declaration in the essay's first paragraph that Du Bois was a genius beyond anyone in the modern black scholarly class is brought in fragments back to earth like a clay pigeon: "[H]e was, in style and substance, a proud black man of letters primarily influenced by nineteenth century Euro-American traditions."[12] Proceeding with the prosecution's case in chief, West arrays evidence of Du Bois's primary crime, which is addressing evil in a way at the very beginning of the twentieth century that West alleges was unsuited to staving off the violence, capitalist exploitation, and ideology of the twenty-first century. The lesser included offense is having formulated the concept of the Talented Tenth. Du Bois has been *seduced* by Enlightenment and Victorian thought, and West is keen to illustrate that Du Bois was not really black enough, despite his genius, because he "did not feel it in his bones deeply enough."[13] Moreover, because Du Bois did not experience the depths of degradation in nineteenth- and early-twentieth-century America, he was incapable of fully learning "fundamental lessons" from the black masses.[14] And in a characteristic coup de grace, just like John Jones in "Of the Coming of John," Du Bois is demonstrated to be outside the influence of the Holy Spirit and practically

outside the reach of *der schwarz volksgeist* that Moses translates for us. At-
torney West asks us to, at the very least, convict Dr. Du Bois of *involuntary
whiteness:*

> Du Bois's intriguing description reminds one of an anthropologist visit-
> ing some strange and exotic people whose rituals suggest not only the
> sublime, but also the satanic. The "awfulness" of this black church ser-
> vice, similar to that of my own black Baptist tradition, signifies for him
> both dread and fear, anxiety and disgust. In short, a black ritualistic ex-
> plosion of energy frightened this black rationalist. It did so not simply
> because the folk seem so coarse and uncouth, but also because they are
> out of control, overpowered by something bigger than themselves.[15]

West draws a sharp distinction between Du Bois's reaction and his
ostensibly more authentic black religious experience—stepping from the
secular podium to the pulpit in what I have argued is a classic move for
African American scholars. However, West is certainly not the only African American man of letters to have had the black Baptist or Methodist
experience, nor is he the only one to have taken his place at the pulpit on
occasion. Any scholar who has been born and bred in the black Baptist
tradition has likely seen and shared the experience of the congregation
as what we know as the Holy Spirit sweeps across a mass of worshippers
attuned to the divine by a skillful and inspired delivery of scripture and
hymnody. However, there is another kind of effusion of spirit that coun-
terfeits that religious ecstasy, and it can be generated by a need on the
part of the masses that meets with a poseur's sometimes stomach-turning
outpouring of gibberish, fragmented doctrine, and personal or local prejudices turned into an exhortation in the name of the Father, the Son, and
the Holy Ghost. Sometimes the differences between the two are hard to
discern, but not often. This is the province of the huckster, the "jack-leg"
preacher, the uneducated teacher, and the less-than-talented shepherd who
needs to keep the flock feeling fed and led, lest he return next Sunday to
find them having fled. Sister Mary needs something to get her through
the week, you know. These practitioners greatly dislike intellectuals, who
might see through them, and there is no end to the intimations and outright claims that education ruins a black mind for the Lord. Du Bois knew
this dangerous kind of faux religion, as did James W. C. Pennington, Daniel
Payne, and Christopher Rush and many of West's predecessors in spirit
and scholarship. Frederick Douglass knew it as well, and he parodied it
in his Slaveholder's Sermon. It is disappointing to see West maneuver Du

Bois into this particular cultural trap and stumbling block, for he *must* know that thing from which Du Bois would have recoiled as mere Pythian ecstasy. More concerning is the fact that this is one of the opening gambits in the set of rhetorical moves that will ostensibly lead to Du Bois being put in check as an intellectual leader, largely because he is not steeped enough in blackness. Like a darker Achilles, I suppose we are to imagine, he has that weakness in the heel where Euro-America held on tightly so as not to let him fall into that black Styx.[16]

True, there is much to compare between Du Bois's view of culture and of education and the European models of manhood and civilization of the Victorian imperial states. Yet, stupidity was not the only great sin Du Bois saw in the world or in the masses of whites and African Americans. It was not merely education—classes and grades and degrees—that Du Bois saw as essential to building in America an enduring black civilization. It was a particular education in the classics that he recommended in *The Souls of Black Folk,* one that looked very much like his Fisk (and Great Barrington) education, to which Harvard and Berlin added. The model for the Talented Tenth is not so much Matthew Arnold, as West suggests, but Cicero, whose men of duty help extend what is the Roman spirit, that thing which makes civilization out of men who are otherwise self-serving, acquisitive, and barbaric. All men are united by that spark of their creator, but Roman citizens are separated from the masses of humanity by their commitment to duty and the higher needs of civilization, against personal interest and even the interest of preserving their own lives.[17] Perhaps West would find similar reasons to decry the establishment of a class of noble, educated men, bound by Romanesque duty, just as he does when he sees it constructed of Victorian paternalism, but the two cultures and circumstances are not the same and deserve distinct analyses. To do that, however, one has to take on the classics directly.

The many treatments of Du Bois certainly leave much to be desired where his classical training and influences are concerned, but little additional detail on Du Bois's classicism has emerged from scholarship more generally sculpted to reflect the classical tradition in American intellectual life. John C. Shields's provocative *The American Aeneas: The Classical Origins of the American Self* (2001) builds on his signal work on Phillis Wheatley's classicism, but even in looking as far ahead as Hawthorne and Melville for evidence of the Virgilian metanarrative, Shields does not discuss any additional African American classical activity in American literature. Caroline Winterer's *The Culture of Classicism: Ancient Greece and Rome in American Intellectual Life, 1780—1910* (2002) is a remarkably revealing and sorely needed examination of the classical tradition in American education, except that it virtually ignores black colleges and curricula, African American writers such as Wheatley, Douglass, Cooper, and Du Bois, or professional black classicists such as James M. Gregory and William Sanders Scarborough. Although she reports that late-nineteenth-century changes in education included access to classical education for blacks (at the urging of missionaries), she relies heavily on a brief note referring readers to James D. Anderson's *Education of Blacks in the South* to support those roughly seven lines on 2 of 244 pages. The most comprehensive examination of Du Bois's life and works has come from David Levering Lewis, whose two-volume critical biography lays bare the scholarly, religious, cultural, and racial influences and experiences in Du Bois's life and will provide a catalyst for scholarly work for many years to come. Lewis is careful to attribute a portion of Du Bois's philosophical understanding of humanity and global politics to his classical education. However, he does not closely examine the classical allusions and the broader implications of the rather heavily classical curriculum at his various collegiate homes. Lewis's limited examination of the classics is more understandable, given its place in the vast context of Du Bois's long life. Still, Lewis offers much more insight into Du Bois's classical background than the majority of his more narrowly focused peers.

The most substantive critical examination of Du Bois's classical education, background, and literary deployments remains Arnold Rampersad's *The Art and Imagination of W. E. B. Du Bois* (1976). Rampersad flatly states the risk scholars run by failing to see Du Bois's complexity, causing them to "misrepresent the major ways in which his art and imagination functioned."[18] The early Du Bois, the writer of *The Souls of Black Folk,* is a complicated fusion of New England moral elitism, curious and stalwart Burghardt and Du Bois blackness, A.M.E. Zion Christianity, and *fin de siecle* classical training at Fisk and Harvard, all dipped ever so briefly but transformingly in the *sturm und drang* of the southern black experience. Rampersad chronicles Du Bois's classical courses at Fisk and Harvard and notes how "[t]he combination of religious and secular, Biblical and classical reference suggests the complexity and confusion of Du Bois's prophetic sense."[19] Rarely have Rampersad's warning and example been heeded, but the implications for scholarship on Du Bois are clear. Recognizing Du Bois as a classicist—a man who was trained to read and write the classical languages and translate and interpret classical texts—demands that scholars be conversant enough in those languages, texts, and traditions of scholarship to accurately assess the nature and implications of Du Bois's allusions and classically grounded educational, political, literary, and philosophical arguments. Moreover, it means that whatever claims and calculations scholars have made about Du Bois's contributions to the understanding of race in the twentieth century (especially in *The Souls of Black Folk*), the project of African American uplift, the black nationalism of the period, or the formation of a black intelligentsia have been underestimated and perhaps misread because their classical foundations have been ignored or unexplored. For instance, Wilson J. Moses argues that scholars readily admit Du Bois's affinity and similarity to German romantics, racial theorists, and nationalists like Bismarck, Du Bois's Berlin professor Heinrich von Treitschke, romantic writer Johann Wolgang von Goethe, and composer Richard Wagner, all of whom were concerned with the *volksgeist* and appeared in Du Bois's writings. But scholars fail to recognize that Du Bois could have gotten his views on race and black nationalism just as easily from classically educated clergymen Edward Blyden and Alexander Crummell, who looked directly to the classics and also appear in Du Bois's writings. He points out that even Marcus Garvey, whom Du Bois disliked, possessed the same personal and rhetorical style as the Germans.[20] While Moses is correct to insist that the Du Bois–Germany nexus is no more evident than the Du Bois–Crummell–Blyden nexus, the classical tradition that was a shared love and educational foundation for the German elite, Blyden, Crummell, and Du Bois is the basic foundation or matrix that creates a broader relationship among black nationalism, German nationalism, German romanticism, and Du Bois.[21]

An actual examination of Du Bois's education reveals remarkable depth and a significant investment in classical texts and subjects. His education was influenced by the same nineteenth-century educational changes that marked Anna Julia Cooper's experience, including the emphasis on "being cultured." Du Bois's early education in Great Barrington, Massachusetts, was followed by a double undergraduate career at Fisk University in Nashville, Tennessee, and Harvard University. Du Bois found similar rhetorical training at both institutions. In *Against Racism* and *W. E. B. Du Bois: Negro Leader in a Time of Crisis*, Herbert Aptheker and Francis Broderick provide a wonderful catalogue of Du Bois's courses of study at Great Barrington, Fisk, Harvard, and Berlin. Broderick notes his standard college preparatory curriculum, which included

> four years of Latin and three of Greek; arithmetic, algebra, and geometry in three of the four years; one year of English; a year of ancient and American history; and scattered bits of geography, physiology, and

hygiene. In addition, like every other student, he presented composi-
tions, declamations, and recitations, and performed occasional exercises
in reading, spelling, and music.[22]

Du Bois's handwritten record of his work at Fisk is particularly interesting: it has much to say to scholars like Winterer about classical activity among African Americans and about the curricula of the colleges and
universities she ignores in her book. Du Bois listed one hundred hours of
English composition with weekly class and annual public rhetorical exhi-
bitions. In addition were six years of Latin, including thirty hours of Latin
composition, as well as the study, in Latin, of the following literary works:
Caesar's *Gallic War,* Books I–IV; Cicero's *Orations,* which included four
against Cataline, *Pro Archia Poeta,* and half of *Pro Marcello;* Virgil's *Eclogues* and books I–VI of *The Aeneid;* four-fifths of Horace's *Odes,* as well
as two of his epodes, three satires, three shorter epistles, and the *Ars Poetica;* Tacitus's *Agricola;* and Livy's Book XXI. In addition to German and
French, he noted considerable work in Greek: thirty hours of Greek composition; Xenophon's *Anabasis* I–IV and *Memorabilia;* Plato's *Phaedo;* and
Thucydides's Book I. He also studied translations of Greek literature, including Sophocles, Aeschylus, Euripides, and others. Included as well were
selections from Herodotus, Demosthenes's *De Corona,* Homer's *Iliad* I–II,
Sophocles's *Antigone,* and another Greek tragedy that was in his course of
study but not yet named by the instructor. Du Bois also listed considerable study in English, political science, history (including Greek history),
mathematics, physical science, natural history, chemistry, and astronomi-
cal drawings.[23] Broderick includes Homer's *Odyssey* and the Greek New
Testament.[24]

Du Bois's Fisk study mirrored the better part of Cooper's St. Augustine curriculum and added a healthy amount of Horatian verse and Greek
drama. Another addition, Tacitus's *Agricola,* drives home the importance
of Roman civic virtue by celebrating Tacitus's father-in-law's careful execution of duty, reluctance to seize honor for himself, and judicious use of
power. He also notes that this was done in the time of Domitian, whose
vicious and murderous reign was one in which literature was burned, authors and other citizens were executed, and many were intimidated into silence for fear of informers, spies, and the possibility of death, enslavement,
or financial ruin. Tacitus's description of Rome under Domitian is curi-
ously similar to the situation described by scholars of the conflict between
Booker T. Washington and his foes, of which Du Bois was one and Cooper
was imagined to be. In *The Souls of Black Folk,* the chapter "Of Mr. Booker T.

Washington and Others" describes the hesitation, doubt, and failure of manliness in the black population that gave rise to Washington, and it outlines the difficulty and necessity of defying his Tuskegee Machine.

Washington's manipulation of education, the nineteenth-century black press, and employment for the professional class of nineteenth-century African Americans exemplifies the oppressive power to which Du Bois alludes. The Tuskegee principal's use of informers, economic blackmail, and even the threat of prison suggests that Du Bois wrote of Washington with a classical precursor in mind. In his *Annals* and *Histories*, Tacitus, to whom both Du Bois and Cooper allude in their work, appears to capture the predicament of those scholars outside Washington's machine: "We witnessed the extreme of servitude when the informer robbed us of the interchange of speech and hearing. We should have lost memory as well as voice, had it been as easy to forget as to keep silence."[25]

Harvard offered an ivy-clad addition to Du Bois's Fisk studies. He spent a significant amount of time in his first year in the sciences, including qualitative analysis, laboratory geology, and advanced geology. In the second year, he took George Santayana's courses in French and German philosophy. William James was his professor in psychology and a man Du Bois called his "favorite teacher and closest friend."[26] F. G. Peabody provided a course in the ethics of social reform, and Alfred Bushnell Hart taught Du Bois American constitutional and political history. Rhetoric, elocution, and economics rounded out his studies. In his first two graduate years, Du Bois threw himself into history and aligned himself more closely with Hart. He also studied Roman law, political economy, and composition. Du Bois attained the B.A. in 1890 and the M.A. in 1892. He spent considerable time perfecting his literary and rhetorical abilities. The basic text of rhetorical instruction at both Fisk and Harvard was Adams Sherman Hill's *The Principles of Rhetoric* (1878). Hill was at that time the Boylston Professor of Rhetoric and Oratory at Harvard. Both Josiah Royce and Barrett Wendell, Du Bois's composition teachers, drew heavily on Hill's theories and advice. "On the subject of oratory," notes Arnold Rampersad, "Hill's work was grounded squarely on the classical tradition of Aristotle's *Rhetoric* and Cicero's speeches. On the writing of prose, Hill drew his examples from British and American writers of his century, from Samuel Taylor Coleridge to F. Marion Crawford."[27] With his study of Roman law, we can see that Du Bois's vision of oratory incorporated the Ciceronian style of executing rhetoric or prosecuting a case. It would have been a matter of presenting the truth, or some version of it, in appropriately affecting and provocative fashion, one that appealed to the reason, hearts, virtues, and vanities of an audience and anticipated the psychology of a jury or audience of educated, aristocratic peers.

Rampersad makes a particularly useful observation about Du Bois that separates him from the earlier tradition of African American writers who obtained an education rich in classical texts and clarifies our view of Du Bois's literary style and sense of audience. Unlike writers in the earlier tradition, Du Bois was not in any way an intellectual product of the church or of the clergy; rather, he was indebted to academe and the classics. He explicitly rejected the ministry when it was suggested to him, and his education at Fisk, Harvard, and Berlin, as well as his faculty position at Wilberforce, thoroughly relieved him of any lingering affinity for the organized church. As Rampersad notes,

> [T]hrough the pages of Hill's *Rhetoric* Du Bois was instructed at both Fisk and Harvard in the *exordium* and the *narratio,* the *probatio* and the *refutatio.* Du Bois has been called a "preacher" by one sympathetic critic, but there is really no resemblance between his style of composition and the tradition of extemporaneous, rhythmical, and often incandescent language of the fundamentalist black preacher. Over the years Du Bois' speeches and his polemical writing became much more direct and unadorned, but for the first fifty years and more of his life he showed the mark of classical principles of rhetoric and of other, more "modern" stylistic criteria. . . . *The Souls of Black Folk* is overwhelming evidence of the influence of Hill and his disciple Wendell.[28]

This is an observation regularly missed by critics who hone in on Du Bois's references to God or his frequently penned prayers or items such as "Litany of Atlanta." Whatever Du Bois's view of God, he was no fan of establishment Christianity. Brian L. Johnson carries on a sustained argument for Du Bois's agnosticism, and David Levering Lewis's work suggests as much.[29] The willingness of scholars to dismiss his observations as mired in religiosity may be partly explained by contemporary hostility toward religion, but the rest is likely an unwillingness to do the work of examining the fusion of Christianity and classics.

Du Bois was a product of the era of academic transformation in colleges and universities. Although the classical languages and rhetoric were less commanding, their influence was still enormous. Moreover, as Rampersad notes, "[T]he stylistic ideals of the literary critic of today—simplicity, directness, and the judicious use of specialized vocabulary—were still in the future. An essential aspect of the age of transition was a decline in the rule of the gentleman of letters, although he still represented a powerful cultural force. The pursuit of literary study was a gentlemanly art, and the gentleman of letters never forgot his links to the past."[30] Du Bois absorbed the style of his professors, and Rampersad argues that this both improved and possibly corrupted Du Bois. The result of Hill's and Wendell's training was that the writer's relationship with the audience

> blended elementary psychology with the manners of an educated gentleman. The way to an audience's mind and feelings was through persuasion and indirection, not accusation or anger. Persuasion combined with substantive argument to capture the audience. Argument was the ordered display of evidence conforming to the rules of logic. Persuasion, in which sense, feeling, and knowledge of human nature were essential, gave ultimate power to cold argument.[31]

Rampersad argues that Du Bois might well have inherited a good deal of his elitism and attitudes about being a man of culture from Wendell and Hill. Moreover, he argues that his scholarly experiences affected the way he viewed African American literature, leaving him ill prepared and not at all disposed to poetry, fiction, and literary criticism. Du Bois was also bereft of tolerance for more modern African American artistic works and what Rampersad terms "earthier forms of expression," forms that were tremendously distant from those found in the classical texts that were part a gentleman's education.[32]

Du Bois's movement between history, composition, psychology, and the sciences also left him rather awkwardly placed between the worlds of gentleman scholar and orthodox, rigorous, and scientific scholarship. The influence of the University of Berlin (1892–94) only complicated Du Bois's intellectual architecture with courses in politics, Prussian state reform, theoretical political economy, industrialism and society, Prussian constitutional history, and jurisprudence. At Berlin, Du Bois also fell under Heinrich Von Treitschke's influence. Von Treitschke understood history as being made by strong men of heroic will, above the masses and without their influence, a view that combined with Du Bois's background of the heroes, gods, and singular political figures prominent in classical writings of Greece and Rome. As Rampersad points out, Von Treitschke's declamation against mulattoes "fell from the same plant that would bear the evil flower of Hitler's genocide."[33] Germany reinforced what so many contemporary scholars decry as Du Bois's elitism, further encouraging him to see his classically inflected world as one substantially above that of the degraded masses. However, this experience also introduced him to socialism and at the same time prompted him to seize his imagined destiny to elevate (and perhaps rule) the masses in an improvised, classically pagan ritual with Greek wine, candles, prayers, and singing. He dedicated his library to his mother and vowed to "make a name in science, to make a name in literature and thus to raise my race. Or perhaps to raise a visible empire in Africa thro' England, France, or Germany."[34] The first step in Du Bois's imperial ascension was tripped up by the Slater Fund, which refused to extend funds for the final semester he needed to earn the Ph.D. from Berlin. Du Bois returned to America and received the Ph.D. from Harvard in 1895.

Du Bois's education suggests that the classics would have had an effect on his work similar to that on Cooper's. The classical texts central to his higher education emphasized the supremacy of virtuous ambition over corrupting luxury, greed, and injustice. The writers he encountered decried tyranny and argued that merit should win one the right to rule over others. Du Bois did not extract a love of democracy from the classical writers, and although he decried race prejudice, the classics did not give him a belief in the absolute equality of men.

Virtue, in a variety of contexts, is a particular concern of Du Bois's. As early as his Harvard commencement address "Jefferson Davis as Representative of Civilization," Du Bois identified heroism and its corruption, Teutonic brutality. Civilization and its corruption, "the rule of might," also developed early in Du Bois's thought, as did culture and its corruption, unenlightened materialism. Although "virtue" appears only three times in *The Souls of Black Folk,* the terms and ideas that he considers virtuous appear often: "culture" occurs forty times, "moral" eighteen times, "morality" three times, "hero" four times, "good" fifty-nine times, "goodness" three times, "righteous" twice, and "righteousness" seven times.[35] Combined with the classical and contemporary texts, heroes, and exemplars he deploys in *Souls,* these terms emphasize a strong sense of civic, moral, intellectual, and spiritual virtue, all in the service of a rich, enlightened culture for blacks and whites. Like Cooper, Du Bois develops understandings of race or gender far different from the predominant thought of his era. His understanding of race and blackness is rooted in antiquity and a long historical view of blacks being active in the formation of the West. Du Bois also employs the classics to produce a view of women as more heroic, powerful, provocative, and influential than his Victorian and Edwardian era traditionally tolerated, importing Sappho, Atalanta, Lachesis, the Amazons, and others directly into *The Souls of Black Folk.* Many of the women in his works are powerful, influential, and ambitious, even if unsuccessful in their ventures, and *The Souls of Black Folk* also suggests that Du Bois imagined an equal education for women and men.[36] From the landmark work *The Souls of Black Folk* to less famous efforts like *Dark Princess*, Du Bois wrote women of potential, ambition and intellect into his works.

Du Bois's commitment to classical reason and disdain for the messy, unfocused, and often thoroughly intellectually stunting religion of the folk drove him away from organized religion and from the masses populating churches. Du Bois would have had little hope that the amorphous mixture of folk passion and Christian doctrine he encountered could be operated upon by his solid classical and contemporary instruments of analysis or the Talented Tenth he hoped to deploy among the people. "The Coming of John" strongly suggests that while he celebrated the passion of the spiritual sorrow songs and the strength of the African American folk, Du Bois did not relish the narrow doctrine and the wild exultation of the people's temples. The limitations and dangers of religion were no more tolerable to him than those of Booker T. Washington's provocative gospel of work, materialism, and accommodation. It is in Du Bois's mixed-genre, highly classicized, and wide-ranging *The Souls of Black Folk* that we see the most direct challenge to the overwhelming force of stark Washingtonian power and white retrenchment. *The Souls of Black Folk* arrays classical elements in combination with African American literary and cultural history and blends with the cultural productions of African American oratory, religion, music, and intellectual critique. Within *The Souls of Black Folk*, Du Bois executes a landmark analysis of African Americans and enunciates the ultimate stakes in the battle between Western virtue and capitalist opportunism and its resulting poverty of culture. Du Bois focuses on the same population emerging from the defeated South that Cooper identifies, and it is into the nature of this focus on the masses that the critics of Du Bois's elitism should look. Despite the fact that he sees the people as strong and promising, he argues that there are serious problems with the culture of the New South. Economic progress is increasingly triumphing over virtue in America—both civic virtue that will honor and defend the rights of all citizens in the republic and the intellectual and spiritual virtue that privileges education, wisdom, and morality over the acquisition of wealth and power. Du Bois fears that blacks and southerners may completely join the throngs of amoral and ignorant money-getters. He puts the question bluntly:

> What if the Negro people be wooed from a strife for righteousness, from a love of knowing, to regard dollars as the be all and end all of life? What if to the mammonism of America be added the rising mammonism of

the reborn South, and the mammonism of this South be reinforced by the budding mammonism of its half-awakened black millions? Whither, then, is the new-world quest of goodness and beauty and truth gone glimmering? Must this, and that fair flower of freedom which, despite the jeers of latter-day striplings, sprung from our fathers' blood, must that too degenerate into a dusty quest of gold—into lawless lust with Hippomenes?[37]

As seductive as the promises of Gilded Age prosperity and Washingtonian progress are to southerners, they are just myths to Du Bois. Accordingly, he combats them with one of his own, the classical myth of Hippomenes and Atalanta. In the ancient tale, Atalanta was exposed to the elements by her father (who wanted a son) and subsequently raised in the wild by a bear. She grew into a remarkable hunter and athlete. Reconciled with her father, virginal Atalanta proceeded to fight off suitors (often literally) and defeat men in every contest of athletic and hunting skill. She eventually agreed that she would marry any man who could best her in a footrace, provided she could kill any losers (she usually speared them at the finish line). Eventually Hippomenes struck on the idea of acquiring the Golden Apples of the Hesperides and tossing them in her path. She stopped to collect the gold and lost her race with him. Consequently, she lost her independence and apparently her piety. According to the myth, she and Hippomenes were caught making love in the temple of Cybele and promptly turned into lions for the indiscretion. Using this myth gives Du Bois a way of describing how virtue and liberty can be destroyed by materialism. It illustrates the choices the wronged, impoverished, but free blacks have for using their strength and freedom. They can expend it for the faint promise of wealth or use it to attain civil liberties, political power, and philosophical or spiritual understanding—civic, moral, and intellectual virtue. Moreover, the Atalanta tale gives Du Bois an oddly progressive illustration of African Americans' predicament, one that also emphasizes what is at stake for women in this cultural choice. Atalanta, the swift, talented, and graceful huntress—clearly the superior of the amorous and frustrated Hippomenes—is felled by her lust for gold. She loses her maidenly freedom and is doomed to the restrictions and limited frontiers of marriage and domestic servitude.[38]

"Of the Wings of Atalanta" deals directly with the crisis of civic virtue, morality, and education that exists for African Americans, but Du Bois implicates the rest of the nation as well. He makes an odd lament in the opening pages of the chapter—for the fall of the South:

It is a hard thing to live haunted by the ghost of an untrue dream; to see the wide vision of empire fade into real ashes and dirt; to feel the pang of the conquered, and yet know that with all the Bad that fell on one black day, something was vanquished that deserved to live, something killed that in justice had dared not die; to know that with the Right that triumphed, triumphed something of the Wrong, something sordid and mean, something less than the broadest and best.[39]

In Atlanta, the new Lachesis, factories and rail lines replaced the old plantation South and greeted "the busy Mercury in his coming."[40] Invoking the name of Lachesis is particularly interesting, because Lachesis was one of the *Moerae*, the three Fates, who spun, allocated, and cut the thread-length of life for humans. Lachesis was the disposer of lots, the apportioner of life.[41] Calling the cotton kingdom of Atlanta the new Lachesis suggests that, as the "spinner of web and woof for the world" and capital of the South, its choices would determine the fate and quality of life for many and the length of the reconstructed civilization's life. Unlike Rome and its seven hills, the kingdom of Atlanta chose to crown its hundred hills with factories and link its fate to industry.[42] Among all the gods the population could reach out to embrace, Atlanta chose Mercury, god of commerce, as its patron.

Du Bois also wonders whether the industrial South, freed of slavery, yoked to business, and filling the plates, pockets, and appetites of African Americans and the "'cracker' third estate," might have lost something virtuous as it shed its vice of slavery. Du Bois argues that the power of the preachers, teachers, elders, and gentlemen to form the character of youth has given way to the workers, artisans, employers, and employees who dispense and acquire money and property. For African Americans, the loss is even more profoundly dangerous. Like Homer and Virgil, who listed heroes on the battlefield and their lineage, in *The Souls of Black Folk* Du Bois provides a genealogy and chronicle of great and virtuous members and acts of a "peculiar dynasty" of historic black leaders. In this primer on black leadership, he insists that revenge or revolt, surrender and acquiescence, or "a determined effort at self-realization and self-development despite environing opinion" may be the response of an oppressed people.[43] Noting the "instructive experience" that African Americans have had in choosing leaders, he continues to list leaders who have advanced the race in each of the categories. Revolution he marks in the Maroons, Danish blacks, and Cato of Stono.[44] Assimilation and the liberalizing tendencies of the eighteenth century produce Phillis Wheatley, Benjamin Banneker, and others.

Insurrection and self-determination mark the nineteenth century, ending with Frederick Douglass championing "assimilation *through* self-assertion, and on no other terms."[45] Even within the broad realm of assimilation, Du Bois counts the actions of past leaders as virtuous and timely: "the earnest songs of Phillis, the martyrdom of Attucks, the intellectual accomplishments of Banneker and Derham, and the political demands of the Cuffes."[46] These are the founding fathers and mothers of African American culture, and they represent personal and civic virtues and cultural accomplishments set to burn as sacrifice on the altar of the temple of Mercury.

To Du Bois, the temptation to trade all of the old virtues and traditions of culture and leadership for the promise of money and property is the modern version of Atalanta's predicament. The possibility that the greed of the industrial North might be joined with the greed of a rebuilding South and an eager, hungry, and impoverished African American population portended the end of virtue and the triumph of the worst of the Old and New South, the celebration of power and the quest for wealth under the leadership of a few powerful but unrefined men. It is because of the source of Du Bois's concern about the masses that critics of his elitism may be wrong. As Carole Lynn Stewart points out in *Re-cognizing W. E. B. Du Bois in the Twenty-first Century,* the Talented Tenth was a population that could come from anywhere.[47] It is easy for contemporary scholars to look on a group of educated and talented leaders, see a given fraction, and immediately with contemporary eyes see a privileged class, a spoiled elite, and oppressors of the "people." But this is not the body of leaders that Du Bois imagined, because it is from the masses that the Talented Tenth will come. It is back into the fight for rights that these leaders are to go. And the idea of a leading group does not end with African Americans. If the American project is to succeed, the nation will need leaders who are talented and educated about the prejudice and ignorance of the masses and the religious and political leaders who would manipulate them. Frederick Douglass decried these politicians and preachers as well, and Phillis Wheatley lectured the young leaders at Du Bois's alma mater about their duties in "To the Students at the University of Cambridge." Du Bois continues the call for righteous leadership in *The Souls of Black Folk.* For a rich, virtuous American civilization to triumph, he maintained, "broad-minded, upright men, both black and white" who are college-bred and committed to peace will have to take the place of these "untrained demagogues."[48] Du Bois is not averse to the idea of an elite class, but their aims and virtue are issues of concern even to him. According to Du Bois, the problem of untrained, unrefined, and generally vicious men gave rise to most of the world's strife and corruption, especially the racism that pervaded American society. The proximate barrier to African American cultural growth was the color line, the issue of the twentieth century that Du Bois clearly understood. But he increasingly seemed to recognize that the ultimate cause of the racial conflict, black cultural stagnation, and disintegration of American cultural virtue was the longstanding battle outlined by his Harvard professor William James:

> Speaking broadly, there are never more than two fundamental parties in a nation: the party of red blood, as it calls itself, and that of pale reflection; the party of animal instinct, jingoism, fun, excitement, bigness; and that of reason, forecast, order gained by growth, and spiritual methods—briefly put, the party of force and that of education.[49]

The greatest obstacles to Du Bois's party of reason and spirituality are the increasingly retrenched racist whites and Booker T. Washington and his economic and political program of industrial education and commercial enterprise for the masses of African Americans. The South had long suffered from a corrupt form of martial virtue, a viciousness that Du Bois called Teutonic. Du Bois's 1890 Harvard commencement address on Jefferson Davis is instructive. In this address, Du Bois argues that Davis is the prime representative of a tragic, southern, corrupted virtue. Judged by the "Teutonic" standard, Du Bois argues that there is something noble about Davis. However, this nobility is incomplete when evaluated "by every canon of human justice." His is not the virtue of Aeneas or even Achilles, nor is it the virtue of the philosophers of antiquity. The error of the antebellum South was that its civilization was built on a false standard of virtue. While it was not the rage of Achilles, it was a sinister "[i]ndividualism coupled with the rule of might." Under this standard of *virtus,* a culture could celebrate "a naturally brave and generous man, Jefferson Davis—now advancing civilization by murdering Indians, now a hero of a national disgrace called by courtesy, the Mexican War, and finally, as the crowning absurdity, the peculiar champion of a people fighting to be free in order that another people should not be free."[50]

Du Bois then notes a fundamental problem of the Western cultural transmission: classical republics and empires were regularly undone by the impulse to tyranny and thus degenerated, subverting, or overtly opposing their enriching founding cultural ideals. With three years of Greek at Great Barrington, followed by Greek composition, literature, and history at Fisk and political philosophy at Fisk, Harvard, and Berlin, Du Bois would have been acquainted with Socrates's and Aristotle's theories of how states collapsed. Neither was fond of empires.[51] Aristotle left Macedon at the outset of his student Alexander's imperial quest, and the Greeks held imperial Persia in great disdain. Also, unlike Cooper, Du Bois is unwilling to fully embrace the barbarian culture that followed Rome, despite its eventual Christian conversion. He sees something brutal and dangerous in the Teutonic strain that mixed with already corrupt Roman imperial tyranny. While he admires German strength, he fears its latent penchant for strong men and violence—a reasonable fear in his era. Both Cooper and Du Bois generally elide Rome's own history of ruthless conquest and brutality, but in romanticizing Rome, Du Bois does identify the strain of imperialist and totalitarian terror that threatens to burst from the Western tradition at its weakest moments—a strain that corrupted the American South.[52] He writes:

> Advance in civilization has always been handicapped by shortsighted national selfishness. The vital principle of division of labor has been stifled not only in industry, but also in civilization, so as to render it well-nigh impossible for a new race to introduce a new idea into the world except by means of the cudgel. To say that a nation is in the way of civilization is a contradiction in terms, and a system of human culture whose principle is the rise of one race on the ruins of another is a farce and a lie. Yet this is the type of civilization which Jefferson Davis represented: it represents a field for stalwart manhood and heroic character, and at the same time for moral obtuseness and refined brutality.[53]

Du Bois goes on to argue that the Teutonic civilization of the strong man, which has been so romantically portrayed by historians, is the same force that crushed an already corrupt and tyrannical Rome and ended for a time all civilization when it "descended golden-haired and drunk from the blue north. . . . The Teutonic met civilization and crushed it—the Negro met civilization and was crushed by it." As early as 1890, Du Bois had identified a sinister element in the cultural transmission to the New World, but at the time he argued that among African Americans one could not find "elements of the Teutonic deification of self and Roman brute force."[54] But, in 1890, Du Bois had yet to encounter Booker T. Washington. By the time of *Souls*, Du Bois knew exactly what to make of Washington and what the strain of Teutonic manliness in American culture meant for African Americans. He found Washington's program no better than the "crazy imperialism of the day," which regarded "human beings as among the material resources of a land to be trained with an eye to future dividends" and used race prejudice to underpin its structure.[55]

Washington's argument that black social and political rights were secondary to their developing a strong industrial infrastructure captured the imaginations of white southerners and black freedmen. Based at Tuskegee Institute and physically advanced by a "machine" of political, economic, and journalistic ventures, Washington's platform of social segregation and commercial servitude, captured in "The Atlanta Exposition Address," struck a harmonious chord with the times:

> As we have proved our loyalty to you in the past, in nursing your children, watching by the sick-bed of your mothers and fathers, and often following them with tear-dimmed eyes to their graves, so in the future, in our humble way, we shall stand by you with a devotion that no foreigner can approach, ready to lay down our lives, if need be, in defense of yours, interlacing our industrial, commercial, civil, and religious life with yours in a way that shall make the interests of both races one. In all things that are purely social we can be as separate as the fingers, yet one as the hand in all things essential to mutual progress.[56]

Du Bois rejected this Atlanta Compromise as a surrender of principles for the dubious promise of material gain and peace. According to Du Bois, "Mr. Washington distinctly asks that black people give up, at least for the present, three things,—First, political power, Second, insistence on civil rights, [and] Third, higher education of Negro youth" for the purposes of industrial growth and conciliation.[57] The result was to Du Bois nothing less than disenfranchisement, legal codification of racism, and the degradation of black educational opportunity. Du Bois was horrified that those trained only to value wealth and material accretion were inclined to compromise their equality and give up their rightful share of the privileges reserved for whites and settle for a role determined by the whims of their political and economic masters, as long as profit was promised. Du Bois suggests that by compromising in the face of late nineteenth-century white retrenchment, Booker T. Washington and many of his followers had given in to despair and greed.

Du Bois not only identifies materialism and despair as destroyers of his people but also employs a eugenics-laced argument of generational decline that echoes Frederick Douglass and Anna Julia Cooper. According to Du Bois, creeping degeneracy has affected the race. A new generation of men exists who are far more likely to value gold than the freedom their fathers desired. Just as Frederick Douglass argued in his Fourth of July oration, these sons are lesser men than their founding fathers. Holding to the true line of descent, Du Bois and others like him would wrest the prizes of racial privilege from whites. Where greed, doubt, and hesitation are the progenitors of Washington's position, the historic black founding fathers of resistance are the line from which Du Bois traces his approach. Washington's plan has no central foundation of virtue and disseminates nothing of virtue to succeeding generations. Such a life philosophy is to Du Bois a guide to the degeneration of a race.

If we consider the manner in which *The Souls of Black Folk* describes Washington, we see that "shrewdness" and "tact" are his distinguishing characteristics of leadership, and they resonate as something less than cardinal virtues. In the chapter "Of Mr. Booker T. Washington and Others," Du Bois lists more of Washington's character and lineage. His heart is the heart of the South, which he knew "from birth and training." Du Bois sardonically refers to him as the "most distinguished Southerner since Jefferson Davis."[58] We might be inclined to read right across this well-worn passage, but with it, Du Bois initiates a significant critique of virtue that recalls his Harvard oration and resonates throughout the rest of the work.

When Du Bois links Washington to the Old South in birth and training, he deftly shifts his lineage from the black and white founding fathers and their ideals to a firm genealogical and intellectual connection to the slaveholders who were willing to undo the American Revolution, a breach of *pietas*. This also removes Washington from the genealogical line of descent shared by other black leaders. Moreover, linking him with Davis in 1903 is more than an easy, back-handed compliment. The conflict and corruption of the South is Washington's inheritance as a nineteenth-century African American who must rule, tyrannically if need be, in order to lead. Other great leaders led by serving or giving something to the people or their cause. As Du Bois's discussion and allusions in *The Souls of Black Folk* suggest, because Washington was so malformed in the civic, moral, and intellectual virtues, he could easily and ruthlessly wield power while conceding the rights and power of his people. Washington's spirit is the cynical spirit of the age, his education is the speech and thought of triumphant commercialism, and his ideals are those of material prosperity. Du Bois reports that Washington's friends are legion—ominous and telling in a biblical sense.[59] The "acme of absurdities" for Washington is the lone black child in the throes of poverty studying French grammar. Du Bois reminds the reader of the wonder and wisdom of the scene, questioning how narrowness can make men great. He puts Washington in direct conflict with the classical world by musing to his readers what Socrates would say of Washington's position.[60]

Not even a lesser son, such as the latter-day striplings of Du Bois's description, but a man descended from another line of founding fathers like Jefferson Davis, Washington comes as a great compromiser, rather than a champion, of principles. Others, like Douglass, had refused to adulterate those principles of equality. In a period of cultural and political retrenchment in the nation, Washington arises as a kind of Dark Age leader, in the moment of crumbling ethical infrastructure and "shifting ideals." He brings a "gospel of work and money" while surrendering the rights, opportunity, and tradition of his people. Ultimately, Washington's philosophy will cause the annihilation of African American culture.

Du Bois illustrates the danger of not protecting and enhancing that rich culture in "Of the Meaning of Progress." The chapter uses Du Bois's rural teaching experience as a foundation. Du Bois proceeds to deconstruct the cultural focus of the Gilded Age, progress. He takes specific issue with the idea that the progress of industrial growth and material accretion is true advancement. Du Bois calls into question not only the reality of progress, but also whether any progress can exist for African Americans at all when American racism constrains and ravages them. Robbed of their cultural heritage of aggressively, heroically, and virtuously pursuing the ideals of liberty and education and stripped of civil rights, blacks are particularly vulnerable to white hostility, despite any native goodness or ambitious economic plans they might possess.

Particularly interesting in "Of the Meaning of Progress" is that Du Bois quickly sets up a classical challenge to the underlying philosophy of work and acquisition. He arrays the lessons of Cicero, both his oratory and its virtuous content, against the value of a philosophy of acquiring land without civil liberty. The schoolmaster Du Bois visits the rural southern hills bearing the word of Cicero's defense of Archias the poet, *Pro Archia Poeta*. Cicero defended Archias, a Greek intellectual living in Rome, in what was essentially a deportation hearing. During one of many periods of active xenophobia in the empire, the aristocratic political faction (*optimates*) in Rome presumed that their defeats were coming at the hands of foreigners who were illegally voting. Consequently, they secured the passage of a *Lex Papia* to allow for deportations, conducted a census in Rome, and attempted to deport the Greek agitator and intellectual by claiming that his influence on Rome as an outsider and noncitizen was a danger to the people. Roman progress would be seriously threatened by having noncitizens influencing the course of the republic. Cicero rather quickly dispensed with the citizenship issue, but he continued to argue Archias's value to Rome. He suggested that beyond the power of money, political influence, and passing cultural acclaim, the very thing that any Roman would most desire was to have his life made immortal, given meaning by being sung in poetry. The fleeting riches of a material life faded in comparison to the richness that one like Archias could provide. To have him around meant to have one's life, the story of Rome, and the values of the nation preserved for posterity and rendered memorable and useful for the true progress of the culture. Du Bois reapplied a version of this argument whenever blacks' resolve to educate youth flagged, and the story suggests both the dangers of being without civil liberties and the substantial value of having an educated population.

The people Du Bois describes in the Tennessee communities are richly all-American in their hardworking simplicity. Nonetheless, there is a running battle to gather the children in the little schoolhouse and keep them "on the rough benches, their faces shading from a pale cream to a deep brown, the little feet bare and swinging, the eyes full of expectation, with here and there a twinkle of mischief, and the hands grasping Webster's blue-back spelling book."[61] The people believe wholeheartedly in the acquisition of land, the production of cash crops, and purchasing commercial items, not the preservation of culture or the discovery of profound philosophical truths. Du Bois reports how the people have committed to the American Dream of pulling themselves up by their own bootstraps. However, the goals and desires they have are for higher culture and richer, fuller lives. Josie, the daughter of the first farm family he encounters, has "about her a certain fineness, the shadow of an unconscious moral heroism that would willingly give all of life to make life broader, deeper, and fuller for her and hers."[62] As Nellie McKay notes, Du Bois "places the strength and courage of a young black woman in the foreground" in the chapter. Moreover, he addresses her courage and determination in the face of the "Sisyphean dimension of the life [she and her family] lived."[63] Du Bois describes Josie's mother in similar terms. They share characteristics of industry and morality and have ambitions for a better life in which they can live "'like folks.'"[64]

Du Bois also deploys the classics to describe the admirable character of the hill folk. Doc Burke's wife is described as a "magnificent Amazon," which invokes its own classical images and mythology of the female warriors, at war against the brutal centaurs, present in the Trojan War and in the text of *The Aeneid*.[65] However, as Page duBois points out in her *Centaurs and Amazons: Women and the Prehistory of the Great Chain of*

Being (1991), the violent, antimarriage, unbridled centaurs and Amazons were creatures that allowed the Greeks to explore the world of opposites surrounding them: women/men, beast/human, and barbarian/Greek. She also illustrates how the Amazon/Centaur fault line was the point at which measuring polar opposites metamorphosed into a determination of superiority and inferiority, a central part of Western thought and philosophy and the progenitor of the great chain of being, and links the hierarchies developed by Plato and Aristotle to this cultural moment of comparison.[66] The noble but ignorant and rough-hewn men and women of the hills had a "certain magnificent barbarism about them that [Du Bois] liked. They were never vulgar, never immoral, but rather rough and primitive."[67] Those rough souls, especially the strong women of the chapter, seem to offer Du Bois his own interpretive tool to settle the hierarchical positions, superior and inferior, of his and Washington's plans for African Americans. What we see in Du Bois's assessment of the masses is not condescension; it is a recognition of their nature, goodness, strength, and potential. What is left is to have some force or some leader open the doors of opportunity to them before the forces of racism, civic exclusion, and economic vulnerability crush them.

Du Bois points out a number of underlying and ultimately fatal problems with the lives of the wholesome but hopelessly doomed aspirants to a better life. Mainstream American economic progress is not accessible to African Americans, despite their individual ambition or talents. Moreover, virtue, where it exists in its seedling form, has little or no nourishment and withers or degenerates into vice. Returning to the area ten years later, teacher Du Bois finds that those students with the most promise—Josie, Jim, and Ben—"whose young appetites had been whetted to an edge by school and story and half-awakened thought," were dulled or destroyed by the racial and economic realities of the Veil.[68]

Du Bois makes clear that Jim especially might have "made a venturous merchant or a West Point cadet" if "cultured parentage and a social caste" had supported him.[69] Instead, his talents and ambitions degenerated into recklessness and anger. Illegitimacy and vice have corrupted others, and even Josie's life ended when she lost her one, remaining, mundane hope of marriage and domestic happiness. Others had reached the pinnacle of their lives as wives with "babies aplenty" or in hardscrabble farming. Of one, Du Bois says that she "married a man and a farm," a striking image of a domestic(ated) Atalanta and a limited life. Still others, like the Burkes, had managed to buy some land but remained in terrible debt. In each case, the people are defenseless and subject to racism, the whims and greed of their white neighbors, and the lack of opportunity for life beyond agriculture and domesticity. Many farms, families, and dreams rest precariously on the backs of aging men and women. Du Bois offers only a thin possibility that some of their progeny will survive the travail of racism to inherit what little they have, and inherited property or capital is the foundation of generational wealth that is so essential to the capitalist materialist project. Moreover, without the presence of a scholar such as Du Bois to chronicle their struggles, their stories will go untold and offer nothing to future generations in terms of guidance, experience, and virtue.

Ultimately, the practical economic and legal realities of racism reduce the commercial, industrial, and agricultural progress that Washington advances as the hope of the race to a dream at best. Du Bois asks, "Is it possible that nine millions of men can make effective progress in economic lines if they are deprived of political rights, made a servile caste, and allowed only the most meager chance for developing their exceptional men? If history and reason give any distinct answer to these questions, it is an emphatic *No.*"[70] It is no evil thing to be of the masses, poor, or undereducated, but those so situated are vulnerable on many fronts. Du Bois is careful not to dismiss the lives of the black masses, who had survived (if only survived) and often had little choice about leaving or transforming. He demonstrates some ambivalence about judging the people by arguing, "How hard a thing is life to the lowly, and yet how human and real! And all this life and love and strife and failure,—is it the twilight of nightfall or the flush of some faint—dawning day?" But an answer lies in the fact that Du Bois rides off to the city of Nashville—with all the promise the city is imagined to hold—in the Jim Crow car of a train.

Du Bois puts no faith in the myth of progress; neither does he trust the myth of the "Methodists and hard-shell Baptist churches" where the people came to "make the weekly sacrifice with frenzied priest at the altar of the 'old-time religion,'" after sacrificing to Mercury during the working week.[71] What he does offer the reader is a resounding claim that what blacks need is culture and the virtues and strength that it brings. The way to refine the "unconscious moral heroism" that the masses like Josie possess and attain the "broader, deeper, and fuller" life she and others desire is to reject the culture of materialism and separate from the white and Washingtonian culture that would both seek to reduce blacks to peonage and devalue nonmaterial gains and the pursuit of higher culture and education.

Du Bois links that greater culture to a virtuous core of leaders who see the complex relationship between the rich culture of the West and the African American struggle in America. In "Of Our Spiritual Strivings," Du

Bois calls double-consciousness a longing to attain "self conscious manhood." This is something subtly but significantly different from manliness,
as it has often been deployed. It immediately implies a refined manliness,
one with profound intellectual and psychological dimensions and embracing the nuanced and refined manhood Cooper suggested. But it also has
a relationship to the rich tradition of education in *virtus*—the search for a
"better, truer, self," which resonates with Cooper's quest for brighter, nobler, and holier attributes. Moreover, Du Bois argues that African Americans have as their goal to be "co-worker[s] in the kingdom of culture."[72]

In elucidating the essential desire to contribute to Western culture,
Du Bois links African Americans to the larger struggle to create civilization. He also argues that it is impossible to work alongside a white American population that does not recognize the value of its own Western past
or has rejected blacks as partners in culture. Du Bois contends that black
leaders of the past have already labored to become cultural partners with
whites only to be disillusioned. He argues that in trying to address their
practical needs, repair the psychological damage of slavery, and achieve
laurels that could undo the stereotypes of blackness, some African Americans fell into despair: "[The struggle] has wrought sad havoc with the courage and faith and deeds of ten thousand thousand people—has sent them
often wooing false gods and invoking false means of salvation, and has
even seemed about to make them ashamed of themselves."[73] Universally,
blacks felt "the weight of [their] ignorance,—not simply of letters, but of
life, of business, of the humanities . . . shackled [their] hands and feet," and
they embarked on Reconstruction-era efforts to address their deficiencies.
Blacks embraced the fundamental tenets of the culture as presented by the
nineteenth-century white population:

> Men call the shadow prejudice and learnedly explain it as the natural
> defense of culture against barbarism, learning against ignorance, purity
> against crime, the "higher" against the "lower" races. To which the Negro
> cries Amen! And swears that to so much of this strange prejudice as is
> founded on just homage to civilization, culture, righteousness, and prog-
> ress, he humbly bows and meekly does obeisance.[74]

Du Bois argues that the attempts to create individual and civic virtue,
contribute to culture, and employ the lessons and tools of education and
the Western transmission were met with cynicism, hostility, and corrupt
manipulation by whites. Whites ignored the progress of blacks, focusing
instead on whatever errors they could find. They proceeded to abridge

blacks' rights and access to civic culture because of those alleged errors. This to Du Bois was a betrayal of the Western tradition, and the crushing weight of this rejection prompted even more African Americans to accept second-class citizenship, abandon their pursuit of virtue and culture, and surrender the cultural and spiritual benefits of the good life. To save the masses of blacks from "second slavery," Du Bois advocates cultural secession:

> Work, culture, liberty—all these we need, not singly, but together, not successively, but together, each growing and aiding each and all striving toward that vaster ideal that swings before the Negro people, the ideal of human brotherhood, gained through the unifying ideal of Race; the ideal of fostering and developing the traits and talents of the Negro, not in opposition to or contempt for other races, but in large conformity to the greater ideals of the American Republic, in order that some day on American soil two world-races may give each to each these characteristics both so sadly lack.[75]

Because African Americans found that they would be excluded from the American version of Western culture, regardless of their accomplishments or virtues, they would have to depend upon their own separate articulation of the Western tradition. The goal of virtue and all it entailed would be the goal of the race, but they would pursue it in a context where their *virtus* was cultivated, celebrated, and rewarded. As Alfred Moss illustrates, African Americans really had little choice but to adopt separation:

> By the mid-1880s blacks of all classes, in the North as well as the South, were coming to feel that the intense and implacable hostility of whites left them no alternative but to accept a separate existence apart from the larger American community. Many continued to protest and agitate for all their rights as citizens, but the impossibility of halting their exclusion had to be acknowledged. Confronted with this situation black Americans began to pour their energies into the creation of cultural, welfare, religious, educational, economic, and social institutions that would be counterparts to the ones from which whites barred them.[76]

Fundamental to building African American culture is "the central problem of training men for life." Du Bois's analysis of the history, life, and future of the "massed millions of the black peasantry" ultimately centers on what he calls in the book's "Forethought" the "struggle of its greater souls" and how those greater souls might be adequately refined for the uplift of the race.[77] How one produces great and virtuous men, great souls, is at the core of Du Bois's intellectual labor. However, Du Bois also infuses his formula for great men and the leading class with a commitment to the value of the culture as a whole, civil generosity, civic duty, solidarity with the folk, and improving their lives.

Etched into the other side of the shield is an alternative destiny for African Americans, one not linked to accommodating white racism but built on classical education. Du Bois never asserts that efforts to become part of the industrial and economic structure of the South and the nation are not useful and necessary. But more important, African Americans must form and maintain a scholarly and spiritual foundation for the race. A "solid, permanent, structure" must be built on the "Negro college" and the classical education it provides. Practical and philosophical problems of civilization must all be answered by "study and thought and an appeal to the rich experience of the past":

> Internal problems of social advance must inevitably come,—problems of work and wages, of families and homes, of morals and of the true valuing of the things of life; and all these and other inevitable problems of civilization the Negro must meet and solve largely for himself, by reason of his isolation; and can there be any possible solution other than by study and thought and an appeal to the rich experience of the past?[78]

The search for higher individualism, a respect for the quest for knowledge, and the world of learning that has created men who "aforetime have inspired and guided worlds" must be an essential part of African Americans' future. Du Bois argues that this intellectual realm is open to those who will enter it (although at first, this fortunate few will be the Talented Tenth), and it represents the education that must be brought to the people. Du Bois, acting as guide, prophet and teacher, insists that others can join him in the company of the great thinkers and their works, where contemporary barriers of race fade:

> I sit with Shakespeare and he winces not. Across the color line I move arm in arm with Balzac and Dumas, where smiling men and welcoming men glide in gilded halls. From out the caves of evening that swing within the strong-limbed earth and the tracery of the stars, I summon Aristotle and Aurelius and what soul I will, and they come all graciously with no scorn nor condescension.[79]

W. E. B. Du Bois and *The Souls of Black Folk*

To create a civilization that will address both the mundane and transcendent experiences of human life, Du Bois pins his hopes on the classics and the educational program he believes has historically formed the most enriching nursery for civilization. He argues that the epics, philosophies, and treatises that form and cultivate a nuanced and thoughtful virtue, manliness, and heroism advance the philosophical search for Truth and contribute to the progress of civilization. They are, in Du Bois's view, the essential educational column for African Americans and the rest of the nation:

> In a half-dozen class-rooms they gather then,—here to follow the love-song of Dido, here to listen to the tale of Troy divine; there to wander among the stars, there to wander among men and nations,—and elsewhere other well-worn ways of knowing this queer world. Nothing new, no time-saving devices,—simply old time-glorified methods of delving for the Truth, and searching out the hidden beauties of life, and learning the good of living. The riddle of existence is the college curriculum that was laid out before the Pharoahs, that was taught in the groves by Plato, that formed the *trivium* and the *quadrivium,* and is to-day laid before the freedmen's sons by Atlanta University. And this course of study will not change; its message will grow more deft and effectual, its content richer by the toil of scholar and sight of seer; but the true college will ever have one goal,—not to earn meat, but to know the end and aim of that life which meat nourishes.[80]

Du Bois's educational program shares much with Anna Julia Cooper's curriculum of racial improvement. Du Bois continues to include Virgil's *Aeneid* and Homer's *Iliad,* with their complicated studies of nations, virtue, manliness, and heroism. Moreover, Du Bois makes sure to sustain the link to Africa, playing modern-day Herodotus by not only characterizing *The Aeneid* as the "love-song of Dido" but also making the "curriculum that was laid out for the Pharoahs" the precursor to that which "was taught in the groves by Plato, that formed the *trivium* and *quadrivium.*" By including the *trivium* and *quadrivium,* Du Bois is quick to broaden the curriculum to reflect the evolved tradition of the West. It also suggests that he would embrace contemporary humanities instruction.

Even as he champions the transforming and enriching power of classical education and envisions a black virtue and heroism that will help rebuild the black masses, Du Bois is fully aware of the strikingly different experiences, challenges, and dangers awaiting the men and women who form the leadership class. In the end, the training of black men is a virtue defined by their commitment to building civilization, a manly project of "higher individualism" (refined to the limits of talent and ability, but with an ambition dedicated to regenerating and leading the masses) and a heroism sculpted to enable individuals to carry civilization into the dangerous "red hideousness of Georgia."[81] In "The Coming of John," the title character experiences the wonder of a world of knowledge, but he also has to face that red hideousness of which Du Bois speaks. The fates of both the hero and his sister are far from desirable. John is transformed by his education at Wells institute, physically and intellectually. Just as his rolling, carefree gait, disheveled look, and visage of happy ignorance disappear, so too is John made stern and determined by his experience with the knowledge of both antiquity and the present:

> He caught terrible colds lying on his back in the meadows of nights, trying to think out the solar system; he had grave doubts as to the ethics of the Fall of Rome, and strongly suspected the Germans of being thieves and rascals, despite his text-books; he pondered long over every new Greek word, and wondered why this meant that and why it couldn't mean something else, and how it must have felt to think all things in Greek. So he thought and puzzled along for himself,—pausing perplexed where others skipped merrily, and walking steadily through the difficulties where the rest stopped and surrendered. He . . . looked now for the first time sharply about him and wondered why he had seen so little before.[82]

When John returns to his home, his words are tinged with profundity, anger, and sarcasm. He is alert to the Veil of race and affronted by the limited world blacks inhabit. At home the transformed John encounters not only the anger of the white community but also scorn from the uneducated black population. He rejects the narrowness of church denominations and the frenzied priesthood that Du Bois disdains. His knowing sternness, commentary on the cultural needs of his community, and curriculum for the youth he teaches discomfit blacks and infuriate whites; and as previous cultivators of virtue and knowledge found, the ground was not easily broken for planting. His sister asks hesitantly if sadness always comes from learning. Hearing that it does, she eventually decides that she wants to learn also. John dies in the battle for the minds of the young blacks in Altamaha, Georgia, and his sister seems destined for solemn, if not deadly, intellectual and social struggles of her own.

In contrast to the deadly conflicts in the bloody South, Du Bois envisions grander forces of cultural change. In 1897, Du Bois participated in founding the American Negro Academy, of which Anna Julia Cooper was also a member. Like many other ethnic and professional groups of the nineteenth century, African Americans also made numerous attempts to focus their collective cultural, political, and intellectual power through formal organizations. The American Negro Academy took on as its weighty cultural and academic mission using its members' "skills and abilities as a means of both leading and protecting their people and as a weapon to secure equality and destroy racism."[83] This task rested on the shoulders of a membership significantly involved with the classics.[84] These men (and, later, women such as Anna Julia Cooper) represented a more glorious aspect of the African American experience with the classical tradition, one that could operate at the lofty levels of academe. But, as Du Bois knew, the masses existed in places that were not the bustling Carthage and fruitful Italy of *The Aeneid* but bloody like the plains of Troy. Worse, they might well be in darker places than even John Jones encountered. In his chapter "Of the Quest of the Golden Fleece," Du Bois describes Dougherty County, Georgia, a land of ignorance, sharecropping, child labor, moral collapse, rampant racism, and little hope of growing virtuous men among the cotton. Here Du Bois identifies a "submerged tenth" of the black population living in squalor, hopeless sharecropping, and moral decay.[85] "Shiftlessness" and the collapse of family structures are the result of despair. In a "revival of the old Roman idea of patronage," outside agitators are kept out, because African Americans not from the area must be vouched for by a white man.[86] In these forbidding frontier zones, a significant part of the struggle would have to be conducted. If ever there were to be a challenge to the value of the classics it would be here. Du Bois recognized the challenge and mused in this chapter and in his 1911 romance *The Quest of the Silver Fleece* (drafted between 1904 and 1906) that surely the ancient quest that Apollonius of Rhodes, Pindar, and Euripides gave us could not have been more daunting than the story of the American South.[87] He writes:

> I have sometimes half suspected that here the winged ram Chrysomallus left that Fleece after which Jason and his Argonauts went vaguely wandering into the shadowy East three thousand years ago; and certainly one might frame a pretty and not far-fetched analogy of witchery and dragon's teeth, and blood and armed men, between the ancient and the modern Quest of the Golden Fleece in the Black Sea.[88]

Of note here is that Du Bois's chapter and fictional creation deploy the first of the heroic epics. By going to the beginning of the epic heroic tradition,

Du Bois places the trials of African Americans firmly in the classical mythological era of most striking terror. Du Bois makes the allusion to dragons' teeth and bloody battle himself, images one can easily imagine as blacks do battle with white opponents literally and figuratively in the cotton field.

Du Bois recognized these dark possibilities for the future, and he looked to classical training in individual and civic virtue, manliness, and culture to provide leaders who could commit themselves to the dangers and death that awaited them in some parts of America. That education also armed these men and women to be the leading class when they took their places not only in the red clay of the South but also in the equally unforgiving terrain of academe. Whether fleeing a burning Troy, building new civilization on some unknown frontier, or embarking on the most dangerous quest, the Talented Tenth would be prepared. The race (and its culture) had no choice: it could either accept a second slavery of mind and body in the increasingly unfriendly culture, or it could strike out on its own quest for civilization.

Du Bois is significant in part because he is the first classically educated African American to discern the ultimate incompatibility of the two American visions of culture and to demand that African Americans assume the mantle of the West and take control of the Western tradition for their own purposes. He prefers to build a separate civilization, cultivate it with a direct transmission of culture and learning from the classical world to twentieth-century African Americans, and give the Western tradition new vitality by employing it in the uplift of his people. It is appropriate that Du Bois should find something strangely familiar in the first of the heroic epics. African Americans at the beginning the twentieth century faced, like Jason and his Argonauts, a world populated by all the monsters yet to die at the hands of heroes and filled with tests of virtue that would plant and uproot nations. The glories of Rome were far away, as were the glories of an older, wiser America, and the world was largely unexplored, untamed, and menacing. For W. E. B. Du Bois in 1910, the quest for the Golden Fleece had only just begun; many of the greatest black heroes of the age were aboard his *Argo;* the gods were perched on Olympus; and the wide, wine-dark sea stretched into the future.

CONCLUSION

ΑΠΟΛΛΩΝ

THE TEMPLE OF APOLLO

How the African American writers I have examined used the classics reflected their individual needs to establish positions of authority or authenticity as writers, scholars, race representatives, or leaders. Moreover, whether or not specific classical texts assumed prominence in their various works and which works emerged as definitive for each writer also reflected the political and social demands of their eras and the lessons and tools they deemed necessary for their readers and the culture to acquire and adopt.

Phillis Wheatley's notable exercise in acquiring voice and transmitting positions on slavery, race, and Christianity is clearly mediated by her precarious position as a slave. We should be quick to note that just as she declares her Christian piety and orthodoxy, she deploys classical writers and texts that were widely known as sources of practical good sense, solid morality, and ageless lessons in heroism and piety. Homer, Virgil, Terence, Horace, and Ovid all support Wheatley's literary adventure in America and Europe. Her writings also adhere to the belletristic expectations of her readership in England, the country in which her book of poems found a publisher. It is also clear that Wheatley initially presents herself as a student, a supplicant, or a hopeful aspirant to the level of the great classical masters. Although she ambitiously sheds this mantle of humble student for the role of teacher, she never fully abandons her image as a follower, talented though she might be, of the even greater masters who have lit her way. The classics tell both her white readers and a black readership that grows over generations not only that the classical world offers evidence of black accomplishment but also that classical writers are suitable guides to living a good life and potentially an emancipated life. Moreover, Wheatley points to classical writers and texts as supplementary guides to goodness and accompaniments to Christianity, which she shows to be flawed in the hands of slaveholders. Where Christian virtue is obscured by the cloud of racism, classical virtue may be a clearer alternative.

Frederick Douglass's experience with the classics, initially through *The Columbian Orator* and later from other sources, illustrates yet another way in which the classics are personally imbibed by writers and then recommended to the masses. While Caleb Bingham's text helps awaken Douglass's mind and animate his thoughts of freedom, this early influence is less obvious than in Wheatley's works. Douglass's speeches reflect the influence of classical oratorical strategies demonstrated in *The Columbian Orator* long before it is certain that he seizes upon the broader body of the classics as a tremendous reservoir of knowledge and cultural and political power. At first, it is his acquisition of personal agency and the heroic seizure of freedom that define Douglass; and the readings from classical sources included in *The Columbian Orator* help him amplify that power, articulate his manhood, and declare the justness of his cause against corrupt slaveholders. When he recognizes that gaining the ability to more carefully and skillfully deploy the classics has extraordinary power to expand his audiences, increase his oratorical range, grant him increased powers of allusion, and even alter his social standing and financial position, such speeches as "The Claims of the Negro Ethnologically Considered" illustrate the powerful result. When Douglass seeks to burnish his image, secure his legacy, and ensure the survival of the accomplishments of African Americans, it is to the writings of the Roman senators he turns as an example of that process of cultural and literary apotheosis. To the masses of African Americans, Douglass offers his Grand Tour of Europe, Greece, and Egypt, as well as the image of himself astride the Pyramid of Cheops, as powerful indicators of leadership, political conquest, and his position as first among his people.

Anna Julia Cooper deployed the lessons of her classical education both within her writing and broadly to the students she taught over the course of her long life. Perhaps more than any of the other writers examined in this project, Cooper maintained the least distance between her intellectual belief in the supremacy of the classics and Western civilization and her direct dealings with the African American masses. Particularly compelling about Cooper's use of the classics is her attempt to adapt the lessons of the classics to practical concerns of educating the masses and reformulating the idea of gender in the West. Nonetheless, Cooper's project of advancing classical education has a particularly Christian component, one that attempts to proselytize as it educates. She seeks a cultural renaissance in America that goes hand in hand with a gently but relentlessly conquering Christianity that is far more optimistically and brilliantly orthodox than Phillis Wheatley's, Frederick Douglass's, or Du Bois's faith. Wheatley may declare her conversion and her piety, but she does not hold high the conquering banner of the church. Douglass wages a pitched battle against the organized church in Europe and America, refusing to excuse the widespread support for slavery among Christian denominations.

W. E. B. Du Bois's outlook is particularly dour, and he does not hold out hope that the faith of the fathers can truly transform the quickly decaying, materialistic, and immoral American civilization. Perhaps because of this darker vision of the future, Du Bois moves beyond Cooper's restyled chivalry and Christian imperialism for a culture and civic virtue explicitly rooted in the study of life, philosophy, and learning found in the ancient writings, the *trivium,* and the *quadrivium.* He sees this intellectual virtue of cultivated insight and wisdom, matched with heroism and civic commitment, as the truly civilizing influence in the world—one that directly challenges the materialist machine of Booker T. Washington. Both Cooper and Du Bois wish to transform the hearts and souls of men and women and cultivate virtue, but for Du Bois the method is less the rejuvenating sunlight of womanhood and more the enriching soil of classical education. The primary threat to civilization is not just that men may degrade women and allow their moral virtue to wither. It is that both may surrender their quest for the meaning of life to the immediate gratification of material wealth and sink forever into ignorance and barbarism as the last intellects and heroes of the race fade into history. So, Du Bois would have us all at youth enter the Temple of Apollo, that versatile god of knowledge, healing, music, and young citizens, to be initiated into our role as citizens, culture builders, scholars, and guardians of the race.

In many ways, the literal and literary journeys of Cooper and Du Bois at the turn of the century are oddly Virgilian in style (and more contemporarily, Dantesque). A recurrent theme in black male writing is the journey of painful understanding, the journey underground, or the "descent into the underworld," which is "primarily political and social in its implications." The traditional journey in the black female novel is one that can be partly political and social, but it is more likely "a personal and psychological journey, the state of becoming 'part of an evolutionary spiral, moving from victimization to consciousness.'"[1] Certainly, literal and figurative journeys into the underworld have a long literary pedigree in the West. Among the early classical myths, Hercules descends to steal Cerberus and rescue Alcestis, Orpheus journeys after Eurydice, and Theseus travels there to help Pirithous steal away Persephone. In *The Republic*, Socrates tells a story of a fallen warrior's trip to the underworld and the rewards of virtue and vice to underpin the superiority of the just life.[2] In the classical epics and Dante, with which at least Cooper and Du Bois were certainly familiar, the journey takes place with the direction of another or accompanying guide. Odysseus journeys to the underworld in Homer's *Odyssey*, learns his fate from Tiresias, and is introduced to some of the horror and waste of the Trojan War and the emptiness of the underworld. Aeneas ventures into the underworld with the Sybil to see his father Anchises once more, and he is enlightened about the future of Rome before being sent out through the gate of false dreams. Dante provides the most famous journey through the underworld in the *Inferno*. We can easily argue about the personal psychological or political and social implications of each trip. But in almost every case we focus on the traveler. We can look to both Wheatley and Douglass as travelers who are transformed by a harrowing journey. Wheatley clearly makes her journey while following Homer and Virgil and Terence. Douglass travels through the horrors of the antebellum underworld and is led out by multiple guides—Sophia Auld, Caleb Bingham, unsuspecting schoolboys, Anna Murray, the East Baltimore Mental Improvement Society, and African American clergy, among others.

Perhaps Cooper and especially Du Bois did not ever perceive of themselves, at least in *A Voice from the South* and *The Souls of Black Folk,* as followers, travelers trailing behind a knowledgeable sage. Both seemed to already know the terrain and the lessons to be found in the landscape. It might be useful to consider that, with the exception of "The Coming of John," neither Cooper nor Du Bois gives us a single character who is transformed by a journey through the underworld.[3] Although they provide personal information, they do not deliver personal narratives of transformation that clearly mark them as towering representative figures. Truthfully, neither gives any indication that they would submit to being directed or led at all—Circe, the Sybil, and Virgil notwithstanding. It is more productive to consider that they perused the roles available in the Western tradition and styled themselves as the guides and sages to journeying heroes, the adventurous readers who can be transformed by what they see and learn or go on to destruction. They lead us through the rich history of the Western world or the harrowing historical landscape of African Americans from colonial slavery to the beginning of the new century. In the end, Cooper, whom Father Felix Klein called his "amiable guide" through Virgil, and the brooding Du Bois both guide their readers through landscapes full of provocative dangers, revelations, and lessons but rich with classical signs, wonders, tools, and weapons for the world above.

The existence of such provocative guides for African Americans raises questions for further investigation. While the publication of the groundbreaking *Souls of Black Folk* provides a reasonable pause in a discussion of classical influence in African American literature, the influence of World War I, the larger African American experience with Europe, and the explosion of literature, economy, and culture in the Harlem Renaissance all demand further evaluation. Merely looking ahead in the career of W. E. B. Du Bois suggests that beyond *The Quest of the Silver Fleece*, his transforming political and intellectual consciousness will raise questions about the usefulness of the classics as tools to interpret the West and the increasing domestic American and international turmoil that characterizes it. As Paul Fussell points out in *The Great War and Modern Memory*, the murderous First World War shattered Victorian and Edwardian ideas of class and culture, leaving the European upper classes and their classically and romantically infused language and sensibilities in the bloody mud of numerous battlefields. African American literature and culture did not escape the transforming power of such events as World War I, and more harrowing journeys through the underworld lay ahead in World War II and the civil rights struggles of the mid-twentieth century. We also know many of the next generation of literary travelers and guides had the classics as part of their education. Writers like Zora Neale Hurston and Jean Toomer, as well as those who peopled Cooper's M Street classrooms and Du Bois's Talented Tenth, all imbibed the classics, but through our current scholarship, we know little or nothing about classical influences in their works and lives. We have yet to ask whether and how the classics actually survived modernism in African America and the global conflicts that transformed African Americans and America more broadly. Moreover, among the many voices that rang out in the civil rights era, who among the orators reached into antiquity for guidance? We know, for instance, that Charles Hamilton Houston was a product of M Street/Dunbar High, and he was the mentor to Thurgood Marshall.

There are yet questions to ask about the contemporary life of the classics in African America, from the work of Alice Walker and Toni Morrison to Percival Everett's return to the pantheon in *Frenzy* (1996) and even *Erasure* (2011), to Randall Kenan, who asks what happens when the hegemony of Judeo-Christian thought among African Americans is challenged by the mythological and philosophical richness of conversations with young Italian classicists.[4] These questions require the depth and attention of a larger study, across a far greater period of time. Ultimately, scholars must answer the question of what it is in the classics that after nearly 240 years, from Phillis Wheatley to Percival Everett and beyond, continues to inspire African American writers.

NOTES

Introduction: A More Than Partial Grace

The title here, "A More Than Partial Grace," draws on a phrase from Phillis Wheatley, "To Maecenas," *The Collected Works of Phillis Wheatley*, ed. John C. Shields (New York: Oxford UP, 1988) 11.

1. Kristen Wilcox, *The Culture of Classicism: Ancient Greece and Rome in American Intellectual Life* (Baltimore: Johns Hopkins UP, 2002) 1.

2. In the American tradition, Addison's *Cato* became the model for American civic duty and *pietas*, adapting the Roman struggle against tyranny to local American concerns. The play ran regularly prior to the American Revolution and was performed by soldiers at Valley Forge. It may even hold the inspiration for famous remarks of the revolutionary era, including Patrick Henry's "Give me liberty or give me death" and Nathan Hale's regret that he had only one life to give for his country. One can also see the influence of other proponents of Roman virtue. Dr. Joseph Warren, before delivering his commemorative speech for the fifth anniversary of the Boston Massacre, changed his clothes and appeared in the pulpit of Boston's Old South Church in a "Ciceronian Toga." James McLachlan, "Classical Names, American Identities," *Classical Traditions in Early America*, ed. John W. Eadie (Ann Arbor: U of Michigan Center for Coordination of Ancient and Modern Studies, 1976) 82–83.

3. Homer, *The Iliad*, trans. Michael Reck (New York: HarperCollins, 1994) I:1–7. Agamemnon angers Achilles by taking his battle prize, the lady Briseis. In I:148–72, Achilles directly questions the virtue of engaging in battle.

4. Naoto Yamagata, *Homeric Morality* (New York: Brill, 1994).

5. Homer, *The Iliad,* trans. Robert Fagles (New York: Penguin, 1998) 82.

6. Virgil [Publius Vergilius Maro], *The Aeneid,* trans. Allen Mandelbaum (New York: Bantam, 1982). Aeneas is continually urged on his way toward Italy by Venus, his mother and patron goddess, when he frequently hesitates to follow his heroic destiny to found Rome. He is tempted most memorably by the luxuries of Carthage and its beautiful Queen Dido, who entices Aeneas to end his quest and stay with her in the city "whose walls already rise" (Bk. I, line 620, p. 14).

7. Carl J. Richard. *The Founders and the Classics: Greece, Rome, and the American Enlightenment* (Cambridge, MA: Harvard UP, 1994) 9.

8. Richard Waswo, *The Founding Legend of Western Civilization: From Virgil to Vietnam* (Hanover, NH: Wesleyan UP, 1997) 2–11.

9. Richard Beale Davis, *Intellectual Life in the Colonial South 1585–1763,* 3 vols. (Knoxville: U of Tennessee P, 1978) 3:1647–48.

10. Davis 3:1639.

11. Carl Richard is keen to note that Jefferson had read Gibbon and even recommended his *History of the Decline and Fall of the Roman Empire* as the "best work of its kind" (97).

12. Edward Gibbon, *The History of the Decline and Fall of the Roman Empire* (London: Plummer & Brewis, 1821) 3:16.

13. Rogers M. Smith, *Civic Ideals: Conflicting Visions of Citizenship in U.S. History* (New Haven, CT: Yale UP, 1997) 33.

14. Smith 18.

15. Martha C. Nussbaum, *Cultivating Humanity: A Classical Defense of Reform In Liberal Education* (Cambridge, MA: Harvard UP, 1997) 153.

16. Mary Church Terrell, *A Colored Woman in a White World* (Washington, DC: Ransdell, 1940) 41.

17. Carter G. Woodson, *The History of the Negro Church* (Washington, DC: Associated Publishers, 1921) 178.

18. Roman manumission of slaves was commonplace (creating labor problems in the first century, for instance), and former slaves could participate in limited civic life. The regularity of manumission distinguished Roman slavery from Athenian and American slavery. J. Albert Harrill, *The Manumission of Slaves in Early Christianity,* Hermeneutische Untersuchungen zur Theologie 32 (Tübingen, Germany: Mohr, 1995) 53–54.

19. In "The Contribution of Antiquity to American Racial Thought" (collected in *Classical Traditions,* ed. Eadie 199), David Weisen notes that this theory prompted sixteenth-century philosopher Jean Bodin, with whom Jefferson was likely acquainted, to assert that heat made southern nations overly affected by black bile, which rendered them moody and thoughtful, leading to the creation of the major arts and sciences.

20. W. E. B. Du Bois, "The Future of the Negro" (1904), rpt. in *The Oxford W. E. B. Du Bois Reader*, ed. Eric J. Sundquist (New York: Oxford UP, 1996) 368.

21. Alexander Pope, *An Essay on Criticism* (London: Lewis, 1711), facsim. ed. (London: Scolar Press, 1970) I:88.

22. Pope, *Essay* I:136.

23. Qtd. in Edwin L. Wolfe, "Classical Languages in Philadelphia," *Classical Traditions*, ed. Eadie 50.

24. Caroline Winterer, *The Culture of Classicism: Ancient Greece and Rome in American Intellectual Life, 1780-1910* (Baltimore: Johns Hopkins UP, 2002) 1.

25. William Kerrigan and Gordon Braden, *The Idea of the Renaissance* (Baltimore: Johns Hopkins UP, 1991) 8.

26. W. E. B. Du Bois, *The Souls of Black Folk*, ed. Henry Louis Gates Jr. and Terri Hume Oliver (New York: Norton, 1999) 58–59.

27. Du Bois, *Souls* 58. Gates and Oliver's note clarifies this educational program: "The seven liberal arts of the Middle Ages. Divided into the *trivium* (grammar, logic, and rhetoric), and the *quadrivium* (arithmetic, music, geometry, and astronomy)."

28. Du Bois, *Souls* 58.

29. James D. Anderson, *The Education of Blacks in the South, 1860–1935* (Chapel Hill: U of North Carolina P, 1988) 29–30.

30. Alexander Keyssar, *The Right to Vote: The Contested History of Democracy in the United States* (New York: Basic, 2000) 93.

31. Keyssar 93.

32. Keyssar 98.

33. Anderson 29–30.

34. In *The Civilization of the Renaissance in Italy* (London: Phaidon, 1951), Jacob Burckhardt notes that since "Cicero offered no model for Latin conversation . . . other gods had to be worshipped beside him. The want was supplied by representations of the comedies of Plautus and Terence, frequent both in and out of Rome, which for the actors were an incomparable exercise in Latin as the language of daily life" (144). Moreover, the age of decadence after the 1527 sack of Rome is indicated by the disappearance of Terence from the stage: "Giovio . . . not impartially, but on the whole correctly, [noted] the causes of this decline: 'The plays of Plautus and Terence, once a school of Latin style for the educated Romans, are banished to make room for Italian comedies'" (152).

35. A notable exception may exist in Plato. In *The Fragility of Goodness* (New York: Cambridge UP, 1986) 3–4n, Martha Nussbaum argues that we may be right to see Plato as the first feminist philosopher. She points out that in *The Republic*, Socrates chastises Glaucon for failing to use both masculine and

feminine participles when they discuss rulers. Socrates fears it will give the false impression that they are discussing only men.

36. Shelley P. Haley, "Black Feminist Thought and Classics: Re-membering, Re-claiming, Re-empowering," *Feminist Theory and the Classics,* ed. Nancy Sorkin Rabinowitz and Amy Richlin (New York: Routledge, 1993) 25.

37. Mary Helen Washington, Introduction, *A Voice from the South* by Anna Julia Cooper (Oxford UP, 1988) xxx (qtd. in Haley 26).

38. Jacques Berlinerblau, *Heresy in the University: The Black Athena Controversy and the Responsibilities of American Intellectuals.* (New Brunswick, NJ: Rutgers UP, 1999).

39. Nancy Sorkin Rabinowitz, introduction, *Feminist Theory and the Classics,* ed. Nancy Sorkin Rabininowitz and Amy Richlin (New York: Routledge, 1993) 1.

40. Irene F. DeJong and J. P. Sullivan, eds., *Modern Critical Theory and Classical Literature* (New York: Brill, 1994) 6–13.

41. Frank M. Snowden Jr., *Blacks in Antiquity* (Cambridge, MA: Harvard UP, 1970) 6.

42. E. A. Hooton, *Up from the Ape,* rev. (New York: Macmillan, 1944) 662 (qtd. in Snowden 6n).

43. Haley 31.

44. Alfred A. Moss Jr., *The American Negro Academy: Voice of the Talented Tenth* (Baton Rouge: Louisiana State UP, 1981) 3, 24. The proposed "African Academy," later the American Negro Academy, was to be "an organization of Colored authors, scholars, and artists." Its goals were:

   a), to promote the publication of literary and scholarly works;

   b), to aid youths of genius in the attainment of the higher culture, at home and abroad;

   c), to gather into its Archives valuable data, historical or literary works of Negro authors;

   d), to aid, by publications, the vindication of the race from vicious assaults, in all the lines of learning and truth;

   e), to publish, at least once a year an "Annual" of original articles upon various Literary, Historical, and Philosophical topics, of a racial nature, by selected members; and by these and diverse other means, to raise the standard of intellectual endeavor among American Negroes.

45. Philip S. Foner and Robert James Branham, *Lift Every Voice: African-American Oratory, 1787–1900* (Tuscaloosa: U of Alabama P, 1998) 790–91.

46. William Sanders Scarborough, "The Theory and Function of the Thematic Vowel in the Greek Verb," *Transactions of the American Philological Association* 15 (1884): vi.

47. In his lecture "Negro English" (published in Anglia [Leipzig, 1884] and in *Transactions of the American Philological Association* 16 [1885]: xxxi–

xxxiii), Harrison purported to provide an understanding of the "baby-talk" of blacks, which he listed among other "Negroisms" of a race of men he found linguistically retarded, superstitious, imitative, and "on intimate terms with the wild animals and birds, the *flora* and *fauna* of the immense stretches of pine woods among which for generations his habitation has been pitched." For Scarborough's lecture, see William Sanders Scarborough, "Fatalism in Homer and Virgil," *Transactions of the American Philological Association* 16 (1885): xxxvi–xxxvii.

48. William Sanders Scarborough, "The Chronological Order of Plato's Dialogues," *Transactions of the American Philological Association* 24 (1892): vi–viii.

49. Moss 38.

50. Davis 3:1639.

51. Davis 3:1639.

52. Haley notes Walker's attention to the myth of Perseus and Medusa in *In Search of Our Mother's Gardens* (29). Madonne M. Miller also explores significant classical resonances in Toni Morrison's *The Bluest Eye*, noting the intersection of Ovid's Tereus and Philomela myth and Homer's version of Hades's rape of Persephone; see "Lady No Longer Sings the Blues: Rape, Madness, and Silence in *The Bluest Eye*," *Conjuring: Black Women, Fiction, and Literary Tradition*, ed. Marjorie Lee Pryse and Hortense J. Spillers (Bloomington: Indiana UP, 1985) 176–84. Cornel West's views on intellectual synthesis were articulated in his lecture, Forum for Contemporary Thought, University of Virginia, 6 Oct. 2000.

1. The Trojan Horse

1. Henry Louis Gates Jr., foreword, Wheatley, *Collected Works* viii.

2. Julian D. Mason Jr., acknowledgments, *The Poems of Phillis Wheatley*, ed. Julian D. Mason Jr. (Chapel Hill: U of North Carolina P, 1966) xiii.

3. Sacvan Bercovitch, *The Puritan Origins of the American Self* (New Haven: Yale UP, 1975) 56–58, 64–66, 86–87, 217n22, 219n34.

4. As Walter J. Ong has exhaustively illustrated, the long tradition of classical education in the West has underpinned government, diplomacy, religion, and professions such as medicine and the law. Moreover, it has largely served to enshrine and enshroud power, as well as define masculinity, virtue, class, and the terms for negotiating each. So the emphasis on the classics in eighteenth-century education that became Wheatley's intellectual foundation was, not surprisingly, an early European import. See Ong, *The Presence of the Word: Some Prolegomena for Cultural and Religious History* (New Haven: Yale UP, 1967).

5. John D. Pulliam and James Van Patten, *History of Education in America*, 6th ed. (Englewood Cliffs, NJ: Prentice Hall, 1991) 16. In 1647, the General Court of Massachusetts passed a law requiring that a town with fifty or more households set up a school or contract with the nearest town for education for their children.

6. Pulliam and Van Patten 22.

7. Pulliam and Van Patten 24.

8. Carl J. Richard, *The Founders and the Classics: Greece, Rome, and the American Enlightenment* (Cambridge, MA: Harvard UP, 1884) 18.

9. In "Of National Characters," *The Philosophical Works of David Hume*, vol. 3 (Boston: Little, Brown, 1854), David Hume opined, "I am apt to suspect the negroes and in general all the other species of men (for there are four or five different kinds), to be naturally inferior to the whites. There never was a civilized nation of any other complexion than white, nor even any individual eminent either in action or speculation. No ingenious manufactures amongst them, no arts, no sciences." (228–29). Specifically addressing Hume's position, Immanuel Kant argued that "[t]he Negroes of Africa have by nature no feeling that rises above the trifling. . . . Father Labat reports that a Negro carpenter, whom he reproached for haughty treatment toward his wives, answered: 'You whites are indeed fools, for first you make great concessions to your wives, and afterward you complain when they drive you mad.' And it might be that there was something in this which perhaps deserved to be considered; but in short, this fellow was quite black from head to foot, a clear proof that what he said was stupid." Kant, *Observations on the Feeling of the Beautiful and Sublime*, trans. John T. Goldthwait (Berkeley: U of California P, 1960) 110–11.

10. Warren H. Button and Eugene F. Provenzo Jr., *History of Education and Culture in America*, 2nd ed. (Boston: Allyn & Bacon, 1989) 44.

11. William H. Robinson, *Phillis Wheatley and Her Writings* (New York: Garland, 1984) 11.

12. Robert E. Bell, *Women of Classical Mythology* (New York: Oxford UP, 1991) 368; Ovid [Publius Ovidius Naso], *The Art of Love* [*Ars Amatoria*], trans. J. H. Mozley, ed. G. P. Goold (1929; Cambridge, MA: Harvard UP, 1979) II:91, III:121, 151. See also Michael Stapleton, ed., *Thomas Heywood's Art of Love: The First Complete English Translation of Ovid's* Ars Amatoria (Ann Arbor: U of Michigan P, 2000) II:88, III:117, 123.

13. "Lodge, Thomas," *Oxford Book of English Verse, 1250–1900*, ed. Sir A. T. Quiller-Couch (Oxford, UK: Clarendon, 1919) 98–99.

14. Wheatley, *Collected Works* 275; Robinson, *Phillis Wheatley and Her Writings* 42.

15. Margaretta Odell, "Memoir," *Memoir and Poems of Phillis Wheatley* (1834; Miami, FL: Mnemosyne, 1969) 13–15.

16. "Hutchinson, Thomas," *Dictionary of American Biography*, ed. Dumas Malone (New York: Scribner's, 1932) 440. In *The Life of Thomas Hutchinson* (New York: Da Capo, 1972), James K. Hosmer includes an August 30, 1765, letter to Richard Jackson in which Hutchinson reported that the mob was ruthlessly thorough in sacking the house, "not leaving a single book or paper in it, and have scattered or destroyed all the manuscripts and other papers I had been collecting for thirty years together" (91–94).

17. As an example of Mather's and other Puritan divines' substantial investment in the classics, Bercovitch points out that Mather's *Magnalia Christi Americana* is rife with Christian and classical parallels, comparisons, and claims of sameness. Mather "alludes to the Roman epic [*The Aeneid*] more frequently, more consistently, than to any other work (except for the Bible), from his opening invocation, a direct paraphrase of Virgil's" to the last section, concerning the wars of Og-Philip, which he titles "Arma Virumque Cano" (66).

18. Arthur Wentworth Hamilton Eaton, *The Famous Mather Byles: The Noted Boston Tory Preacher 1707–1788* (Boston: Butterfield, 1914) 101–6.

19. Wheatley's private copies of Pope's works, including his translation of *The Odyssey*, are currently held in special collections at the University of North Carolina at Charlotte.

20. As one early admirer of Wheatley wrote to a friend, "It is about two months since I subscribed for Phillis's poems, which I expected to have sent you long ago, but the want of spirit to carry on anything of the kind here has prevented it, as they are not yet published." John Andrews to William Barrell," 29 May 1772, Andrews-Barrell Letters, Massachusetts Historical Society, Boston.

21. Wheatley, "Sir [David Wooster] October 18, 1773," *Collected Works* 170.

22. Wheatley, *Collected Works* 170–71.

23. Andrews to Barrell, 28 Jan. 1774.

24. Robinson, *Phillis Wheatley and Her Writings* 35.

25. Kirsten Wilcox, "The Body into Print: Marketing Phillis Wheatley," *American Literature* 71.1 (Durham: Duke UP, 1999): 11.

26. Wilcox 17.

27. Benjamin Franklin, *The Works of Benjamin Franklin*, ed. John Bigelow, 12 vols. (New York: Putnam, 1904) 6:172–73.

28. Wilcox 18.

29. Wilcox 11–12.

30. Wilcox 11–12.

31. Wilcox 8.

32. Thomas Wooldridge to the Earl of Dartmouth, 24 Nov. 1772, County Record Office, Stafford, England, *Critical Essays on Phillis Wheatley*, ed. William H. Robinson (Boston: G. K. Hill, 1982) 20.

33. Benjamin Rush, *An Address to the Inhabitants of the British Settlements in America Upon Slave Keeping* (Philadelphia: Dunlap, 1773) 2n.

34. *Gentleman's Magazine and Historical Chronicle* 43 (Sept. 1773): 456.

35. *London Monthly Review; or, Literary Journal from June, 1773 to January, 1774,* vol. 49 (Oct. 1774): 457–59.

36. Robinson, *Critical Essays* 33–36.

37. Thomas Jefferson, *Notes on the State of Virginia,* Literary Classics of the United States, ed. Merrill D. Peterson (1785; New York: Library of America, 1984) 266–67.

38. Jefferson 264.

39. Jefferson 264.

40. Jefferson 268.

41. Voltaire, *Oeuvres Completes,* ed. Louis Moland, 52 vols. (Paris: Garnier, 1882–85) 48:594–95 (as translated in Robinson, *Critical Essays* 33).

42. Evert A. Duyckinck and George L. Duyckinck, *Cyclopaedia of American Literature* (New York: Scribner, 1856) 1:368.

43. Mason 13.

44. Henry Louis Gates Jr., *Figures in Black: Word, Signs, and the "Racial" Self* (New York: Oxford UP, 1987) 4.

45. John C. Shields, "Phillis Wheatley's Use of Classicism," *American Literature* 52.1 (1980): 102.

46. Meyer Reinhold, *Classica Americana: The Greek and Roman Heritage in the United States* (Detroit: Wayne State UP, 1984) 151.

47. Reinhold 26–28.

48. Shields, "Phillis Wheatley's Use of Classicism" 100.

49. Horace [Quintus Horatius Flaccus], *The Odes of Horace,* trans. David Ferry (New York: Farrar, 1997) 112–13.

50. "Maecenas," *The Oxford Classical Dictionary,* 3rd ed. rev., ed. Simon Hornblower and Antony Spawforth (Oxford, UK: Oxford UP, 2003).

51. Horace, *Odes* I.1.

52. Translations of *The Aeneid* appeared regularly and were of varying quality. Dryden's translations appeared in 1697 and Christopher Pitt's translation, dedicated to Frederick, Prince of Wales, and borrowing "fifty or sixty entire lines from Mr. Dryden," appeared in 1743 (London: J. Hughs). It might well have been among the texts available to Phillis Wheatley. My own citations are from the Mandelbaum edition (see ch. 1, n. 6, above).

53. Mandelbaum, Introduction, Virgil vii.

54. J. C. Rolfe, ed., *Suetonius,* 2 vols., Loeb Classical Library (London: Heinemann; New York: Macmillan, 1914) 2:460, accessed 15 Mar. 2003 <http://www.fordham.edu/halsall/ancient/suet-viribus-rolfe.html#De%20Vita%20Terenti>.

55. Terence [Publius Terentius Afer], *The Comedies,* trans. Betty Radice (New York: Penguin, 1976) 12, 342–43.

56. Reinhold 151.

57. Betty Radice takes special care to deny Terence's racial Africanity, oddly pursuing the question of race in the introduction to her edition of the comedies. She even denies that he is of North African origin: "Even the surname Afer is no proof that Terence was of North African origin; witness the distinguished orator, Gnaeus Domitius Afer. Terence has been conjectured to be a Semitic Carthaginian, a Berber, or the son of one of Hannibal's captives from South Italy, and so racially either Greek or Italian" (12–13).

58. Joel Augustus Rogers, *World's Great Men of Color,* ed. John Henrik Clarke, 2 vols. (New York: Simon & Schuster, 1996) 1:118–20. Robert Graves challenges the idea of Terence's black Africanity; in the introduction to his edition of *The Comedies of Terence* (Chicago: Aldine, 1962), Graves classifies him as "probably a Berber" (ix). The 1896 *Harper's Dictionary of Classical Literature and Antiquities* (New York: American Book Co., 1896) states, "Terence was a native of Carthage (though his cognomen, Afer, suggests that he was of African [Libyan], not Phoenecian heritage." Elsewhere, the dictionary classifies Libyans and Aethiopians and the two indigenous African peoples, but Libyans are imagined to be "Caucasian."

59. Houston A. Baker Jr., "'There Is No More Beautiful Way': Theory and Poetics of Afro-American Women's Writing," *Afro-American Literary Study in the 1990s,* ed. Houston A. Baker Jr. and Patricia Redmon (Chicago: U of Chicago P, 1989) 137.

60. On occasion, there is confusion about Publius Cornelius Scipio and Publius Cornelius Scipio (Aemilianus), Africanus [the Younger]. The son of Aemilius Paulus, Scipio Aemilianus was adopted as a child by Publius Cornelius Scipio Africanus's son, Publius Cornelius Scipio. Publius Cornelius Scipio did not ascend to lofty Roman notoriety like his father, although he was an augur and minor orator. After razing Carthage with his armies and selling the inhabitants into slavery, Scipio Aemilianus was honored by Rome with the name "Africanus" (like that of his grandfather by adoption) and later honored as Numantinus for other military exploits. Publius Cornelius Scipio Aemilianus Africanus Numantinus, or Scipio Africanus the Younger, was the leader of the Scipionic Circle, which supported many other literary figures such as Terence. "Cornelius, Scipio Aemilianus Africanus Numantinus, Publius," *Oxford Classical Dictionary,* ed. Hornblower and Spawforth.

61. The all-too-early deaths of the two figures are as ironically similar as their beginnings. Terence died at about the age of twenty-six, and Wheatley was approximately thirty-one at her death.

62. Shelley P. Haley, "Black Feminist Thought and Classics: Re-Membering, Re-Claiming, Re-empowering," *Feminist Theory and the Classics,* ed. Nancy Sorkin Rabinowitz and Amy Richlin (New York: Routledge, 1993) 23–43.

208

63. Wilson Jeremiah Moses, *The Golden Age of Black Nationalism, 1850–1925* (Hamden, CT: Archon, 1978) 10–11.

64. Alexander Pope, *Poems of Alexander Pope*, vol. 7, ed. Maynard Mack (New Haven, CT: Yale UP, 1967) 252–53.

65. John Shields uses the term "epyllion," or short epic, to describe "Goliath of Gath" and "Niobe in Distress." He notes that this is a contested term among classical scholars, but it helps describe the longer poems that display similar, if truncated, characteristics of their long epic cousins. The idea of the short epic seems quite useful in describing Wheatley's long poems, which use cultural stories of Greece and Rome, their heroes, their moral and political lessons, and their literary devices. Shields, "Phillis Wheatley's Use of Classicism" 104n.

66. Virgil 234–35.

67. Pope, *Poems* 259.

68. Byles's lines in the style of Lucan and his poems and letters to Alexander Pope present us with earlier conversations between generations of poets. We have one line of influence from Pope to Byles to Wheatley, but Wheatley also took inspiration directly from Pope's work.

69. Shields, "Phillis Wheatley's Use of Classicism" 103–4.

70. Richard Steele, *The Tatler*, ed. George A. Aitken, vol. 2 (London: Ballantyne, 1898); see issue dated 13 Dec. 1709 (p. 378).

71. For further discussion, see Benjamin J. Sadock, M.D., and Virginia A. Sadock, M.D., eds., *Comprehensive Textbook of Psychiatry*, vol. 1 (Philadelphia: Lippincott, 2000) 620–24.

72. Mandala-type forms appear in a number of world cultures, giving the Jungian theory a special place in historical, spiritual, and other projects that seek to find unifying themes across human communities.

73. Sadock and Sadock 807–9.

74. See Martin H. Teicher, "Scars That Won't Heal: The Neurobiology of Child Abuse," *Scientific American* 286.3 (Mar. 2002): 68–75, for a generally accessible description of the medical findings at a number of research sites around the nation. For more in-depth research analyses, see M. D. De Bellis, M. S. Keshavan, D. B. Clark, B. J. Casey, J. N. Giedd, A. M. Boring, K. Frustaci, and N. D. Ryan, "Developmental Traumatology, Part 2: Brain Development," *Biological Psychiatry* 45.10 (15 May 1999): 1271–84; and Martin H. Teicher, "Wounds That Time Won't Heal: The Neurobiology of Child Abuse," *Cerebrum* 2.4 (2000): 50–67.

75. Carla Williard, "Wheatley's Turns of Praise: Heroic Entrapment and the Paradox of Revolution," *American Literature* 67.2 (1995): 223–56.

76. Mason 48.

77. Ovid [Publius Ovidius Naso], *Metamorphoses*, trans. Sir Samuel Garth, John Dryden, Alexander Pope, Joseph Addison, and William Congreve (1742; New York: Heritage, 1961) 177.

2. The Virtuous Voice of Frederick Douglass

1. Unnamed reporter, qtd. by John W. Blassingame, introduction to series one, *The Frederick Douglass Papers*, ed. John W. Blassingame, vol. 1 (New Haven, CT: Yale UP, 1979) xlvii. This source is cited hereafter as *Douglass Papers*; all references are to series one, *Speeches, Debates, and Interviews* (5 vols.).

2. Frederick Douglass, *My Bondage and My Freedom* (New York: Miller, 1855) 359.

3. James M. Gregory, *Frederick Douglass: The Orator* (1893; Chicago: Afro-Am, 1969) 19–20.

4. Ruggles argued that unless they were educated, blacks would be "*depressed and degraded.*" With education blacks could demonstrate to whites that they were equally capable of "indefinite Expansion." David Ruggles to Gerrit Smith, 22 Apr. 1836, Gerrit Smith Papers, Syracuse University Library, Syracuse, NY.

5. "When the white abolitionist Samuel J. May visited New Bedford in 1835, he observed that Johnson 'has conciliated the respect of the community in which he dwells . . . by his uniformly upright conduct and modest manners.' May said that through industry and thrift Johnson had built up 'a very pretty estate, and has found time to attend to the cultivation of his mind.'" Kathryn Grover and Carl J. Cruz, "Nathan Johnson Set Abolitionist's Course," *South Coast Today*, 6 Feb. 2000, accessed 13 July 2010 <http://www.s-t.com/daily/02–00/02–06–00/a01lo211.htm>.

6. Gregory 92.

7. Gregory 210. We might note that although Douglass and Gregory do not specify which of "Rome's ancient senators and statesmen" Douglass is reading, the senators who left writings of note include Cicero, Cato the Elder, and both Pliny the Elder and the Younger.

8. Qtd. in Gregory 210.

9. In volume 2 of *The Frederick Douglass Papers* (1982), there are nine references to African languages, people, and locations, including Abyssinia, Ethiopia, and Egypt. Twelve references to ancient Greece or Rome exist, including discussions of classical slavery, the works of Herodotus, the works of Aeschylus, and the Oracle of Dodona. The depth and scope of references increases through the Civil War and Reconstruction periods.

10. *Douglass Papers* 2:508.

11. Caleb Bingham, *The Columbian Orator*, ed. David Blight (New York: New York UP, 1998), xiii–xxvii.

12. *Douglass Papers* 1:xxix–xxx. Editor John W. Blassingame notes a variety of classically tinged descriptions of Douglass.

13. *Douglass Papers* 1:lxix, xxxv.

14. For an introduction to the discussion, see the previously cited volumes by John W. Eadie, Richard Beale Davis, Meyer Reinhold, Carl J. Richard, and Carolyn Winterer, as well as John C. Shields, *The American Aeneas: The Classical Origin of the American Self* (Knoxville: U of Tennessee P, 2001).

15. See, for example, Philip S. Foner, ed., *Frederick Douglass on Women's Rights* (Westport, CT: Greenwood, 1976).

16. Deborah E. McDowell, "In the First Place: Making Frederick Douglass and the Afro-American Narrative Tradition," *Critical Essays on Frederick Douglass*, ed. William L. Andrews (Boston: G. K. Hall, 1991) 192–214.

17. Winterer, *Culture* 44.

18. Winterer, *Culture* 45.

19. Winterer, *Culture* 2.

20. Winterer, *Culture* 47.

21. Even Jackson eventually imported classical and Greek Revival themes into his fire-damaged and reconstructed mansion, The Hermitage.

22. Winterer, *Culture* 42.

23. Winterer, *Culture* 36.

24. Winterer, *Culture* 60.

25. Winterer, *Culture* 1.

26. Colonization, the plan to solve slavery and race problems by shipping blacks back to Africa, offered a convenient outlet for those slaveholders and whites disenchanted or morally opposed to slavery but unwilling to tolerate social equality with blacks. As Henry Wiencek observes, "Some abolitionists such as those organized by William Lloyd Garrison, denounced the group as a fraud, a mere sop to the consciences of slaveholders willing to free a few people, but unwilling to part with slavery itself." But to many slaveholders, like Robert Hairston, who felt misgivings over slavery, the American Colonization Society's program seemed to be the only reasonable and practical way to bring an end to the "peculiar institution." Henry Wiencek, *The Hairstons: An American Family in Black and White* (New York: St. Martin's, 1999) 87.

27. In the case of *Scott v. Negro London* (3 Cranch 324, 7 U.S. 324, 2 L.Ed. 455 [U.S.Dist.Col.,1806]), a slave was brought into Virginia by a man who claimed ownership. However he did not take the oath of ownership required by law. Eleven months afterward, the actual owner of the slave came to Virginia and took the necessary oath. The court held that the ownership fraud did not mean that the slave was entitled to his freedom. In *Scott v. Negro Ben* (6 Cranch 3, 10 U.S. 3, 3 L.Ed. 135 [U.S.Dist.Col., 1810]), it was held that the freedom detailed under Act Md.1783, which prohibited bringing slaves into Maryland, was not secured if the master failed to prove, "to the satisfaction of the naval officer or collector of the tax, that such slave had resided three years in the United States," even though such proof was required by the act.

28. *Dred Scott v. Sandford* (60 U.S. [19 How.] 393 [1857]) effectively dismantled the Missouri Compromise, with Chief Justice Roger B. Taney determining that African Americans could not be considered citizens of the United States and that the Negro "had no rights which the white man was bound to respect." Importing slaves was banned in the United States after June 1, 1808, and legislation in 1820 made importation a form of piracy with the penalty of death. Nonetheless, in *The Antelope* (25 U.S. 546, 6 L.Ed. 723, 12 Wheat. 546 [U.S. Ga.,1827]), the U.S. Supreme Court ruled that the international slave trade did not violate U.S. law, and slave trading was not piracy unless the laws of another country made it so. Even if slavery or transportation were illegal in the United States, a ship transporting slaves on the high seas could not be seized merely on that count. Although Chief Justice John Marshall argued in *The Antelope* that slavery was contrary to natural law, the court continued to affirm state sovereignty on the issue of slavery and to uphold fugitive slave codes.

29. The *Amistad* case (15 Pet. 518, 40 U.S. 518, 10 L.Ed. 826 [U.S.Conn.,1841]), helped rally abolitionist sentiment, drew prominent black and white figures into the spotlight in the antislavery cause, and focused international attention on American slavery.

30. In *Ableman* (21 How. 506, 62 U.S. 506, 16 L.Ed. 169 [US Wis 1858]), the court upheld the validity of the 1850 Fugitive Slave Act, confirming the supremacy of slaveholders' right to conduct fugitive manhunts over northern state sovereignty and establishing yet another touchstone for national and international foment over slavery.

31. David Walker's 1829 *Appeal* boldly defined the cultural choice for America as one of African American rights or revolution and illustrated the antidemocratic and counterrevolutionary nature of American racism. Nat Turner's 1831 revolt underscored African Americans' resistance to white American oppression, but it also galvanized the American South to apply even more restrictive slave codes. Increasingly harsh laws effectively eliminated the last vestiges of black humanity and rights, including education. South Carolina passed legislation in 1835 that made it a crime to educate African Americans.

32. Roderick M. Stewart, "The Claims of Frederick Douglass Philosophically Considered," *Frederick Douglass: A Critical Reader*, ed. Bill E. Lawson and Frank M. Kirkland, (Malden, MA: Blackwell, 1999) 145–72.

33. Benjamin Quarles, "Letters from Negro Leaders to Gerrit Smith," *Journal of Negro History* 27.4 (Oct. 1942): 435, accessed 20 Nov. 2003 <http://links.jstor.org/sici?sici=0022-2992%28194210%2927%3A4%3C432%3ALFNLTG%3E2.0.CO%3B2-A>; Daniel A. Payne, *Recollections of Seventy Years* (New York: Arno, 1968) 325.

34. Frederick Douglass, *My Bondage and My Freedom*, ed. William L. Andrews (Champaign: U of Illinois P, 1987) 23. *Valeo (-ere)* generally translates as

212

to be strong, vigorous, or healthy; to have force, prevail, and so on. *Vale* or *valeas* operates as a farewell, with the obvious attributes of being well or vigorous.

35. Douglas Blane, "Created Equal," *Avenue—The University of Glasgow* 32 (May 2002), accessed 18 Nov. 2003 <http://www.gla.ac.uk:443/avenue/32/na2. html, 20 >.

36. It would be incorrect to suggest that only African American clergy and scholars were engaged in endeavors that served to combat the prevalent feeling among whites that blacks were ignorant or barbaric. Edmonia Lewis, an Oberlin graduate and accomplished sculptor of neoclassical, African-American, and Native American subjects, moved to Rome in 1864 and began to sculpt in a studio once occupied by Antonio Canova. She periodically returned to the United States to display works, including the famous *Cleopatra,* now in the Smithsonian. Frederick Douglass and Helen Pitts Douglass visited her in Rome in 1887. Douglass's diary noted that speaking Italian for so long had "impaired" her English, and Benjamin Quarles also notes that she "was delighted to see them and lent Helen some books." Douglass was clearly aware of her classically influenced creations. See Benjamin Quarles, *Frederick Douglass* (Washington, D.C.: Associated Publishers, 1948) 310.

37. Winterer, *Culture* 14.

38. For instance, unlike other Gospels, Mark 15:16 explains: "And the soldiers led [Jesus] away into the hall, called Praetorium; and they call together the whole band."

39. Matthew 3:9 and Luke 3:8 both detail John the Baptist's admonition to Jewish listeners: "And think not to say within yourselves, We have Abraham to *our* father: for I say unto you, that God is able of these stones to raise up children unto Abraham." Douglass uses this on more than one occasion to drive home the failings of the descendants of the Founding Fathers in pursuing and protecting liberty and the virtues of the American Revolution. "What to the Slave is the Fourth of July?" contains the most notable incidence of this: "It was fashionable, hundreds of years ago, for the children of Jacob to boast, we have 'Abraham to our father,' when they had long lost Abraham's faith and spirit."

40. Wilson J. Moses, *Alexander Crummell* (New York: Oxford UP, 1989) 26.

41. James W. C. Pennington, *The Fugitive Blacksmith; or, Events in the History of James W. C. Pennington, Pastor of a Presbyterian Church, New York, Formerly a Slave in the State of Maryland, United States,* 3rd ed. (1850; London: Gilpin; Westport, CT.: Negro UP, 1971) 56–57. Pennington writes, "My dear friend, W.W., . . . cited to me various instances of coloured persons, of whom I had not heard before, and who had distinguished themselves for learning, such as Bannicker [*sic*], Wheatley, and Francis Williams." Author Anne Plato, a parishioner and literary protégé of Pennington's goes so far as

to appropriate Wheatley's verses in her *Essays; Including Biographies and Miscellaneous Pieces, in Prose and Poetry.*

42. Woodson 178. Pennington also wrested more classical training and refinement in seminary at Yale in 1835. He was not allowed to join the classes at Yale, but he was permitted to sit outside the windows of the classrooms. At Heidelburg, Pennington enlisted the help of a Professor Carové to lobby the faculty. Carové argued to his colleagues that Pennington's astonishing strides since slavery in pursuit of his own education were reason enough to award the doctor of divinity degree. Pennington made it clear to the faculty that he sought the degree to use as a symbolic weapon in the fight for the freedom of his people in America.

43. Herman E. Thomas, *James W. C. Pennington: African-American Churchman and Abolitionist* (New York: Garland, 1995) 48.

44. Beverley J. F. Shaw, *The Negro in the History of Methodism* (Nashville: Parthenon, 1954) 38; Payne, *Recollections* 15.

45. "Then, on a Thursday morning, I bought a Greek grammar, a lexicon, and a Greek Testament. On the same day, I mastered the Greek alphabet; on Friday I learned to write them; on Saturday morning I translated the first chapter of Matthew's Gospel from Greek into English. My very soul rejoiced and exulted in this glorious triumph. Next came the Latin and the French" (Payne 22).

46. Frederick Douglass, "This is Not a Layman's Day, but a Bishop's Day: An Address Delivered in Baltimore, Maryland on 21 May 1894," *Douglass Papers* 5:613–16.

47. Alexander Crummell to John Jay, 12 Sept. 1851, Jay Family Papers, Butler Library, Columbia University, qtd. in Moses, *Alexander Crummell* 73.

48. Moses, *Alexander Crummell* 8.

49. Moses, *Alexander Crummell* 75.

50. Christopher Rush, *A Short Account of the Rise and Progress of the African M.E. Church in America* (New York: Zuille, 1866) 93–106, accessed 1 July 2003 <http://docsouth.unc.edu/church/rush/rush.html>.

51. Dorothy B. Porter, "The Organized Educational Activities of Negro Literary Societies, 1828–1846," *Journal of Negro Education* 5, no. 4 (Oct. 1936): 565.

52. Gregory Lampe, *Frederick Douglass: Freedom's Voice, 1818–1845* (Lansing: Michigan State UP, 1998) 34; Porter 565–66.

53. Porter 566.

54. In 1843, Payne and his compatriots rejected a man's ordination on educational grounds, which prompted an angry churchman to "demand violently whether one must read Greek, Hebrew, and Latin before he could be ordained." Later, Payne did press through a rigorous educational program for ministerial aspirants. Shaw 37–38.

55. Payne 64.

56. As Caleb Bingham insists in the opening words of his *Columbian Orator,*
a primary rhetoric manual of the nineteenth Century, the Roman orator
Cicero was emphatic that all other elements of oratory gain their power from
sound and tone: "All the former [aforementioned parts of oratory] have their
effect as they are pronounced. It is the action [pronunciation] alone which
governs in speaking; without which the best orator is of no value: and is often
defeated by one, in other respects, much his inferior." Bingham, *The Columbian Orator,* ed. David W. Blight (1797; New York: New York UP, 1998) 5.

57. Homer immediately comes to mind, but even Socrates's commentary on
education in Book II of *The Republic* depends on a specific oral exercise
within the discussion to arrive at the lesson of the best education: "Come
then, and let us pass a leisure hour in storytelling, and our story shall be the
education of our heroes." Plato, *Republic,* trans. Benjamin Jowett (New York:
Barnes & Noble, 1999) II:56.

58. Lampe 7.

59. Frederick Douglass, *Life and Times of Frederick Douglass* (1892; New York:
Collier, 1962) 90–91; William A. McFeely, *Frederick Douglass* (New York:
Norton, 1991) 37–38.

60. Frank Towers, "African-American Baltimore in the Era of Frederick Douglass,"
ATQ [*American Transcendental Quarterly*] 9.3 (Sept. 1995): 172–73.

61. Towers 173.

62. Towers 173–74.

63. The New England self-improvement societies were particularly active. The
Boston society included a series of lectures in the humanities and sciences,
including the subject "Athens." Porter 570.

64. Bingham 3.

65. Bingham's *Orator* was a companion text to his earlier work *The American
Preceptor* (1794), which was dedicated to the teaching of moral virtues to
young men and included one hundred selections of prose and poetry. *The
Columbian Orator* went through twenty-three editions and became a cen-
terpiece of education throughout rural America and the South. Bingham's
text was influential not only for Douglass but also for Abraham Lincoln.
The *Orator* reflects the American peculiarity of eschewing aristocratic
language while reaching back for Greek and Roman models of oratory.

66. Douglass, *Bondage* (1855 ed.) 156–58.

67. Bingham xiv.

68. Cicero, *De Oratore,* LIX, trans. J. S. Watson (New York: Harper, 1895) 258.

69. Cicero, LIV, LXXXIII.

70. Walter J. Ong. *The Presence of the Word: Some Prolegomena for Cultural
and Religious History* (New Haven, CT: Yale UP, 1967).

71. Canova's 1821 sculpture of George Washington depicted the first President in the garb of a Roman general, reclining with a gold stylus in hand and inscribing a tablet. It was purchased by the State of North Carolina and resided in the State Capitol until a fire destroyed the work in 1831. The king of Italy graciously donated a copy, made from Canova's original models, which presently stands in the North Carolina State Capitol. That a southern state government possessed a Canova sculpture suggests the level of classicism in the early nineteenth-century South and illustrates the pretensions to classical republicanism that Douglass would later assail.

72. Bingham 30.

73. Bingham 30.

74. Bingham 59.

75. Bingham 211.

76. Bingham's selections for *The Columbian Orator* reflect distinctly abolitionist sentiments. The "Dialogue Between a Master and a Slave" was a favorite of Douglass's, and "A Slave of Barbary" provided a dramatic exploration of slavery. Douglass declared that the *Orator* had laid out for him "the principles of liberty, and poured floods of light on the nature and character of slavery." Douglass, *Bondage* (1987 ed.) 99–100.

77. *Douglass Papers* 1:xl.

78. *Douglass Papers* 1:3.

79. Lampe 67.

80. Marcus Tullius Cicero, *On the Parts of Oratory,* trans. H. Rackham, 2 vols., Loeb Classical Library (Cambridge, MA: Harvard UP, 1982), 2:viii, 28.

81. Cicero, *On Invention,* trans. H. M. Hubbell, 2 vols., Loeb Classical Library (London: William Heinemann, 1960) I:xvi. 22–xvii. 23, 45–47.

82. "During the first three or four months my speeches were almost exclusively made up of narrations of my own personal experience as a slave. 'Let us have the facts,' said the people. So also said Friend George Foster, who always wished to pin me down to my simple narrative. 'Give us the facts,' said Collins, 'we will take care of the philosophy.' Just here arose some embarrassment. It was impossible for me to repeat the same old story, month after month, and to keep up my interest in it. It was new to the people, it is true, but it was an old story to me; and to go through with it night after night, was a task altogether too mechanical for my nature. 'Tell your story, Frederick,' would whisper my revered friend, Mr. Garrison, as I stepped upon the platform. I could not always follow the injunction, for I was now reading and thinking. New views of the subject were being presented to my mind. It did not entirely satisfy me to *narrate* wrongs; I felt like *denouncing* them. I could not always curb my moral indignation for the perpetrators of slaveholding villainy, long enough for a circumstantial statement of the facts which I felt almost sure everybody must know. Besides, I was growing,

and needed room. 'People won't believe you ever was a slave, Frederick, if you keep on this way,' said friend Foster. 'Be yourself,' said Collins, 'and tell your story.' 'Better have a little of the plantation speech than not,' it was said to me; 'it is not best that you seem too learned.' These excellent friends were actuated by the best of motives, and were not altogether wrong in their advice; and still I must speak just the word that seemed to *me* the word to be spoken *by* me." Frederick Douglass, *Life and Times of Frederick Douglass* (Hartford, CT: Park, 1881) 218–19, accessed 1 May 2010 <http://docsouth. unc.edu/douglasslife/douglass.html#douglass236>.

83. *Douglass Papers* 1:3.

84. *Douglass Papers* 1:4.

85. In some of the same sections that filtered through to Bingham, Cicero is also particularly careful to emphasize that undermining the opponent is a multifaceted process. The orator gains good will from carefully recounting his own virtuous acts, but he can also gain by emphasizing the vices of his opponents, the good deeds and wisdom of the audience, and the facts of his case. Douglass's attacks on his opponents run close to Cicero's advice: "Good-will is acquired from the person of the opponents if we can bring them into hatred, unpopularity, or contempt. They will be hated if some act of theirs is presented which is base, haughty, cruel, or malicious; they will become un-popular if we present their power, political influence, wealth, family connex-ions, and their arrogant and intolerable use of these advantages, so that they seem to rely on these rather than on the justice of their case. They will be brought into contempt if we reveal their laziness, carelessness, sloth, indolent pursuits or luxurious idleness." Cicero, *On Invention* I:xvi. 22–xvii. 23, 45–47.

86. Bingham 1: 8.

87. *Douglass Papers* 1:3–4.

88. As other scholars such as Henry Louis Gates have noted, autobiographical texts gained prevalence in the late eighteenth century, with martial, court, and religious intrigue forming the core plot lines. French and English texts that promised insider tales of the upper echelons of society captured the attention of European and American readerships. Mystical and miraculous experiences of deliverance characterized the spiritual tales of this genre. A ready audience for both Douglass's powerful and provocative insider expo-sés existed by the time he emerged. Gates also argues that the picaresque genre and the sentimental novel provided even more technical convention for the slave narrative to exploit and therefore amplified its effect. Henry Louis Gates Jr., *Figures in Black: Words, Signs, and the "Racial" Self* (New York: Oxford UP, 1989), 80–83.

89. Edward E. Hairston, "A Profile of Positive Role Models for Young African-American Males," diss., Virginia Polytechnic Institute and State University, 1995, 16–17.

90. McDowell, "In the First Place" 201.

91. Bingham 10. Also, in *The Republic,* Socrates emphasizes that the guardians' training will have to be closely monitored, and music will have to be regulated and censored because individual tones and rhythms produce corresponding emotional effects that might not be desirable in the guardians.

92. *Douglass Papers* 1:4. We can only imagine the particular sounds and gestures involved in Douglass's delivery, but good, suggestive evidence exists in the known structure of slave preachers' sermons and contemporary scholarly examinations of the sermonic tradition in African-American Christianity. As a licensed A.M.E. Zion exhorter, Douglass would have known these techniques. Moreover, both A.M.E. Zion directives on preaching and *The Columbian Orator* address the appropriate and effective use of the body to excite the emotions of listeners.

93. Lampe 316.

94. Lampe 316.

95. Lampe 316.

96. Lampe 317.

97. Bingham 41–42.

98. *Douglass Papers* 1:12–13.

99. James Monroe, *Oberlin Thursday Lectures Addresses and Essays* (Oberlin, OH: Edward J. Goodrich, 1897) 84–90.

100. *Douglass Papers* 1:11.

101. Drema R. Lipscomb. "Sojourner Truth: A Practical Public Discourse," *Reclaiming Rhetorica: Women in the Rhetorical Tradition,* ed. Andrea A. Lunsford (Pittsburgh: U of Pittsburg P, 1995) 230.

102. Andrea A. Lunsford, "On Reclaiming Rhetorica," *Reclaiming Rhetorica: Women in the Rhetorical Tradition,* ed. Andrea A. Lunsford. (Pittsburgh: U of Pittsburg P, 1995) 6.

103. *Douglass Papers* 1:42.

104. Lampe 41.

105. Bingham 27–28.

106. Bingham 42.

107. *Liberator* 3 Dec. 1841: 193; Lampe 82.

108. *Herald of Freedom* 3 Dec. 1841: 162–63.

109. Bingham 27.

110. *National Anti-Slavery Standard* 2 Sept. 1841: 50; Lampe 64.

111. *Liberator* 27 Aug. 1841: 138.

112. *Douglass Papers* 1:xxix.

113. *Douglass Papers* 1:xxxiv.

114. In 71 B.C., Spartacus, a Thracian slave trained at the gladiatorial school of Batiatus in Capua, escaped with seventy to eighty gladiators and raised an army of seventy thousand slaves. Among other exploits, he turned the slaves into an impressive fighting force and defeated two consular armies and the proconsul of Cisalpine Gaul in 72 B.C. The Roman senate sent Marcus Licinius Crassus to deal with Spartacus. Spartacus had hoped to escape south from Italy over the Alps, to the South through Sicily, or to the Roman East, but Crassus and other legions under Marcus Licinius Lucullus trapped him in Southern Italy. After defeating part of Crassus's force with an army that had grown to 120,000, he was eventually defeated and assumed killed in the final battle with Crassus. The Romans crucified approximately six thousand captured slaves along the road from Rome to Capua. Spartacus has long been popularly imagined as a leader of a social revolution in a Rome torn by corruption, political infighting, and republican collapse, even though contemporary scholars have tempered their enthusiasm because Spartacus seemed more interested in escape than in changing Rome. Charles Freeman, *Egypt, Greece, and Rome* (New York: Oxford UP, 1996) 346–48; Erich Gruen, *The Last Generation of the Roman Republic* (Berkeley: U of California P, 1974) 20–22.

115. *Herald of Freedom*, 3 Dec. 1841: 162.

116. *Liberator*, 3 Dec. 1841: 197.

117. Douglass, Helen Pitts, *In Memoriam: Frederick Douglass* (Philadelphia: Yorston, 1897) 44.

118. *Douglass Papers* 1: 26–27.

119. One of the more provocative examples of this comes in the form of an 1876 sermon by A.M.E. minister Benjamin Arnett, who gave a centennial thanksgiving address at St. Paul A.M.E. Church in Urbana, Ohio, exhorting, "[W]e call on all American citizens to love their country, and look not on the sins of the past, but arming ourselves for the conflict of the future, girding ourselves in the habiliments of Righteousness, march forth with the courage of a Numidian lion and with the confidence of a Roman Gladiator, and meet the demands of the age, and satisfy the duties of the hour. Let us be encouraged in our work, for we have found the moccasin track of Righteousness all along the shore of the stream of life, constantly advancing, holding humanity with a firm hand." See "African-American Perspectives: Pamphlets from the Daniel A. P. Murray Collection, 1818 – 1907," *American Memory: Historical Collections for the National Digital Library*, Library of Congress, accessed 18 May 2009 <http://lcweb2.loc.gov/cgi-bin/query/r?ammem/murray:@field(FLD001+26022912+):@@@REF>.

120. E. Cobham Brewer, *Dictionary of Phrase and Fable*, "Lion" (Philadelphia: Altemus, 1898).

121. Lampe 192.

122. Lampe 75.

123. Rafia Zafar, "Franklinian Douglass: The Afro-American as Representative Man," *Frederick Douglass: New Literary and Historical Essays,* ed. Eric J. Sundquist (New York: Cambridge UP, 1990) 99–117.

124. In the *Magnalia Christi Americana* chapter titled *"Nehemias Americanus,"* Mather argues that John Winthrop has the virtues of Lycurgus and other classical lawgivers and could stand equal to them, but it is his combination of classical values and Christianity that makes him a superlative man. Mather starts with a quotation from Cicero and then employs Lycurgus, Numa, Plutarch, Plato, Cato, Alexander, Hannibal, and Caesar, among others, to demonstrate his virtues. Cotton Mather, *Magnalia Christi Americana: or, The Ecclesiastical History of New-England from Its First Planting, in the Year 1620, Unto the Year of Our Lord 1698* (1702; New York: Russell, 1967).

125. Jane Marsh Parker, "Reminiscences of Frederick Douglass," *Outlook* 51 (Apr. 1895): 553.

126. Douglass, *Life and Times* 384.

127. Quarles 336.

128. Maria Diedrich, *Love Across Color Lines: Ottilie Assing and Frederick Douglass* (New York: Hill & Wang, 1999) 121–27.

129. Diedrich 190–92.

130. Diedrich 223. Douglass sought a U.S. passport before acquiring a French visa. There is suspicion that he might have contemplated a long-term exile in Germany or France with Assing, had not his daughter Annie died in 1860, prompting his mournful return.

131. Ottilie Assing to Frederick Douglas, 5 Jan. 1877, *Radical Passion: Ottilie Assing's Reports from America and Letters to Frederick Douglass,* ed. Christoph Lohmann (New York: Lang, 1999) 333–34.

132. Diedrich 190–92.

133. Douglass asserts in 1843 to the Worcester County Slavery Society that abolition is "virtually and essentially a *Christian* enterprise, and is, therefore, imperative in its claims on the regard, sympathy and cooperation of the professedly Christian churches of our land." Moreover, Douglass proposed and argued a resolution in the meeting that "the hands of the American church are full of blood, and that she is not, while she continues thus, what she assumes to be, the heaven-appointed instrumentality for reforming the world." In the succeeding month, Douglass returned to Rhode Island and established a long-running Sunday evening lecture series. While illustrating and decrying the heresy of slavery within the church, Douglass seems to initiate his own abolitionist reformation—complete with Sunday services. Douglass even goes so far as to say, "[T]his society [the American Anti-Slavery Society] is above either Church or State; *it is moving both,* daily, more and more." *Douglass Papers* 1:22.

134. Zafar 114.

135. Henry Louis Gates Jr., "From Wheatley to Douglass: The Politics of Displacement," *Frederick Douglass: New Literary and Historical Essays,* ed. Eric Sundquist (New York: Cambridge UP, 1990) 48.

136. Frederick Douglass, "The Claims of the Negro Ethnologically Considered: An Address Delivered in Hudson, Ohio, on 12 July 1854," *Douglass Papers* 2:499.

137. Surely we must recall Mr. Severe and other overseers of Douglass's past, his detailed and much reported narrative, and what he and abolitionists called his graduation from the peculiar institution with his diploma written on his back.

138. *Douglass Papers* 2:516.

139. *Douglass Papers* 2:517.

140. *Douglass Papers* 2:517–18. Douglass paraphrases an argument of British scholar and physician, Robert G. Latham, whose *Man and His Migrations* (New York, 1852), details a relationship between the Tumali language and languages in Palestine and the Arabian Peninsula.

141. *Douglass Papers* 2:522.

142. Henry Louis Gates Jr., *Figures in Black: Word, Signs, and the "Racial" Self* (New York: Oxford UP, 1987) 14.

143. However, as his life progressed, Douglass sought to gain personal experience in most of these roles, acquiring or seeking to acquire the foundation and imprimatur to address a wide variety of virtues. He sought a commission in the United States Army but was denied, in addition to being shabbily treated in the process. His sons summed that count for him. He possessed federal appointments during his lifetime and addressed many of the most significant national and international political issues of his era, traveling around the world as a public citizen and virtual statesman.

144. In his famous "What to the Slave is the Fourth of July?" oration, Douglass tells the auditors that although they rejoice in the Founding Fathers' accomplishments, their current generation is a lesser one. They are diminished by their unwillingness to complete the establishment of liberty for all.

145. *Douglass Papers* 3:193.

146. *Douglass Papers* 3:193.

147. *Douglass Papers* 3:299–300.

148. *Douglass Papers* 3:474.

149. Again, we should recall the orations listed in *The Columbian Orator.* Douglass frequently picked up the strain of Cicero, Cato, and others who spoke out against those who looted the allies, citizens, and legacy of Rome. Both Douglass and Cato made a particular target of those who "lived by stealing" but gilded their actions by calling them something more honorable.

150. *Douglass Papers* 3:432.

151. *Douglass Papers* 3:608.

152. *Douglass Papers* 3:432–33.

153. Scholars generally accept that Nero did not set the fire of Rome but raced back from coastal leisure to direct firefighting efforts. However, the record suggests that he did lounge in full dramatic garb with his lyre to sing his original composition "The Sack of Troy." It is accurate to say that Nero used the fire to his personal and political advantage, as the succeeding persecution of Christians demonstrates. Ultimately, the question is inconsequential in determining the decadence and vileness of Nero; sufficient evidence exists of those qualities.

154. Henry Wiencek, *The Hairstons: An American Story in Black and White* (New York: St. Martin's Press, 1999) 141.

155. Douglass, *Narrative* 22.

156. Jefferson 190–91.

157. Women run the risk of being circumscribed by two particular extremes of classically influenced thought. On one hand, the most cursory investigation of history suggests that the idea that women are incapable of pure reason, remain hopelessly controlled by emotion, and present sexual and intellectual threats to the reason and piety of men has seriously restricted the position of women in Western society. The Protestant and Catholic branches of Christianity have and continue, in whole or in part, to resist including women in the church hierarchy. As late as the 1970s, some flagship American universities resisted coeducation, with many suggesting (as it had been throughout U.S. history), that coeducation would corrupt young men and masculinize young women. On the other hand, the defense of female virtue has presented other problems, particularly in the American South. As W. J. Cash illustrates in *The Mind of the South* (New York: Knopf, 1941), the "proto-Dorian" ideal of the alabaster goddess of white feminine purity had the extraordinary and endlessly troublesome effect of placing white womanhood on a pedestal. This succeeded in restricting the realm of the belle and the lady to a narrow zone of sexual purity and inaccessibility, physical inactivity, political nonagency, and virtual voicelessness. Moreover, the proto-Dorian ideal amplified the violence visited on African-Americans: black women were regarded as sexual surrogates for the inaccessible belle, while black men were seen as bestial and barbaric threats to white female purity, which had to be vanquished by the legions of virtuous and heroic southern men.

158. This calls into question whether Douglass could possibly have resisted the urge to persist in his early oratorical joust with an African American named Julius Caesar in a public forum in New York.

159. Barbara E. Johnson, "Euphemism, Understatement, and the Passive Voice: A Genealogy of Afro-American Poetry," *Reading Black, Reading Feminist*, ed.

222

Henry Louis Gates Jr. (New York: Meridian, 1990) 208. We might also read
her excessive compliance in terms of her mirroring the response of Virgil to
the demands of the state. In the midst of oppression, he writes the national
myth of Rome.

160. *Douglass Papers* 5:279–80.

161. *Douglass Papers* 5:280.

162. *Douglass Papers* 5:281.

163. *Douglass Papers* 5:306.

164. *Douglass Papers* 5:306.

165. *Douglass Papers* 5:307.

166. *Douglass Papers* 5:308.

167. *Douglass Papers* 5:322.

168. *Douglass Papers* 5:331.

169. *Douglass Papers* 5:337–38.

3. *Sine Qua Non*

1. Educator and activist Fannie Barrier Williams spearheaded the effort, and
the organizers invited a formidable group. Anna Julia Cooper (1858?–1964),
was an author, orator, educator, and activist in racial politics and the Episcopal Church. Educator and activist Frances Jackson Coppin (1837–1913)
was the first black woman to receive a college degree (from Oberlin) and
founded and headed the Philadelphia Institute for Colored Youth. Sarah
Woodson Early (1825–1907) was a notable early black educator, feminist,
and black nationalist. Hallie Quinn Brown (1845–1949), an educator and
social activist, was one of the founders of the National Association of Colored Women.

2. Shirley Wilson Logan, *We Are Coming: The Persuasive Discourse of Nineteenth Century Black Women* (Carbondale: Southern Illinois UP, 1999) 103.

3. Logan 103.

4. Logan 103.

5. Harper attended Baltimore's Academy for Negro Youth and studied Greek
and Latin there.

6. Emerson muses, "Each man is, by secret liking, connected with some district
of nature, whose agent and interpreter he is, as Linnæus, of plants; Huber, of
bees; Fries, of lichens; Van Mons, of pears; Dalton, of atomic forms; Euclid,
of lines; Newton, of fluxions." See Ralph Waldo Emerson, "Representative
Men: Seven Lectures," *Emerson: Essays and Lectures,* ed. Joel Porte (New
York: Library of America, 1983) 618. Politically, Douglass and some of his
popularly acknowledged and self-proclaimed cultural descendants became
the agents and interpreters of African Americans, if only because white

political and business leaders deemed reductionist politics expedient and the representative men suitable for use or impossible to ignore.

7. Logan 112.

8. Louis G. Harlan, *Booker T. Washington: The Making of a Black Leader, 1856–1901* (New York: Oxford UP, 1972); *Booker T. Washington: The Wizard of Tuskegee, 1901 –1915* (New York: Oxford UP, 1983).

9. William L. Andrews, "Slavery and Afro-American Literary Realism," *Slavery and the Literary Imagination,* ed. Deborah E. McDowell and Arnold Rampersad (Baltimore: Johns Hopkins UP, 1991) 73.

10. Deborah E. McDowell, "'The Changing Same': Generational Connections and Black Women Novelists," *Reading Black Reading Feminist,* ed. Henry Louis Gates Jr. (New York: Meridian, 1990) 94–95.

11. Frances E. W. Harper, *Iola Leroy, or Shadows Uplifted,* 3rd ed. (Boston: Earle, 1892) 258.

12. Starting in the late nineteenth century, middle- and upper-class African American women banded together in a variety of social, religious, and educational clubs that independently undertook the project of uplifting African American women and men in terms of middle-class propriety, including Christian morality, higher education, literary ventures, the arts, music, manners, and social and political aspirations. Like the mutual aid and self-improvement organizations that Frederick Douglass encountered, these groups linked spiritual, intellectual, and racial improvement to expanded reading; and they continued the growth of literature and literacy encouraged by such black exemplars as Wheatley, whom they lionized. Unlike Cooper and Du Bois, the societies were not fundamentally committed to critiquing or transforming Victorian morality and culture. The content of their reading was not primarily composed of classical texts; as Elizabeth McHenry's *Forgotten Readers* suggests, they often read texts that were classical in the broader sense of eighteenth- and nineteenth-century literary productions of popularly recognized merit. While such groups as the Clio Club of Denver might sustain historical discussions of the impact of barbarian invasions on Europe, they were not committed to classical study. This is not to say that the classics did not have a place in men's and women's reading societies. The Female Literary Association of Philadelphia compared its cache of books to the vault created by Demosthenes. The Boston Literary engaged in animated discussions about the best kind of literature, with a number of the male members arguing that one should "know something about the really great literature of Homer, Virgil, Dante, and Shakespeare." Some of the women members argued for more attention to books of recent vintage, and still others among the members argued for books of value rather than books of period or fame. Elizabeth McHenry, *Forgotten Readers: Recovering the Lost History of African American Literary Societies* (Durham: Duke UP, 2002) 56, 172–73, 227.

13. See Lemert's introductory chapter in Anna Julia Cooper, *The Voice of Anna Julia Cooper*, ed. Charles Lemert and Esme Bhan (New York: Rowman, 1998) 15n26, 16–17, 30.

14. Ann duCille, *The Coupling Convention* (New York: Oxford UP, 1993) 52–53, 144.

15. Vivian May, *Anna Julia Cooper, Visionary Black Feminist* (New York: Routledge, 2007) 49–51.

16. May 50.

17. Stephanie Y. Evans, *Black Women in the Ivory Tower, 1850–1954: An Intellectual History* (Gainesville: UP of Florida, 2007) 28–33.

18. Evans 144.

19. Evans 144.

20. Lemert, in Cooper 27.

21. Claudia Tate, *Domestic Allegories of Political Desire* (New York: Oxford UP, 1996) 150–60.

22. Julia Ringwood Costin, "The Women Who are Loved are Those Who are Women," rpt. in Tate 158–59.

23. Tate 156.

24. Hazel Carby, "'On the Threshold of Women's Era': Lynching, Empire, and Sexuality in Black Feminist Theory," *Race, Writing, and Difference*, ed. Henry Louis Gates Jr. (Chicago: U of Chicago P, 1985) 304.

25. Ann duCille notes Cooper's defense of the "classical" training of women, pointing out that she put her "own classical training in play" against "Lord Byron, as well as black men who would be lords" (51–52). There are no specific allusions at play in the Byron-Wordsworth passage, although Cooper is discussing women's influence on genius (see Cooper 59). DuCille neither indicates that there is anything particularly noteworthy about the classics nor discusses the potential the classics have for aiding our interpretation of Cooper. To some extent, it remains unclear whether duCille intends "classical" to mean the classics or "traditional."

26. Winterer, *Culture* 22.

27. Elizabeth Alexander, "'We Must Be About Our Father's Business': Anna Julia Cooper and the In-Corporation of the Nineteenth-Century African-American Woman Intellectual," *Signs* 20.2 (1995): 344.

28. Alexander 337.

29. Alexander 339.

30. Cooper 238–47.

31. Winterer, *Culture* 100.

32. Winterer, *Culture* 100.

33. Winterer, *Culture* 101–2.

34. Winterer, *Culture* 103.

35. Winterer, *Culture* 110–11. Noah Porter, Yale president from 1871 to 1886, argued that liberal culture was "that kind of culture which tends to perfect the man in the variety and symmetry and effectiveness of his powers, by reflection and self-knowledge, by self-control and self-expression" (qtd. in Winterer, *Culture* 111). Even a professional scientist would be improved in his science by cultural attainments in the classics.

36. Winterer, *Culture* 112.

37. Winterer, *Culture* 119.

38. Winterer, *Culture* 119.

39. Basil Gildersleeve, "The Creed of the Old South" *Atlantic Monthly* 69.411 (Jan. 1892): 75–87.

40. African Americans increasingly sought higher education from the growing number of black colleges. Wilberforce University (founded 1856), Atlanta University (1865), Fisk University (1866), St. Augustine's College (1867), Morehouse College (1867), Hampton Normal and Agricultural Institute (1868), and Tuskegee Institute (1880–81) provided a growing range of educational opportunities for African Americans and some Native Americans. Some, like Tuskegee, focused on industrial education, but the vast majority of private and church-sponsored colleges provided a mixture of humanities and classics, sciences, and sometimes industrial and agricultural topics. African Americans also increasingly found spaces in white colleges and universities. Dartmouth graduated its first black student in 1828, a Martinique native, but Oberlin College was the first American college formally to open its doors to African Americans in 1835. Richard Greener graduated Harvard in 1870. Yale's first black graduate, Edward Alexander Bouchet, came in 1874. Wellesley's first black graduate came in 1887. Radcliffe College graduated its first African-American in 1898, Smith in 1900, Mt. Holyoke's seminary in 1883, and the college in 1898. Linda M. Perkins, "The African American Female Elite: The Early History of African American Women in the Seven Sister Colleges, 1880–1960," *Harvard Educational Review* 67.4 (Winter 1997): 718–56.

41. Leona C. Gabel, *From Slavery to the Sorbonne and Beyond: The Life and Writings of Anna Julia Cooper* (Northampton, MA: Smith College, 1982) 12.

42. Cooper 86.

43. Cooper 85–86.

44. Louise Daniel Hutchinson, *A Voice from the South* (Washington, D.C.: Smithsonian, 1981) 32.

45. Hutchinson 34.

46. In Book VI, Aeneas and the Sybil descend into the underworld to visit the shade of Aeneas's father. Anchises reveals a glorious future for Rome, a

vision full of heroes and deceptively empty of scoundrels. He ends their trip through the underworld by sending Aeneas out into the world to realize the dream of Rome. Oddly enough, Anchises sends him out through a polished ivory, glittering gate—"that way the Spirits send false dreams into the world above" (lines 1196–97, p. 160). The troubling suggestion in the underworld episode is also that *pax* comes after you have slaughtered all of your enemies, foreign and domestic.

47. Sallust [Gaius Sallustius Crispus], *The War with Jugurtha*, trans. J. C. Rolfe (Cambridge, MA: Harvard UP, 1921) 4.

48. Sappho of Lesbos was renowned for the power of her very personal lyric and was likely the leader of a circle of women poets. Aspasia was the mistress of Pericles of Athens and regularly conversed with Socrates. The Amazons were a legendary race of women warriors of the age of heroes and appear in Greek lore, including *The Iliad* and as recently in history as the exploits of Alexander the Great. Their kingdom is variously located but always on the frontier or the edge of the known world.

49. In "Victorian Antigone: Classicism and Women's Education in America, 1840–1900" (*American Quarterly* 51.1 [2001]: 70–88), Caroline Winterer writes, "Heroic, ultrafeminine Antigone, however, carried at her core an enormous difficulty for Victorian writers: in rebelling against Creon, she ultimately acted alone. In contrast to the ideal woman, who was forever tethered to her web of family obligations, rebellious Antigone became 'alone,' 'anarchic,' and 'secluded.' Characteristically, Victorian commentators resolved the dilemma by defusing its political implications, stressing instead its intrinsically feminine and religious significations. For one thing, Antigone's trajectory of doom fulfilled Victorian expectations for the childless woman. Respected medical opinion in the mid-nineteenth century held that childless women—'maiden ladies'—courted physical and emotional disaster by spurning their maternal destinies. By renouncing motherhood and wifehood, maidenly Antigone had invited calamity. Authors also stressed that her solitary action, culminating in proto-Christian martyrdom, vaulted her safely beyond masculinity into hyperfemininity. While her aggressive public action, argued Woolsey, made her 'masculine,' her selflessness again rendered the gesture 'exquisitely tender and feminine.' 'Verily she is the man' rather than Creon, agreed Augustus Taber Murray (1866–1940), professor of classical literature at Stanford University, speaking of Antigone at the moment she defies the king. The moments of Antigone's masculinity in fact made her most feminine because they ended in death for her cause—they catapulted her beyond masculinity into heroic, true womanhood because they were done for family and religion. Antigone was 'no virago,' affirmed E. S. Shuckburgh in 1902, 'but a true woman' for 'doing a deed for which she knows she must die.' Biology and religion conspired to make Antigone's solitary suicide a fitting, feminine conclusion to her rebellion."

50. Cooper 51.

51. Music is equally intriguing, because a number of classical theorists, including Plato and Aristotle, discussed the effect of music on the emotions and on virtue. In Plato's *Republic,* with which Cooper was undoubtedly familiar, Socrates goes into intricate detail about the effect of the absence or presence of a variety of tones, chords, and rhythms. He linked some to virtue and others to vice and eventually established the range of music that would enhance the civilization of the city-state and provide maximum virtue for the guardian class. Cooper's "muffled chord" and "silent note" suggest that American civilization cannot be whole or virtuous without the proper tones and rhythms of the Negro—and the black woman in particular.

52. The riddle of the Sphinx has become familiar to the contemporary world: "Which creature walks on four legs in the morning, two legs in the afternoon, and three legs in the evening?" Ironically, it was Oedipus who correctly answered "man" to gain entrance into the city where his life would ultimately be ruined.

53. Cooper 51.

54. And this is no great leap even in contemporary law, much less in literary allusion. Chief Justice Warren Burger argued from the Justinian and Theodosian codes to establish historic legal roots for American law in a concurrence in *Bowers v. Hardwick* (478 U.S. 186 [1986]), and Justices Kennedy and Scalia picked up the heated discussion about the roots and nature of American law nearly twenty years later in *Lawrence v. Texas* (539 U.S. 558 [2003]).

55. Cooper 55.

56. To the extent that Cooper uses an Orientalist vehicle to arrive at an illustration of those ideas, philosophies, treatments, and abuses of women that are anti-Western, anti-Christian, and therefore barbaric, Ann duCille's criticism of her work is fitting.

57. Cooper 54.

58. Cooper 54.

59. Cooper uses the metaphor elsewhere. The unheard, unshielded women who can offer so much to the world are a "fatally beautiful class that stand shivering like a delicate plantlet before the fury of the tempestuous elements, so full of promise and possibilities, yet so sure of destruction" (60–61).

60. Helene P. Foley, "'Reverse Similes' and Sex Roles in the Odyssey." *Women in the Ancient World: The Arethusa Papers,* ed. John Perdotto and J. P. Sullivan (Albany: State U of New York P, 1984) 63.

61. Waswo 6.

62. Alexander Crummell was a thoroughly Anglican colonial missionary in Liberia. As Wilson J. Moses illustrates in *The Golden Age of Black Nationalism*

1850–1925 (41), Crummell crusaded against African cultural expressions in West Africa and ruthlessly attacked all attempts to adapt Anglican doctrine and liturgy to the African culture in Liberia.

63. Cooper 57.

64. Cooper 57.

65. Cooper argues that the church "took advantage of the barbarian's sensuous love of gaudy display and put all her magnificent garments on. She could not capture him by physical force, she would dazzle him by gorgeous spectacles. It is said that Romanism gained more in pomp and ritual during this trying period of the Dark Ages than throughout all her former history" (58).

66. Cooper 56.

67. "Says Chaucer with characteristic satire, speaking of the Friars, 'Women may now go safely up and doun, / In every bush, and under every tree, / Ther is non other incubus but he, / And he will don hem no dishonour'" (Cooper 56).

68. Cooper 55.

69. Many discussions of Cooper mention *Le Pelerinage de Charlemagne,* but scholars do not regularly describe the relatively humorous twelfth-century epic poem or *chanson de geste,* which has an intriguing similarity to the folk tales of one-upsmanship and comeuppance that were common to the African American and Appalachian folk traditions. Bawdiness, piety, supernatural elements, redemption, and the tall tale are all present. *Le Pelrinage* recounts the story of Charlemagne, who asks his queen if he is not the greatest king she knows. He hears from his wife that Hugo the Strong of Constantinople might surpass him, and he grows angry with her. In irritation, he travels to Constantinople with twelve peers—by way of Jerusalem, where the Patriarch gives him holy relics and the title of emperor. He reaches Constantinople to find that the city is at peace and beautiful and that Hugo is strong and handsome. Hugo treats them as guests and lodges them in luxury. While in their rooms, Charlemagne and his men become intoxicated and start telling tall tales: Charlemagne says he can cut a man and a horse in half in one blow; one peer says he can blow all the gates and doors open with the blow of a horn; and so on. Unknown to the group, Hugo has a spy listening and reports back. The men are embarrassed before Hugo, and on pain of death they are prompted to do all their boasted acts. They retire to pray to God before the relics, an angel appears, and God gives them the power to do their deeds. Hugo allows them to go free, with peace between the kingdoms and Charlemagne reconciled to his queen.

70. Cooper 58.

71. William Kerrigan and Gordon Braden, *The Idea of the Renaissance* (Baltimore: Johns Hopkins UP, 1989) 5.

72. Cooper 61.

73. Cooper 62.

74. Cooper 78.

75. Cooper also sidestepped the individual politics of her black women contemporaries and retained full control over the image of black women she constructed. Black club women and intellectuals of the era occupied a number of positions on the political spectrum, not all of which Cooper embraced. For instance, at the Columbian Exposition, Cooper responded to Fannie Barrier Williams's speech in her own "The Intellectual Progress of Colored Women in the United States Since Emancipation." As Lemert and Bhan point out, Williams was of the affluent classes, fair-skinned, temperate, and spoke of the moral and intellectual importance of black women to America. However, Cooper seems to have interpreted Williams's position as far too elitist, for she was careful to take a more provocative position and argue for broader consideration for her "constituency," the poor black women of the South.

In *Voice*'s chapter "Status of Woman in America," Cooper does pause to list black women of substantial achievement: Frances E. W. Harper, Sojourner Truth, Amanda Smith, Sarah Early, Martha Briggs, Charlotte Forten Grimke, Hallie Q. Brown, and Fanny Jackson Coppin. However, she is careful to point out that "these women represent all shades of belief and as many departments of activity" but have in common their "sympathy to the oppressed race in America and the consecration of their several talents in whatever line to the work of its deliverance and development" (Cooper 115–16).

76. Cooper 62.

77. In Book IX of *The Aeneid*, Ascanius, or Iulus, the son of Aeneas and Cruesa's and the young hope of the new Rome, takes as his first battle kill the boasting Numanus, who "stalked before the front lines, shouting things / both worthy and unworthy to be spoken." Interestingly, Numanus goads the Trojan/Romans regarding their fluffy robes of satin and purple, sleeves on their tunics, and ribboned helmets, observing also that they enjoy dancing and other unmanly things. He compares them to his Latin "sturdy race," who expose their children to the elements and train in warfare, frugality, and industry and who are also superior to "fable-babbling Ulysses" and the Greeks. After Ascanius sends an arrow through Numanus's "hollow temples," Apollo descends and cautions him, "enough of war," and not to take up the tools of war. His fate is to build civilization, under which all wars will end. Virgil 236.

78. Virgil's *Aeneid* also raises the question of the nature of human suffering, ambition, and progress. In Book IX, Nisus and Euryalus ponder the nature of their ambitions: "And Nisus says: 'Euryalus, is it / the gods who put this fire into our minds/or is it that each man's relentless longing / becomes a god to him? Long has my heart/been keen for battle or some mighty act; / it cannot be content with peace or rest'" (lines 243–48, p. 218).

79. Cooper 59.

80. In Book XI of *The Odyssey,* Odysseus travels to the underworld and sees a variety of warriors fallen in the Trojan War. Among them are Agamemnon and Achilles. Achilles argues that Odysseus should not gild the lily in describing his death as glorious. The fame means nothing to Achilles; he cares only to know that his son is alive and well. According to Achilles, he would rather be alive as the servant of some poor man than be in the underworld as the shade of a famous but dead warrior.

81. Cooper 62.

82. Cooper 64.

83. Cooper 121. Oddly enough, Cooper does employ the language of conquest in her discussion of Christianity. The only aggressive, imperialist project Cooper will tolerate is that of Christian conquest: "We believe in the Holy Catholic Church. We believe that however gigantic and apparently remote the consummation, the Church will go on conquering and to conquer till the kingdoms of this world, not excepting the black man and the black woman of the South, shall have become the kingdoms of the Lord and of his Christ" (70).

84. Hutchinson 59.

85. Cooper 86–87.

86. Cooper 62. Critics may chafe at the idea of the educated elites uplifting the masses, but escaped slaves, from William Wells Brown to Frederick Douglass to Harriet Jacobs to Solomon Northup, painstakingly revealed the traumatic physical, psychological, moral, and intellectual damage done to the black masses in slavery. A mere twenty-seven years beyond emancipation, it was more than reasonable for Cooper to suggest that a mass of former slaves only one generation away from whips and chains would need intracultural intervention by its small but active educated population. Even contemporary analyses of such traumatic damage would suggest a necessary course of multilayered intervention to restore victims, even for those who were resilient enough to be functional.

87. Cooper 80.

88. Cooper 79.

89. Cooper 79.

90. Cooper 87.

91. Cooper 82.

92. Cooper 82.

93. Cooper 83.

94. Grant Allen, "Plain Words on the Woman Question," *Fortnightly Review* 52 (Oct. 1889): 448–58.

95. Cooper 175.

96. Cooper 174.

97. W. E. B. Du Bois, "The Talented Tenth," qtd. in Alexander 341.

98. Cooper 63.

99. Anderson 30.

100. Unfortunately for many, including Cooper, that program of training which elucidated the rights of humanity and encouraged virtue, heroism, and a thoughtful masculinity ran quite afoul of the virtual surrender of civil rights and political power advocated by black male leaders such as Booker T. Washington. The highly political Washington, D.C., school board accused her of insubordination, stemming from her refusal to accept new, inferior curriculum and texts for M Street students. According to Sharon Harley, Congress had determined to provide the students with "a course of study commensurate with their alleged inferior abilities," and the school board was more than happy to comply. Cooper was determined to defend the depth and scope of subjects provided to African-American students. See Sharon Harley, "Anna J. Cooper: A Voice for Black Women," *The Afro-American Woman: Struggles and Images,* ed. Sharon Harley and Rosalyn Terborg-Penn (Port Washington, NY: Kennikat, 1978) 78.

Cooper's commitment to the scope and rigor of this classical education and her understanding of the classics as the cultural province of both African Americans and whites were the primary reasons for her suffering. In 1905–06, Cooper found herself under assault at M Street and in danger of losing her job. Washington's agents and white Washington, D.C., school board members who were inclined to diminish the curriculum attempted to have her removed as principal by whatever means were required. She was first accused of scholarly and administrative failings and then rumored to have had a sexual affair with one of her adult foster children, a scandal that played out in the pages of the *Washington Post.*

The kind of persecution and political intimidation that Cooper experienced during her years in Washington, D.C., was nothing extraordinary in the age of Booker T. Washington. Washington's Atlanta Compromise address of 1895, the same year as Frederick Douglass's death, heralded the heyday of the theory and practice of industrial education and racial submission. Moreover, Washington's great power and influence within an increasingly retrenched white society created an opportunity for him to exert an oppressive, if not vicious influence on the entirety of African America. According to Louis Harlan, Washington used his power to "keep them [southern blacks] down on the farm," own and influence the black press, intimidate black college professors and administrators, and control the white funds that supported black artists of all varieties. He regularly used informants and spies to infiltrate other black organizations and report to him, and he used the white press and law enforcement to further intimidate foes. "In all the activity of this Tuskegee Machine," writes Harlan, "was a determination to crush rash militants who were more and more openly denouncing him as a traitor to his race." Louis R. Harlan, *Booker T. Washington in Perspective*, ed. Raymond W. Smock (Jackson, MS: UP of Mississippi, 1988) 7–8.

101. Alexander 338.

4. *Quo Vadis?*

1. The *trivium* (grammar, logic, and rhetoric) and the *quadrivium* (arithmetic, music, geometry, and astronomy) composed the liberal arts of the Middle Ages.

2. Francis L. Broderick, *W. E. B. Du Bois: Negro Leader in a Time of Crisis* (Stanford, CA: Stanford UP, 1959) 9–18.

3. Keith E. Byerman, *Seizing the Word: History, Art, and Self in the Work of W. E. B. Du Bois* (Athens: U of Georgia P, 1994) 20–22.

4. Byerman 21.

5. Zhang Juguo, *W. E. B. Du Bois: The Quest for the Abolition of the Color Line* (New York: Routledge, 2001) 6.

6. Wilson J. Moses, *Black Messiahs and Uncle Toms: Social and Literary Manipulations of a Religious Myth* (University Park: Pennsylvania State UP, 1982) 114–15.

7. Wilson J. Moses. *Afrotopia: The Roots of African American Popular History* (Cambridge, UK: Cambridge UP, 1998, 2008) 27–40.

8. Moses, *Afrotopia* 138.

9. Moses, *Afrotopia* 151.

10. *On Duties* has already been introduced; but additionally, *Against Verres* suggests Cicero's incredulity that such rapacious liquidation of the assets of the Roman people in Sicily (to be converted into personal gain and numerous bribes) could occur under the governorship of one man, Verres, without the level of wholesale abandonment of civic duty registering as insanity.

11. Cornel West, "Black Strivings in a Twilight Civilization," rpt. in *The Cornel West Reader* (New York: Basic, 1999) 88.

12. West 88.

13. West 90.

14. West 90.

15. West 90–91.

16. It is a false dichotomy to suggest, as West does, that one must either embrace the rough masses and see them as having the wherewithal to teach the lessons of life worth learning or see them as degraded masses, full of folk faith and ignorance and needing strong leadership by their betters. There was, and remains, good reason to see some of the impoverished and

uneducated population as possessing virtues and insights, but there is no doubt that some in the same population have odious qualities that must be rooted out. One of the very elements West charges that Du Bois is philosophically unusable for is the gangsterization of life in the contemporary era. Gangsterization certainly exists in its own way on Wall Street and in Washington, D.C., but in its common iteration, it has been unrelentingly destructive of black civilization. Little about it is edifying.

17. West 92; Cicero, *On Duties.*

18. Arnold Rampersad, *The Art and Imagination of W. E. B. Du Bois* (Cambridge, MA: Harvard UP, 1976) vii.

19. Rampersad 173.

20. Moses, *Golden Age* 133–34.

21. The influence of German classicism in the nineteenth century is well noted. Du Bois's and Crummell's classical training is apparent in their educational history and writings. Blyden was a professor of classics at Liberia College.

22. Broderick 3.

23. W. E. B. Du Bois, *Against Racism: Unpublished Essays, Papers, Addresses, 1887–1961,* ed. Herbert Aptheker (Amherst: U of Massachusetts P, 1985) 6, 10–12.

24. Broderick 9. Livy's *History of Rome,* Book 21, examines the Second Punic War and the nature and character of the major actors in the political and military conflict, including Hannibal.

25. P. Cornelius Tacitus, *The Annals and Histories,* trans. Alfred Church and J. Brodribb (Chicago: University of Chicago P, 1952), v.

26. Broderick 24; W. E. B. Du Bois, *Dusk of Dawn: An Essay Toward the Autobiography of a Race Concept* (New York: Harcourt, 1940) 38.

27. Rampersad 36.

28. Rampersad 36.

29. Brian L. Johnson, *W. E. B. Du Bois: Towards Agnosticism, 1868–1934* (New York: Rowman, 2008).

30. Rampersad 37.

31. Rampersad 37.

32. Rampersad 39.

33. Rampersad 45.

34. Broderick 29.

35. In *Souls,* Du Bois insists that civic virtue, political activism, and interest in civil rights must be highly recommended to masses.

36. In *Souls,* Du Bois's women characters are not necessarily triumphant, but they are largely characterized as having inclinations toward lofty social, intellectual, or political goals. Josie, like her mother, is formidable in the

household and wants to live "like folks," hungering for something more than the economic progress being discussed in the chapter. Her sad end is, like those of other characters, a result of not having received the opportunity to pursue more than just economic improvement. The futility of the struggle of blacks who have great intellectual or heroic potential to build the mundane and unlikely Washingtonian economic dream is the point of the chapter. John Jones's sister in "The Coming of John" asks John about the sadness that seems to come from education and enlightenment about the state of blacks in America. She tells him that she wants to be sad as well, clearly choosing to pursue dangerous and burdensome knowledge instead of staying blissfully ignorant. After John's death, she remains the one possible hope for enlightening and liberating the blacks of Altamaha, Georgia.

37. Du Bois, *Souls* 57–58.

38. This mythological touchstone opens at least one other portal for criticizing Washington's industrial education and material accretion platform. The intellectual freedom, advancement, and professional expertise demonstrated by Cooper and enabled by the higher education of women comes under serious pressure, if not into certain danger, by Washington's concentration on domestic skills and lower clerical and industrial training for women. If Washington finds no value in a male classicist or linguist, a comparable female scholar must hold even less worth for him.

39. Du Bois, *Souls* 55.

40. Du Bois, *Souls* 55.

41. "Lachesis," *A Classical Dictionary: containing an account of the principal proper names mentioned in ancient authors and intended to elucidate all the important points connected with the geography, history biography, mythology, and fine arts of the Greeks and Romans: together with an account of coins, weights, and measures, with tabular values of the same,* by Charles Anthon (New York: Harper, 1841); "Lachesis," *Harpers Dictionary of Classical Literature and Antiquities,* ed. Harry Thurston Peck (New York: Harper, 1896).

42. Du Bois, *Souls* 55.

43. Du Bois, *Souls* 37.

44. Cato's Conspiracy or the Stono Rebellion, as it was variously called, was an attempt by about eighty slaves to arm themselves and march to Spanish Florida from Stono, South Carolina. They fought an engagement with a South Carolina militia before the rebellion was crushed.

45. Du Bois, *Souls* 39.

46. Du Bois, *Souls* 37–39.

47. Carole Lynn Stewart. "Challenging Liberal Justice: The Talented Tenth Revisited," *Re-cognizing W. E. B. Du Bois in the Twenty-first Century,* ed. Mary Keller and Chester J. Fontenot Jr. (Macon, GA: Mercer UP, 2007) 117–23.

48. Du Bois, *Souls* 73.

49. Rampersad 29.

50. W. E. B. Du Bois, "Jefferson Davis as a Representative of Civilization," *W. E. B. Du Bois: A Reader,* ed. David Levering Lewis (New York: Holt, 1995) 17.

51. In Book VIII of *The Republic,* Socrates examines four forms of government and how the perfect form, aristocracy, deteriorates into the worst form, democracy. In Book V of the *Politics,* Aristotle also addresses the decline of states. In both Socrates's and Aristotle's examinations, greed, perversions of liberty, and the reliance on force are apparent.

52. Wilson J. Moses, *Alexander Crummell* (New York: Oxford, 1989) 294–95. Moses rightly notes that Du Bois's "antidemocratic, authoritarian, racial chauvinistic strain was always at war with his proletarian sentiments." He had an affinity for strong men, elitism, and the prospect of enlightened despotism that was clearly in conflict with the democratic ideals he championed.

53. Du Bois, *Souls* 18.

54. Du Bois, *Souls* 18.

55. Du Bois, *Souls* 65.

56. Booker T. Washington, "The Atlanta Exposition Address," rpt. in Gates and Oliver's edition of Du Bois, *Souls* 169.

57. Du Bois, *Souls* 40.

58. Du Bois, *Souls* 34–35.

59. In Mark 5:8–13, Jesus heals the Gadarene Demoniac: "For he said unto him, Come out of the man, *thou* unclean spirit. / And he asked him, What *is* thy name? And he answered, saying, My name *is* Legion: for we are many. / And he besought him much that he would not send them away out of the country. / Now there was there nigh unto the mountains a great herd of swine feeding. / And all the devils besought him, saying, Send us into the swine, that we may enter into them. / And forthwith Jesus gave them leave. And the unclean spirits went out, and entered into the swine; and the herd ran violently down a steep place into the sea (they were about two thousand), and were choked in the sea."

60. Du Bois, *Souls* 35.

61. Du Bois, *Souls* 48.

62. Du Bois, *Souls* 47.

63. Nellie McKay, "W. E. B. Du Bois: The Black Women in His Writings—Selected Fictional and Autobiographical Portraits," *Critical Essays on W. E. B Du Bois,* ed. William L. Andrews (Boston: G. K. Hall, 1985) 237.

64. Du Bois, *Souls* 47.

65. Amazon queen Penthelisea joined the Trojan cause, but she fell at the hands of Achilles. The Greek hero looked into her eyes at her death; and, tragically, only then did they fall madly in love.

236

66. Page duBois, *Centaurs and Amazons: Women and the Prehistory of the Great Chain of Being* (Ann Arbor: U of Michigan P, 1991).

67. Du Bois, *Souls* 52.

68. Du Bois, *Souls* 51.

69. Du Bois, *Souls* 51.

70. Du Bois, *Souls* 41.

71. Du Bois, *Souls* 50.

72. Du Bois, *Souls* 11.

73. Du Bois, *Souls* 12.

74. Du Bois, *Souls* 14.

75. Du Bois, *Souls* 15–16.

76. Moss 10.

77. Du Bois, *Souls* 5.

78. Du Bois, *Souls* 73.

79. Du Bois, *Souls* 74. Remarkably, Du Bois's statement and his imagined visit to the "gilded halls" somewhere between earth and the stars recall Dante's journey in the *Inferno*. In Canto IV, Dante enters the first Circle of Hell where all those of the pagan world who were virtuous but lived before Christ and those afterward who were without baptism exist in the lands and great castle of Limbo. Among the great minds there, the five greatest writers—Homer, Virgil (Dante's guide), Horace, Ovid, and Lucan—greet and converse with Dante. In a moment of historic self-promotion, Dante writes that they "invited me to join their ranks— / I was the sixth among such intellects." Socrates, Plato, Cicero, Seneca, Ptolemy, Saladin, Camilla, Penthelisea, Caesar, Hector, and Aeneas (but no Achilles) also resided there. Dante Alighieri, *Inferno*, trans. Allen Mandelbaum (New York: Bantam, 1982).

80. Du Bois, *Souls* 64.

81. Du Bois, *Souls* 73–74.

82. Du Bois, *Souls* 145.

83. Moss 3.

84. Moss 24.

85. Du Bois, *Souls* 101.

86. Du Bois, *Souls* 99.

87. In its 1910 manuscript form, the title of Du Bois's romance referred, as one might expect, to the *Golden* Fleece of classical myth (as retold by Apollonius of Rhodes, Pindar, and Euripides) but similarities with another title already in print necessitated the change.

88. Du Bois, *Souls* 89.

Conclusion: The Temple of Apollo

1. Deborah E. McDowell, *"The Changing Same": Black Women's Literature, Criticism, and Theory* (Bloomington: Indiana UP, 1995) 14.

2. The story of Er, the son of Armenius the Pamphylian, is told in Book X of *The Republic*.

3. It is arguable that in his later novels, outside the temporal scope of this volume, an older, more sage Du Bois does provide us with that transformative journey. His romantic *Dark Princess* is one example. Both Matthew Towns and Princess Kautilya have personal and transformative experiences before becoming ready for their revolutionary roles.

4. Randall Kenan, lecture, Department of English, North Carolina State University, 22 Oct. 2002.

WORKS CITED AND CONSULTED

Ableman. 21 How. 506. 62 U.S. 506, 16 L. Ed. 169. U.S. Wis., 1858.

Alexander, Elizabeth. "'We Must Be About Our Father's Business': Anna Julia Cooper and the In-Corporation of the Nineteenth Century African-American Woman Intellectual." *Signs* 20.2 (1995): 336–56.

Alighieri, Dante. *Inferno.* Trans. Allen Mandelbaum. New York: Bantam, 1982.

Allen, Grant. "Plain Words on the Woman Question." *Fortnightly Review* 52 (1889): 448–58.

The Antelope. 25 U.S. 546. 6 L. Ed. 723, 12 Wheat. 546. U.S. Ga., 1827.

Anderson, James D. *The Education of Blacks in the South, 1860–1935.* Chapel Hill: U of North Carolina P, 1988.

Andrews, John. Letters to William Barrell. 29 May 1772, 28 Jan. 1774. Andrews-Barrell Letters. Massachusetts Historical Society, Boston.

Andrews, William L. "Slavery and Afro-American Literary Realism." *Slavery and the Literary Imagination.* Ed. Deborah E. McDowell and Arnold Rampersad. Baltimore: Johns Hopkins UP, 1991.

Assing, Ottilie. "To Frederick Douglass." 5 Jan. 1877. *Radical Passion: Ottilie Assing's Reports from America and Letters to Frederick Douglass.* Ed. Christoph Lohmann. New York: Peter Lang, 1999.

Baker, Houston A., Jr. "'There Is No More Beautiful Way': Theory and the Poetics of Afro-American Women's Writing." *Afro-American Literary Study in the 1990s.* Ed. Houston A. Baker Jr. and Patricia Redmon. Chicago: U of Chicago P, 1989. 135–54.

Bell, Robert E. *Women of Classical Mythology.* New York: Oxford UP, 1991.

Bercovitch, Sacvan. *The Puritan Origins of the American Self.* New Haven: Yale UP, 1975.

Berlinerblau, Jacques. *Heresy in the University: The Black Athena Controversy and the Responsibilities of American Intellectuals.* New Brunswick, NJ: Rutgers UP, 1999.

Bingham, Caleb. *The Columbian Orator.* Ed. David W. Blight. New York: New York UP, 1998.

Broderick, Francis L. *W. E. B. Du Bois: Negro Leader in a Time of Crisis.* Stanford, CA: Stanford UP, 1959.

Burckhardt, Jacob. *The Civilization of the Renaissance in Italy.* London: Phaidon, 1951.

Button, Warren H., and Eugene F. Provenzo, Jr. *History of Education and Culture in America.* 2nd ed. Boston: Allyn, 1989.

Byerman, Keith E. *Seizing the Word: History, Art, and Self in the Work of W. E. B. Du Bois.* Athens: U of Georgia P, 1994.

Carby, Hazel. "'On the Threshold of Women's Era': Lynching, Empire, and Sexuality in Black Feminist Theory." *Race, Writing, and Difference.* Ed. Henry Louis Gates, Jr. Chicago: U of Chicago P, 1985.

Cash, W. J. *The Mind of the South.* New York: Knopf, 1941.

Cicero. *De Oratore.* Trans. J. S. Watson. New York: Harper, 1895.

———. *On Duties.* Ed. M.T. Griffin and E.M. Atkins. Cambridge: Cambridge UP, 1991.

———. *On Invention.* Trans. H. M. Hubbell. 2 vols., Loeb Classical Library. London: Heinemann, 1960.

———. *On the Parts of Oratory.* Trans. H. Rackham. 2 vols. Loeb Classical Library. Cambridge: Harvard UP, 1982.

Cook, William, and James Tatum. *African American Writers and Classical Tradition.* Chicago: U of Chicago P, 2010.

Cooper, Anna Julia. *The Voice of Anna Julia Cooper.* Ed. Charles Lemert and Esme Bhan. New York: Rowman, 1998.

"Cornelius, Scipio Aemilianus Africanus Numantinus, Publius," *The Oxford Classical Dictionary.* 3rd ed. rev. Ed. Simon Hornblower and Antony Spawforth. New York: Oxford UP, 2003.

Crummell, Alexander. "To John Jay." 12 Sept. 1851. Jay Family Papers. Butler Library. Columbia University.

Davis, Richard Beale. *Intellectual Life in the Colonial South, 1583–1763.* 3 vols. Knoxville: U of Tennessee P, 1978.

De Bellis, M. D., M. S. Keshavan, D. B. Clark, B. J. Casey, J. N. Giedd, A. M. Boring, K. Frustaci, and N. D. Ryan. "Developmental Traumatology, Part 2: Brain Development." *Biological Psychiatry* 45.10 (1999): 1271–84.

DeJong, Irene F., and J. P. Sullivan, eds., *Modern Critical Theory and Classical Literature.* New York: Brill, 1994.

Diedrich, Maria. *Love Across Color Lines: Ottilie Assing and Frederick Douglass.* New York: Hill & Wang, 1999.

Douglass, Frederick. *The Frederick Douglass Papers.* Ser. 1: *Speeches, Debates, and Interviews.* ed. John W. Blassingame. 5 vols. New Haven, CT: Yale UP, 1979–92.

———. *Life and Times of Frederick Douglass.* Hartford: Park Publishing, 1881. 10 Mar. 2004 <http://docsouth.unc.edu/douglasslife/douglass.html#douglass236>.

———. *Life and Times of Frederick Douglass.* 1892. New York: Collier, 1962.

———. *My Bondage and My Freedom.* New York: Miller, 1855.

———. *My Bondage and My Freedom.* Ed. William L. Andrews. Urbana: U of Illinois P, 1987.

Douglass, Helen Pitts. *In Memoriam: Frederick Douglass.* Philadelphia: Yorston, 1897.

Dred Scott v. Sandford. 60 U.S. 19 How. 393. 1857.

duBois, Page. *Centaurs and Amazons: Women and the Prehistory of the Great Chain of Being.* Ann Arbor: U of Michigan P, 1991.

Du Bois, W. E. B. *Against Racism: Unpublished Essays, Papers, Addresses, 1887–1961.* Ed. Herbert Aptheker. Amherst: U of Massachusetts P, 1985.

———. *Dark Princess.* Jackson: Banner/UP of Mississippi P, 1995.

———. *Dusk of Dawn: An Essay Toward the Autobiography of a Race Concept.* New York: Harcourt, 1940.

———. "Jefferson Davis as a Representative of Civilization." *W. E. B. Du Bois: A Reader.* Ed. David Levering Lewis. New York: Holt, 1995.

———. "The Future of the Negro." Rpt. in *The Oxford W. E. B. Du Bois Reader.* Ed. Eric J. Sundquist. New York: Oxford UP, 1996.

———. *The Souls of Black Folk.* Ed. Henry Louis Gates Jr. and Terri Hume Oliver. New York: Norton, 1999.

———. *The Quest of the Silver Fleece.* 1911. Millwood, NY: Kraus-Thompson, 1974.

duCille, Ann. *The Coupling Convention: Sex, Text, and Tradition in Black Women's Fiction.* New York: Oxford UP, 1993.

Duyckinck, Evert A., and George L. Duyckinck. *Cyclopaedia of American Literature.* New York: Scribner, 1856.

Eadie, John W., ed. *Classical Traditions in Early America.* Ann Arbor: U of Michigan Center for Coordination of Ancient and Modern Studies, 1976.

Eaton, Arthur Wentworth Hamilton. *The Famous Mather Byles: The Noted Boston Tory Preacher 1707–1788.* Boston: Butterfield, 1914.

Emerson, Ralph Waldo. "Representative Men: Seven Lectures." *Emerson: Essays and Lectures.* Ed. Joel Porte. New York: Library of America, 1983.

Everett, Percival. *Frenzy.* St. Paul, MN: Graywolf, 1997.

Evans, Stephanie Y. *Black Women in the Ivory Tower 1850–1954: An Intellectual History*. Gainesville: UP of Florida, 2007.

Franklin, Benjamin. *The Works of Benjamin Franklin*. Ed. John Bigelow. 12 vols. New York: Putnam's, 1904.

Foley, Helene P. "'Reverse Similes' and Sex Roles in the *Odyssey*." *Women in the Ancient World: The Arethusa Papers*. Ed. John Perdotto and J. P. Sullivan. Albany: State U of New York P, 1984.

Freeman, Charles. *Egypt, Greece, and Rome*. New York: Oxford UP, 1996.

Foner, Philip S., and Robert James Branham. *Lift Every Voice: African-American Oratory*. Tuscaloosa: U of Alabama P, 1998.

Foner, Philip F., ed., *Frederick Douglass on Women's Rights*. Westport, CT: Greenwood, 1976.

Freeman, Charles. *Egypt, Greece, and Rome*. New York: Oxford UP, 1996.

Gabel, Leona C. *From Slavery to the Sorbonne and Beyond: The Life and Writings of Anna Julia Cooper*. Northampton, MA: Smith College, 1982.

Gates, Henry Louis, Jr. Foreword. *The Collected Works of Phillis Wheatley*. Ed. John C. Shields. New York: Oxford UP, 1988. vii–xxii.

———. *Figures in Black: Words, Signs, and the "Racial" Self*. New York: Oxford UP, 1987.

———. "From Wheatley to Douglass: The Politics of Displacement." *Frederick Douglass: New Literary and Historical Essays*. New York: Cambridge, 1990.

Gentleman's Magazine and Historical Chronicle 43 (1773): 456.

Gildersleeve, Basil. "The Creed of the Old South." *Atlantic Monthly* 69.411 (1892): 75–87.

Graves, Robert, ed. *Comedies of Terence*. Chicago: Aldine, 1962.

Gregory, James M. *Frederick Douglass: The Orator*. Chicago: Afro-Am, 1969.

Grover, Kathryn, and Carl J. Cruz. "Nathan Johnson set abolitionist's course." *South Coast Today.com* 6 Feb. 2000. Accessed 10 May 2009 <http://www.southcoasttoday.com/apps/pbcs.dll/article?AID=/20000206/NEWS/302069998&cid=sitesearch >.

Gruen, Erich. *The Last Generation of the Roman Republic*. Berkeley: U of California P, 1974.

Hairston, Edward E. "A Profile of Positive Role Models for Young African-American Males." Diss., Virginia Polytechnic Inst. and State U, 1995.

Hairston, Eric Ashley. "The Ebony Column: Classics and the African-American Literary Tradition, 1772–1910." Diss., U of Virginia, 2004.

Haley, Shelley P. "Black Feminist Thought and Classics: Re-membering, Re-claiming, Re-empowering." *Feminist Theory and the Classics*. Eds. Nancy Sorkin Rabinowitz and Amy Richlin (New York: Routledge, 1993.

Harlan, Louis R. *Booker T. Washington in Perspective*. Ed. Raymond W. Smock. Jackson, Mississippi: UP of Mississippi, 1988.

———. *Booker T. Washington: The Making of a Black Leader. 1856–1901.* New York: Oxford UP, 1972.

———. *Booker T. Washington: The Wizard of Tuskegee. 1901–1915.* New York: Oxford UP, 1983.

Harley, Sharon. "Anna J. Cooper: A Voice for Black Women." *The Afro-American Woman: Struggles and Images.* Ed. Sharon Harley and Rosalyn Terborg-Penn. Port Washington, New York: Kennikat, 1978.

Harper, Frances E.W. *Iola Leroy, or Shadows Uplifted.* 3rd Ed. Boston: Earle, 1892.

Harrill, J. Albert. *The Manumission of Slaves in Early Christianity. Hermeneutische Untersuchungen zur Theologie* 32. Tübingen, Germany: Mohr, 1995. 53–54.

Harrison, James A. "Negro English." *Transactions of the American Philological Association* 16 (1885): xxxi–xxxiii.

Herald of Freedom, 3 Dec. 1841, 162–63.

The Holy Bible. King James Version. Iowa Falls, IA: World Bible Publishers, 1989.

Homer. *The Iliad.* Trans. Michael Reck. New York: HarperCollins, 1994.

Horace. *The Odes of Horace.* Trans. David Ferry. New York: Farrar, 1997.

Hosmer, James K. *The Life of Thomas Hutchinson.* New York: Da Capo, 1972.

Hume, David. "Of National Characters." *The Philosophical Works of David Hume.* Vol. 3. Boston: Little, Brown, and Company, 1854. 228–29.

Hutchinson, Louise Daniel. *A Voice from the South.* Washington, DC: Smithsonian, 1981.

"Hutchinson, Thomas." *Dictionary of American Biography.* Ed. Dumas Malone. New York: Scribner, 1932.

Jefferson, Thomas. *Notes on the State of Virginia.* Literary Classics of the United States. Ed. Merrill D. Peterson. New York: Library of America, 1984.

Johnson, Barbara E. "Euphemism, Understatement, and the Passive Voice: A Genealogy of Afro-American Poetry." *Reading Black, Reading Feminist.* Ed. Henry Louis Gates, Jr. New York: Meridian, 1990.

Johnson, Brian L. *W. E. B. Du Bois: Towards Agnosticism 1868–1934.* New York: Rowman, 2008.

Kant, Immanuel. *Observations on the Feeling of the Beautiful and Sublime.* Trans. John T. Goldthwait. Berkeley: U of California P, 1960.

Kelley, Mary, and Chester J. Fontenot, eds. *Re-cognizing W. E. B. Du Bois in the Twenty-first Century.* Macon, GA: Mercer UP, 2007.

Kenan, Randall. Address. Dept. of English. North Carolina State U, Raleigh. 22 Oct. 2002.

Kerrigan, William, and Gordon Braden. *The Idea of the Renaissance.* Baltimore: Johns Hopkins UP, 1989.

Keyssar, Alexander. *The Right to Vote: The Contested History of Democracy in the United States.* New York: Basic, 2000.

King, William. *An Historical Account of the Heathen Gods and Heroes; Necessary for the Understanding of the Ancient Poets: Being An Improvement of whatever has been hitherto written, by the Greek, Latin, French, and English Authors, upon that Subject.* London: Lintot, 1750.

"Lachesis." *A Classical Dictionary: containing an account of the principal proper names mentioned in ancient authors and intended to elucidate all the important points connected with the geography, history, biography, mythology, and fine arts of the Greeks and Romans : together with an account of coins, weights, and measures, with tabular values of the same,* by Charles Anthon. New York: Harper, 1841.

"Lachesis." *Harpers Dictionary of Classical Literature and Antiquities.* Ed. Harry Thurston Peck. New York: Harper, 1898.

"Lachesis." *Oxford Classical Dictionary.* 3rd ed. rev. Ed. Simon Hornblower and Antony Spawforth. New York: Oxford UP, 2003.

Lampe, Gregory. *Frederick Douglass: Freedom's Voice, 1818–1845.* Lansing: Michigan State UP, 1998.

Lewis, David Levering. *W. E. B. Du Bois, 1868–1919: Biography of A Race.* New York: Henry Holt, 1994.

——. *W. E. B. Du Bois, 1919–1963: The Fight for Equality and the American Century.* New York: Henry Holt, 2000.

Liberator, 27 Aug. 1841, 138; 3 Dec. 1841, 193–97; 10 Mar. 1843, 38.

Library of Congress. *American Memory: Historical Collections for the National Digital* Library. "African-American Perspectives: Pamphlets from the Daniel A. P. Murray Collection, 1818–1907." <http://lcweb2.loc.gov/cgi-bin/query/r?ammem/murray:@field(FLD001+26022912+):@@@REF>.

"Lion." *Dictionary of Phrase and Fable.* Ed. E. Cobham Brewer. Philadelphia: Altemus, 1898.

"Lodge, Thomas." *Oxford Book of English Verse, 1250–1900.* Ed. Sir A. T. Quiller-Couch Oxford, UK: Clarendon, 1919.

Logan, Shirley Wilson. *We Are Coming: The Persuasive Discourse of Nineteenth Century Black Women.* Carbondale: Southern Illinois UP, 1999.

London Monthly Review; or Literary Journal from June, 1773 to January 1774, vol. 49 (Oct. 1774): 457–59.

Lunsford, Andrea A., ed. *Reclaiming Rhetorica: Women in the Rhetorical Tradition.* Pittsburgh: U. of Pittsburg P, 1995.

"Maecenas." *The Oxford Classical Dictionary.* 3rd ed. rev. Ed. Simon Hornblower and Antony Spawforth. New York: Oxford UP, 2003.

May, Vivian. *Anna Julia Cooper, Visionary Black Feminist.* New York: Routledge, 2007.

McDowell, Deborah E. *"The Changing Same": Black Women's Literature, Criticism, and Theory.* Bloomington: Indiana UP, 1995.

——. "'The Changing Same': Generational Connections and Black Women Novelists." *Reading Black Reading Feminist.* Ed. Henry Louis Gates Jr. New York: Meridian, 1990.

——. "In the First Place: Making Frederick Douglass and the Afro-American Narrative Tradition." *Critical Essays on Frederick Douglass.* Ed. William L. Andrews. Boston: G. K. Hall, 1991.

McFeely, William A. *Frederick Douglass.* New York: Norton, 1991.

McHenry, Elizabeth. *Forgotten Readers: Recovering the Lost History of African-American Literary Societies.* Durham: Duke UP, 2002.

McKay, Nellie. "W. E. B. Du Bois: The Black Women in His Writings—Selected Fictional and Autobiographical Portraits." *Critical Essays on W. E. B Du Bois.* Ed. William L. Andrews. Boston: G. K. Hall, 1985. 230–52.

Miller, Madonne M. "Lady No Longer Sings the Blues: Rape, Madness, and Silence in *The Bluest Eye.*" *Conjuring: Black Women, Fiction, and Literary Tradition.* Ed. Marjorie Lee Pryse and Hortense J. Spillers. Bloomington: Indiana UP, 1985. 176–84.

Monroe, James. *Oberlin Thursday Lectures, Addresses, and Essays.* Oberlin: Edward J. Goodrich, 1897.

Moorhead, Scipio. Frontispiece. *Poems on Various Subjects Religious and Moral,* by Phillis Wheatley. Library of Congress, Prints and Photographs Division. 21 July 2004 <http://memory.loc.gov/service/pnp/cph/3a40000/3a40000/3a40300/3a40394r.jpg>.

Moses, Wilson Jeremiah. *Afrotopia: The Roots of African American Popular History.* Cambridge, UK: Cambridge UP, 1998.

——. *Alexander Crummell.* New York: Oxford UP, 1989.

——. *Black Messiahs and Uncle Toms: Social and Literary Manipulations of a Religious Myth.* University Park: Pennsylvania State UP, 1982

——. *The Golden Age of Black Nationalism, 1850–1925.* Hamden, CT: Archon, 1978.

Moss, Alfred A., Jr. *The American Negro Academy: Voice of the Talented Tenth.* Baton Rouge: Louisiana State UP, 1981.

National Anti-Slavery Standard, 2 Sept. 1841: 50.

Nussbaum, Martha C. *Cultivating Humanity: A Classical Defense of Reform in Liberal Education.* Cambridge, MA: Harvard UP, 1997.

——. *The Fragility of Goodness.* New York: Cambridge UP, 1986.

Odell, Margaretta. "Memoir." *Memoir and Poems of Phillis Wheatley.* Boston: George W. Light, 1834. 9–29.

Ong, Walter J. *The Presence of the Word: Some Prolegomena for Cultural and Religious History.* New Haven, CT: Yale UP, 1967.

Ovid. *The Art of Love [Ars Amatoria].* Trans. J. H. Mozley, ed. G. P. Goold. 1929; Cambridge, MA: Harvard UP, 1979.

———. *Metamorphoses.* Trans. Sir Samuel Garth, John Dryden, Alexander Pope, Joseph Addison, and William Congreve. Amsterdam, 1742. New York: Heritage, 1961.

Parker, Jane Marsh. "Reminiscences of Frederick Douglass." *Outlook* 51 (1895): 553.

Payne, Daniel Alexander. *Recollections of Seventy Years.* New York: Arno, 1968.

Pennington, James W. C. *The Fugitive Blacksmith; or, Events in the History of James W. C. Pennington, Pastor of a Presbyterian Church, New York, Formerly a Slave in the State of Maryland, United States,* 3rd ed. 1850; London: Gilpin; Westport, CT: Negro UP, 1971.

Perkins, Linda M. "The African American Female Elite: The Early History of African American Women in the Seven Sister Colleges, 1880–1960." *Harvard Educational Review* 67.4 (1997): 718–56.

Plato. *Republic.* Trans. Benjamin Jowett. New York: Barnes & Noble, 1999.

Pope, Alexander. *An Essay on Criticism.* London: Lewis, 1711. Facsim. ed. London: Scolar, 1970.

———. *The Poems of Alexander Pope.* 10 vols. Ed. Maynard Mack. New Haven: Yale UP, 1967.

Porter, Dorothy B. "The Organized Educational Activities of Negro Literary Societies, 1828–1846." *Journal of Negro Education* 5.4, (1936): 565–76.

Porter, Noah. "Greek and a Liberal Education." *Princeton Review* 14 (July–Dec. 1894): 195–218.

Pulliam, John D., and James Van Patten, *History of Education in America.* 6th ed. Englewood Cliffs, NJ: Prentice, 1991.

Quarles, Benjamin. *Frederick Douglass.* Washington, DC: Associated Publishers, 1948.

———. "Letters from Negro Leaders to Gerrit Smith." *Journal of Negro History* 27.4 (1942): 432–53. Accessed 20 Nov. 2003 <http://links.jstor.org/sici?sici=0022–2992%28194210%2927%3A4%3C432%3ALFNLTG%3E2.0.CO%3B2-A>.

Rabinowitz, Nancy Sorkin. Introduction. *Feminist Theory and the Classics.* Ed. Nancy Sorkin Rabininowitz and Amy Richlin. New York: Routledge, 1993.

Rampersad, Arnold. *The Art and Imagination of W. E. B. Du Bois.* Cambridge, MA: Harvard UP, 1976.

Rankine, Patrice. *Ulysses in Black: Ralph Ellison, Classicism, and African American Literature.* Madison: U of Wisconsin P, 2008.

Reinhold, Meyer. *Classica Americana: The Greek and Roman Heritage in the United States.* Detroit: Wayne State UP, 1984.

Richard, Carl J. *The Founders and the Classics: Greece, Rome, and the American Enlightenment.* Cambridge, MA: Harvard UP, 1994.

Richardson, Joe M. "Francis L. Cordozo: Black Educator During Reconstruction." *Journal of Negro Education* 48.1 (Winter 1979): 73–83.

Robinson, William H, ed. *Critical Essays on Phillis Wheatley.* Boston: G. K. Hall, 1982.

———. *Phillis Wheatley and Her Writings.* New York: Garland, 1984.

Rogers, Joel Augustus. *World's Great Men of Color.* Ed. John Henrik Clarke. 2 vols. New York: Simon, 1996.

Rolfe., J. C., ed. *Suetonius.* 2 Vols. The Loeb Classical Library. London: Heinemann; New York: Macmillan, 1914. 2:460. Accessed 10 Mar. 2003 <http://www.fordham.edu/halsall/ancient/suet-viribusrolfe.html#De%20Vita%20Terenti>.

Ruggles, David. "To Gerrit Smith." 22 Apr. 1836. Gerrit Smith Papers. Syracuse U Library, Syracuse, NY.

Rush, Benjamin. *An Address to the Inhabitants of the British Settlements in America Upon Slave Keeping.* Philadelphia: Dunlap, 1773.

Rush, Christopher. *A Short Account of the Rise and Progress of the African M. E. Church in America.* New York: Zuille, 1866. Accessed 1 July 2003 <http://docsouth.unc.edu/church/rush/rush.html>.

Sadock, Benjamin J., M.D., and Virginia A. Sadock, M.D., eds. *Comprehensive Textbook of Psychiatry.* Vol. 1. Philadelphia: Lippincott, 2000.

Sallust. *The War With Jugurtha.* Trans. J. C. Rolfe. Cambridge, MA: Harvard UP, 1921.

Scarborough, William Sanders. "Fatalism in Homer and Virgil." *Transactions of the American Philological Association* 16 (1885): xxxvi–xxxvii.

———. "The Chronological Order of Plato's Dialogues." *Transactions of the American Philological Association* 24 (1892): vi–viii.

———. "The Theory and Function of the Thematic Vowel in the Greek Verb." *Transactions of the American Philological Association* 15 (1884): vi.

Scott v. Negro Ben. 6 Cranch 3, 10 U.S. 3, 3 L. Ed. 135. U.S. Dist. Col., 1810.

Scott v. Negro London. 3 Cranch 324, 7 U.S. 324, 2 L. Ed. 455. U.S. Dist. Col., 1806.

Shaw, Beverley J. F. *The Negro in the History of Methodism.* Nashville: Parthenon, 1954.

Shields, John C. *The American Aeneas: Classical Origins of the American Self.* Knoxville: U of Tennessee P, 2001.

———. "Phillis Wheatley's Use of Classicism." *American Literature* 52.1 (1980): 97–111.

Smith, Rogers M. *Civic Ideals: Conflicting Visions of Citizenship in U.S. History.* New Haven, CT: Yale UP, 1997).

Snowden, Frank M., Jr. *Blacks in Antiquity.* Cambridge, MA: Harvard UP, 1970.

Stapleton, Michael, ed. *Thomas Heywood's Art of Love: The First Complete English Translation of Ovid's* Ars Amatoria. Ann Arbor: U of Michigan P, 2000.

Steele, Richard. *The Tatler.* Ed. George A. Aitken. Vol 2. 13 Dec. 1709. London: Ballantyne, 1898.

Stewart, Roderick M. "The Claims of Frederick Douglass Philosophically Considered." *Frederick Douglass: A Critical* Reader. Ed. Bill E. Lawson and Frank M. Kirkland. Malden, MA: Blackwell, 1999: 145–72.

Tacitus. *The Annals and Histories.* Trans. Alfred Church and J. Brodribb. Chicago: U of Chicago P, 1952.

Tate, Claudia. *Domestic Allegories of Political Desire.* New York: Oxford UP, 1996.

Teicher, Martin H. "Scars That Won't Heal: The Neurobiology of Child Abuse." *Scientific American* 286:3 (2002): 68–75.

———. "Wounds That Time Won't Heal: The Neurobiology of Child Abuse." *Cerebrum* 2.4 (2000): 50–67.

Terrell, Mary Church. *A Colored Woman in a White World.* Washington, DC: Ransdell, 1940.

Terence. *The Comedies.* Ed. Betty Radice. New York: Penguin, 1976.

"Terence." *Harper's Dictionary of Classical Literature and Antiquities.* New York: American Book Co., 1896.

Thomas, Herman E. *James W. C. Pennington: African-American Churchman and Abolitionist.* New York: Garland, 1995.

Towers, Frank. "African-American Baltimore in the Era of Frederick Douglass," *ATQ [American Transcendental Quarterly]* 9 (1995): 165–81.

United States v. Amistad. 15 Pet. 518. 40 U.S. 518, 10 L. Ed. 826. U.S. Conn., 1841.

Virgil. *The Aeneid.* Trans. Allen Mandelbaum. New York: Bantam, 1982.

———. *The Aeneid.* Trans. Christopher Pitt. London: J. Hughs, 1743.

Voltaire. *Oeuvres Completes.* Ed. Louis Moland. 52 vols. Paris: Garnier, 1882–85.

Walters, Tracey. *African American Literature and the Classicist Tradition: Black Women Writers from Wheatley to Morrison.* New York: Palgrave, 2007.

Waswo, Richard. *The Founding Legend of Western Civilization: From Virgil to Vietnam.* Hanover, NH: Wesleyan UP, 1997.

West, Cornel. Address. Forum for Contemporary Thought. U of Virginia, Charlottesville. 6 Oct. 2000.

———. "Black Strivings in a Twilight Civilization." Rpt. in *The Cornel West Reader.* New York: Basic, 1999.

Wheatley, Phillis. *The Collected Works of Phillis Wheatley.* Ed. John C. Shields. New York: Oxford UP, 1988.

———. *The Poems of Phillis Wheatley.* Ed. Julian D. Mason Jr. Chapel Hill: U of North Carolina P, 1966.

Wiencek, Henry. *The Hairstons: An American Family in Black and White.* New York: St. Martin's, 1999.

Wilcox, Kirsten. "The Body into Print: Marketing Phillis Wheatley." *American Literature* 71.1 (1999): 1–29.

Williard, Carla. "Wheatley's Turns of Praise: Heroic Entrapment and the Paradox of Revolution." *American Literature* 67.2 (1995): 223–56.

Winterer, Caroline. *The Culture of Classicism: Ancient Greece and Rome in American Intellectual Life, 1780 –1910.* Baltimore: Johns Hopkins UP, 2001.

———. "Victorian Antigone: Classicism and Women's Education in America, 1840–1900." *American Quarterly* 51.1 (2001): 70–88.

Woodson, Carter G. *The History of the Negro Church.* Washington, DC: Associated Publishers, 1921.

Wooldridge, Thomas. "To the Earl of Dartmouth." 24 Nov. 1772. County Record Office, Stafford, Eng. *Critical Essays on Phillis Wheatley.* Ed. William H. Robinson. Boston: G. K. Hall, 1982. 20.

Yamagata, Naoto. *Homeric Morality.* New York: Brill, 1994.

Zafar, Rafia. "Franklinian Douglass: The Afro-American as Representative Man." *Frederick Douglass: New Literary and Critical Essays.* Ed. Eric J. Sundquist. New York: Cambridge UP, 1990.

Zhang, Juguo. *W. E. B. Du Bois: The Quest for the Abolition of the Color Line.* New York: Routledge, 2001.

INDEX

256